PRAISE FOR *THE ATTRACTOR FACTOR*

"Whatever you want to attract to your life, Joe Vitale has the secret to make it happen. I highly recommend you get this book and get started today."

—MORRIS GOODMAN, author, *The Miracle Man*

"I got enough by the end of chapter one to create a major energy shift in my life! Joe's easy, direct, and knowledgeable presentation allowed me to embrace important principles effortlessly."

—DEE WALLACE, actress and star of *ET*

"Joe Vitale not only appeared in *The Secret,* he is one of the few who knows and lives attraction! Contained in the five steps that Joe maps out in *The Attractor Factor* are the keys to endless abundance. This book instructs you on how to take control of your beliefs and focus, ultimately attracting the life of your dreams. If you just do what Joe tells you, you will create an abundance far beyond what you can currently imagine. *The Attractor Factor* is the secret that *The Secret* doesn't tell you."

—DAVID SCHIRMER, wealth coach and star of *The Secret*

"Just when you think you understand how the world works, Joe Vitale comes along and takes you to a whole new place. He's engaging, entertaining, enlightening, and—oh boy—does he ever stretch your thinking."

—IAN PERCY, registered psychiatrist and member of both the U.S. and Canadian public speaker halls of fame

"This book has the potential to change humanity."

—DR. RICK BARRETT, author, *Healed by Morning*

THE
ATTRACTOR
FACTOR

THE
ATTRACTOR FACTOR

SECOND EDITION

5

Easy Steps for
Creating Wealth
(or Anything Else)
from the Inside
Out

JOE VITALE

WILEY

John Wiley & Sons, Inc.

Published by John Wiley & Sons, Inc., Hoboken, New Jersey
Published simultaneously in Canada

For general information on our other products and services or for technical support, please contact our Customer Care Department within the United States at (800) 762-2974, outside the United States at (317) 572-3993 or fax (317) 572-4002.

Wiley also publishes its books in a variety of electronic formats. Some content that appears in print may not be available in electronic books. For more information about Wiley products, visit our web site at www.wiley.com.

ISBN: 978-0470-28642-5

Printed in the United States of America

10 9 8 7 6 5 4 3 2 1

For Bonnie
and
For Marian

I love you

Spirit is substance which forms itself according to your demands, and must have a pattern from which to work. A pan of dough is as willing to be formed into bread as biscuit. It makes as little difference to Spirit what we demand.

—Frances Larimer Warner,
Our Invisible Supply: Part One, 1907

CONTENTS

ACKNOWLEDGMENTS   xiii

FOREWORD   *Dr. Robert Anthony*   xv

PREFACE   The Author's True Confession   xix

CHAPTER 1   Miracles Never Stop   1

CHAPTER 2   What's Your Attractor Factor IQ?   7

CHAPTER 3   An Attractor Factor Case Study   17

CHAPTER 4   The Truth about the Law of Attraction   21

CHAPTER 5   The Proof   25

CHAPTER 6   What Are You Dismissing?   55

CHAPTER 7   How to Attract Money   61

CHAPTER 8   It Can Be Another Way   67

CHAPTER 9   A Shortcut to Attracting Whatever You Want   73

CHAPTER 10   An Introduction to the Attractor Factor   77

CHAPTER 11   What's Your Prosperity IQ?   81

CHAPTER 12   Step One: The Springboard   83

CHAPTER 13   Step Two: Dare Something Worthy   91

CHAPTER 14   Step Three: The Missing Secret   135

CONTENTS

CHAPTER 15   Step Four: Nevillize Your Goal   183

CHAPTER 16   Step Five: The Ultimate Secret   207

CHAPTER 17   The Million Dollar Secret Formula   239

CHAPTER 18   The Shocking True Story of Jonathan   243

CHAPTER 19   The Experiment: Intentional Meditation Foundation   247

CHAPTER 20   Common Questions (with Answers)   257

BIBLIOGRAPHY   267

INDEX   279

ABOUT THE AUTHOR   295

SPECIAL OFFER   297

BEYOND THE ATTRACTOR FACTOR   298

ACKNOWLEDGMENTS

I am grateful to my friends Jerry and Esther Hicks for their insights into the process of attracting whatever you want. I am, of course, grateful to Jonathan Jacobs for his work as a healer, miracles coach, and friend. I am also grateful for Bill Ferguson's magic. Linda Credeur was the first to believe in this project, maybe even before me. I want to thank Bob Proctor for his support and belief in me and in this book. A few special friends read early versions of this material and gave me priceless feedback. They deserve a round of applause: Jonathan Morningstar, Jennifer Wier, Blair Warren, David Deutsch, Bryan Miller, Nerissa Oden, Rick and Mary Barrett, and the late Marian Vitale. Jenny Meadows helped with early editing. Matt Holt at Wiley sought me out and convinced me to create this book for you. My mastermind group gave me support and advice. They include Bill Hibbler, Pat O'Bryan, Nerissa Oden, Jillian Coleman, Craig Perrine, Irma Facundo, Bryan Caplovitz, and Jay McDonald. Nerissa, my life partner and love, is always there for me, and always feeding the critters so I can keep writing. I thank Rhonda Byrne, creator of the movie *The Secret*, for putting me in her amazing film. Suzanne Burns, my key assistant, makes my daily life easier so I can focus on writing. Her husband, Bruce, often helps me, never asking for payment. My fellow crusader of the light, Mark Ryan, is always supportive. Victoria Schaefer is a priceless friend. I also want to thank Cyndi Smasal and my Miracles Coaches team over at www.miraclescoaching.com. Finally, I am grateful to the Divine for guiding me in every moment.

Having been in the business of personal development for most of my life, the question I most frequently hear is, "How do I go about getting what I want?"

The answer to that question is clearly defined and answered in this amazing new book by my dear friend, Dr. Joe Vitale.

When I first read *The Attractor Factor*, I was stunned by the insight and clarity it reveals about the hidden and often ignored creative power within us. What is this power? How can we use it to create the life we desire? More importantly, how can we do it in a way that allows us to live our life in an easy, stress-free manner?

These questions have propelled Joe Vitale to research and write this book, and subsequently arrive at a totally new perspective on manifesting your grandest desires.

Joe has harnessed this power to create a life that most people would envy. He's got the homes, the cars, the success, the love, the health—all that anyone would want. He is one of the few people that "walks his talk." He's probably the most lovable marketing specialist alive today. His life is a living testimonial that what he teaches actually works!

Throughout this book he will tell you about his life—the good, the bad, and the ugly. He holds nothing back. He will share with you how, through trial and error, he discovered the five-step formula that took him from poverty, unhappiness, frustration, and sometimes despair, to a life of abundance, happiness, contentment, and, unparalleled success. You'll find it inspiring and unforgettable.

What about you? Do you feel restless and unsatisfied in certain areas of your life? Are you ready to learn about and apply a simple five-step formula that will change your life forever?

Joe "Mr. Fire!" Vitale encompasses a belief that we can find spiritual solutions to problems and create the life we desire through this "Attractor Factor." This book will help you to understand how easy it is to use that formula in your own life and how to live a life without stress, strain, and struggle. It will help you to discover that you have more control over your life and destiny than you ever imagined possible.

Everyone has the desire to discover the great secrets of success, to reach total contentment, and to find the path to personal fulfillment. Joe shows us how to do this through the Attractor Factor.

The secret to attracting the things we truly desire are in the pages of this book. However, I want to warn you that you will be shocked at how simple it is to apply this formula. The simplicity may surprise you, but do not be fooled by it. Our minds love to complicate things, but you cannot complicate the truth. Truth by its very nature is always simple. All we need to do is to apply these simple truths, and our lives can be miraculously changed in an instant.

You will find, as you go through this book, that you may be reintroduced to ideas or strategies you are already familiar with. Again, don't be fooled. As Oliver Wendell Holmes Sr. said, "We all need an education in the obvious."

What Joe has done is to reawaken us to what we already know at a deeper inner level. Then, he encourages us to apply what we know in a simple five-step formula that *cannot fail*!

Imagine what it would be like if we knew the cause of all the things we attract in our life and how we could change our magnetic point of attraction to attract *only* the things we truly desire?

Once you learn the secret of the Attractor Factor, you will be free from worry and self-doubt. You will no longer have to wonder what the future will bring, because you will be able to deliberately create the future you desire by using the simple five-step formula.

You have already made a decision to invest in this book, which is an investment in yourself. You have the power to do great things. The difference between ordinary and *extraordinary* is the "extra." You have already demonstrated that you are willing to go the extra mile by reading this book.

After incorporating the Attractor Factor and the five-step formula into your life you will be able to use it in any situation . . . wherever you are . . . whomever you are with . . . whatever's happening.

The best news of all is you can't screw this up! You can't make a mistake or move in the wrong direction because the Attractor Factor shows you how to flow with the universe instead of against it. Your magnetic point of attraction will always be toward what you want.

So join with me now and allow Joe Vitale to lead you on the journey of self-discovery that will change your life forever.

—Dr. Robert Anthony
www.totalsuccess4u.com

GOT MONEY WORRIES?

A little birdie just came my way and
mentioned a deep, soulful desire of yours.
Heavens no, not that one!
She said that you'd be eternally grateful if, once and for all,
you never, ever had to worry about money again.
Well, I couldn't resist.
Wish granted!
You never, ever have to worry about money again.
Anything else? Anything at all?
—The Universe www.tut.com

The Author's True Confession

I admit it.

I never wanted to publish this book or make it available to a wide audience.

I was scared.

I wrote this book for one person: my sister. Bonnie had three kids, was unemployed, and was on welfare. It hurt me to see her suffer. I knew her life could be different if she knew the five-step process I developed for creating whatever you wanted. I wrote this material for her, and only for her, in 1997. She's now off welfare and doing fine. She's got a house, a car, a job, and a loving family. She's not rich yet, but I think I've shown her a new way to live life.

I never wanted to make this book public, because I was nervous about how the world would perceive me. I've written 17 books so far, for such well-known and conservative organizations as the American Marketing Association and the American Management Association. I also have an audiotape program with Nightingale-Conant. I figured if I told the world about my interest in spirituality, people would ridicule me, clients would fire me, and these organizations would shun me. So I played it safe and kept this book a secret.

But in June 1999, I felt the inner urge to give a copy of the rough manuscript to Bob Proctor, at the beginning of one of his Science of Getting Rich seminars. Bob read it and loved it. And then he did something shocking.

There were 250 people in that seminar in Denver. They all wanted to know how to create wealth. Bob stood before them and read off all of my book titles, and then introduced me to the crowd. I stood and the crowd applauded. They treated me like a celebrity and I loved the attention.

But then Bob told everyone about my new book, my unpublished book, about *this* book. I was surprised. I wasn't ready for this. I held my breath. And then Bob told them the title, which at that time was *Spiritual Marketing.*

There was such a hush throughout the crowd that chills went up my spine. Not only did people favorably react to the book, but they all wanted it—right then. At least 50 people came up and said they wanted to buy the book on the spot. Bob Proctor later said he wanted to record it. And one publisher in the seminar said he wanted to publish the book, sight unseen!

My concerns about publishing this book vanished. I could see that the timing was right to release these ideas, and I saw that I would be safe in doing so.

So here I am.

As with most things in life, there's little to be afraid of, and wealth and glory await right around the corner. All you have to do is step forward and do the things you're being nudged to do from within.

Bob Proctor nudged me in front of 250 people.

As a result, I released the e-book called *Spiritual Marketing* in 2001. The book was an instant success. It became a number one best seller at Amazon on June 4 and 5, 2001, which are my parents' birthdays. The book was translated into seven languages. People wrote me from all over the world, attesting that the five steps explained in the book helped them to get a job, or heal something "incurable," or raise money, or find true love, and more.

It was pretty staggering feedback.

I began to think, "If this material really changes lives, then I must get it out to the world in a bigger way. I need to expand the book and better explain the five steps, and I need a strong publisher, too."

I set that statement as my intention.

And now you're reading this book. Obviously, I expanded it, updated the information, and found the right publisher as well.

That's how the Attractor Factor works.

But before I explain the five-step process, let me say a few things . . .

Within each life lies the causes of whatever enters it.
—F.W. SEARS, *How to Attract Success,* 1914

CHAPTER 1

Miracles Never Stop

More miracles have happened to me since writing the little booklet in 1997 that evolved into what you are now holding. Here are a few of them:

- When I first wrote this book and described the car of my dreams, the car of my dreams at that time was a Saturn. I still love Saturns, but I've upgraded my dream and my car several times since then. I went on to manifest a BMW Z3 2.8 Roadster. It was showcased in an early James Bond movie. I have never in my life had so much fun driving. But as I grew in my life and became bolder about going for my dreams, I also naturally wanted a different vehicle. I was then led to Francine, my beloved 2005 Panoz Esperante GTLM exotic sports car. Whew! What a ride it is! I then went on and attracted a rare 1998 Panoz AIV Roadster. It was once owned by Steven Tyler of the rock band Aerosmith. While attracting cars isn't what this book is about, these new cars symbolize major changes in my life. It's also a message for you: You truly can have anything you can imagine.

- When I first wrote this book, I was still married to Marian, whom I had been with for more than 20 years. Since then we decided we had grown apart. There was nothing negative about the experience or the decision. Marian decided she preferred being alone. I decided to look for another partner. I found one, too, in Nerissa, who I am deeply in love with. I remained friends with Marian right till her death in 2004, and I miss her even now. Still, I'm a lucky man. Major changes in life can truly be easy and effortless.

- When I first wrote this book, I set a goal to generate a passive income stream. I wanted money to come to me easily and effortlessly, always, consistently—no matter where I was or what I was doing. I was then led to meet Mark Joyner, then CEO of Aesop Marketing, who asked if he could put one of my books online as an e-book. I was skeptical. But I gave him *Hypnotic Writing*, a manuscript I wrote many years ago. Mark put it online, marketed it, and the sales blew my socks off. Even now, years after the book went online at www.HypnoticWriting.com, orders keep coming in. Since there is no book to print, stock, or mail, all the money is passive income. Every month I receive a check, sometimes for staggering amounts. And since I now have over three dozen e-books out there, including the best-seller *How to Create Your Own E-book in Only 7 Days* at www.7dayebook.com, the checks are even bigger. I also have many audios online for instant download, including *Money Beyond Belief* with Brad Yates at www.moneybeyondbelief.com and of course *How to Attract a New Car* at www.attractanewcar.com. These sites, and many more, bring me large checks on a regular basis. It's all passive income. Now I smile a lot. I know that when you set an intention, you set the forces of life to bring it to you, and you to it.

- When I first wrote this book, I was living in Houston, Texas. After I met Nerissa, I moved to Austin. I then began the process of attracting our dream home. After a few months, we found a beautiful two-acre, two-story, Hill Country property with wandering wild deer and rabbit, and an outside pool, between Austin and San Antonio, in a small spiritual-artistic community called Wimberley, Texas. Finding this home was a matter of having a clear image of what I wanted while following every intuitive impulse I had. The result was a miracle. We're now looking at buying 377 acres near here and building our own city on it. I'm kidding about the city part, but you get the idea. Think big and big things happen.

- As my career evolved, I ended up in many movies, including the staggering hit, *The Secret,* as well as *The Opus* and *The Leap.* This led to appearances on Larry King's television show, Donny Deutsch's CNBC TV show *The Big Idea,* and much more. This also led to my writing more books, including *The Key* and *Zero Limits,* and recording more audio programs, such as *The Missing Secret.* Obviously, when you do what you love, wealth and fame follow.

I could go on. For example, a man I studied some 20 years ago was Dr. Robert Anthony. His famous books and tapes changed my life. After I came out with an early version of this material, he read it and contacted me. Now the man who was once one of my gurus is now one of my business partners. I ended up producing, recording, and marketing his terrific audio program, *Beyond Positive Thinking.* I think it's the greatest self-improvement material of all time, and I am involved with it! And, if you didn't notice, Dr. Anthony wrote the introduction to the book you are holding.

But wait. There's more. Now people in Hollywood want me to have my own television show. I've gone from homeless to having my own weekly TV show? Talk about mind-blowing. But this is the wild, wonderful life you get when you tune into the ideas in this book.

Just think what wonders are ahead for *you!*

Attraction Works

I just sat down with Nerissa and talked to her about the ongoing miracles in my life. "It happens to you all the time," she said.

She mentioned that just the other day I wanted to book us a flight to Ohio to see my family. Tickets were nearly $1,000. I simply expected to get a better deal while being willing to accept the going fare. When I called the airline back, they told me I had enough frequent flyer miles to get both tickets for just over $100. Way cool.

And Nerissa reminded me of the time I wanted to complete my collection of rare books by P. T. Barnum, a marketing genius and religious man I had studied and written a book about (*There's a Customer Born Every Minute*). I found the last book I needed. But my intuition said not to pay the high price the bookseller was asking. I let it go. I waited. A few days later, the bookseller lowered his price. That's almost unheard of. And, yes, I bought the book.

And she reminded me of the time I looked for one book for nearly seven years and couldn't find it. I gave up. But I decided I would attract it, somehow, some way. Then, out of the blue, an e-mail friend in Canada wrote me that he had the book. I begged to buy it. He declined. But a few days later, he suddenly decided to just send me the book—at no charge!

And she remembered that a year or so ago, when I couldn't find a friend of mine that I loved and missed, I gave up and hired a private investigator. He couldn't find my friend, either. I quit looking. But I made a decision to attract her back into my life. Then one day, simply following my intuition, I walked right up to my friend at a yoga class. I found her without breaking a sweat.

Nerissa also reminded me to tell you what happened just yesterday, while writing this very preface.

I have been practicing the Sedona Method for months now. It's a very simple method for releasing any emotion or negative experience in the way of your being happy right now. I like the method and have told many people about it through my monthly e-newsletter.

I was reading a book by Lester Levenson, the founder of the Sedona Method, just yesterday morning. I sat in my easy chair, reading, feeling happy, wondering how I might learn more about

Sedona and Lester. I remember thinking, "Gee, it sure would be nice to meet some Sedona people and learn more about what they do."

That *same day* I checked my e-mail and to my delighted surprise, there was a message from the director of the Sedona Institute. He had heard about me through the grapevine and wanted to talk to me about how I could help promote their web site at www.sedona.com. Wow!

And then there are the countless times when I want more money for something or other, and I get a brainstorm that pulls in an abundance of money fast.

One time when I needed to raise $20,000, I almost created a seminar on "Spiritual Marketing" to get it. Instead, I felt inspired to see if anyone would sign up for the same class online. This was unheard of at the time I thought of it. But boldness brings magic. And money. I announced that the class would only be conducted by e-mail, would last five weeks, and would cost $1,500 per person. Fifteen people signed up, bringing me a whopping sum of money in one day. Very nice. I have since taught my e-class system to others. They have made upwards of a quarter of a million dollars per year with it. In most cases, I received almost half as payment for my consulting. You know I like that.

Another time I donated $15,000 to the mother of a child who had had a pediatric stroke. She needed the money for a machine to help her child learn how to move his little body. I didn't know her or her child. I gave her a check for the full amount. It was the largest donation I had ever made up to that time. Later the same day I received a check for twice the amount from an unexpected source. Miracles like this are not rare or impossible once you soak up these principles.

"You have miracles happen all the time," Nerissa repeated.

"Why do you think that is?" I asked her. "It certainly wasn't always like that."

"Because you now practice the Attractor Factor," she explained. "You make yourself a magnet for whatever you want. Once you decide you want something, you get it, often almost instantly."

There's no question about it. If I tried to document all the miracles that keep occurring in just my life alone because of the Attractor Factor, I'd never stop writing this book and never get around to releasing it to the public.

My point is this: The five-step formula you are about to discover works.

And because it works, I want you to have it.

I once told Nerissa that there is an easy path through life and a hard path. When I first met her, she was crawling up the rocky side of the mountain. I pointed out that there is an escalator through life, too. You can take the hard path or the easy path. It's all your choice.

When I first met Nerissa, she was unhappy, battling a lawsuit against construction workers who messed up her roof, fighting with her mother almost every day, hating her job, and more. Within a few months of discovering the Attractor Factor, she ended the lawsuit, found common ground with her mother, quit her job, and now has two e-books out and a growing Internet business. And she lives with me in our country estate. She says she is happier now than at any other time in her life, *ever*.

Again, there is a rocky road through life, and then there's an escalator. Which do you prefer? The Attractor Factor shows you the way to glide through life. Why not step up and enjoy the ride?

Remember that things are symbols, and that the thing symbolized is more important than the symbol itself.

—JUDGE THOMAS TROWARD, QUOTED IN
ATTAINING YOUR DESIRES BY GENEVIEVE BEHREND.

CHAPTER 2

What's Your Attractor Factor IQ?

"If you would like the world to be happier, healthier, and wealthier, begin by contributing one happy, healthy, and wealthy person to it: You."

—Dr. Joe Vitale, star of the movies *The Secret* and *The Opus*

Let's begin by checking your IQ when it comes to attracting what you want. The following quiz was created by Ann-Marie Caffrey and used here with her kind permission. Just taking this test will illuminate areas you may want to focus on as you read this book. To see your results, go online and take the test at www.smart-attractor.com.

1. The Target

Q1. When you think about what you would like to manifest in your life, is it something you could easily and without hesitation put down in writing?

a. Yes. I know exactly what it is that I want. I have given it a lot of thought and could describe it clearly in writing.

b. I have a pretty strong vision of what would make me happy but it would probably take me a little while to put the specifics into writing.

c. Well, I know that I want more money because I want to drive a luxury car and live in a fabulous house. I can't say I have spent a lot of time working that out—I haven't thought about specifics much.

Q2. Are the dreams and goals that you have today very different from those you had a few years ago?

a. No. I've had the same dreams and goals for as long as I can remember.

b. They have evolved over the years, but in essence I still want the same things.

c. Yes. I've changed a lot over the years and so have my dreams and goals.

Q3. Think for a moment about achieving something that you believe you really want. Say it to yourself in the present tense— for example, I am earning $200,000 per year in a job I love. Now, become aware of your body's physical responses. Which below best describes the sensation?

a. Relaxed, good, positive feeling totally desiring this outcome with all my being.

b. When I focus on my physical sensations, I get a vague feeling of headache/chest pressure/tightened abdomen/and so forth.

c. Anytime I imagine having this scenario, it causes an unmistakable and negative physical sensation somewhere in my body.

Q4. We all know of individuals who are clearly very driven and motivated to succeed. Where would you rate yourself on that scale of ambition, determination, and drive to succeed?

a. I think I would be toward the top end. I work hard and feel a constant burning ambition to make something good of my life and achieve what I want.

b. About average. I am capable of achieving a lot when I really apply myself. But doing that continually would burn me out.

c. I've never felt hugely motivated about anything in particular. The simple fact is that life isn't fair and it isn't always the hardest workers who get rewarded—so why bother?

Q5. One key trait that many successful people share is persistence. If your friends and family were describing you, which description comes closest to what they might say?

a. He/she is incredibly persistent. Even when things are going wrong, he/she just keeps on going.

b. He/she puts a lot of energy into achieving goals but sometimes gets derailed after a hard knock.

c. He/she starts everything with great enthusiasm but then loses interest once the going gets tough.

2. Positive Mental Attitude

Q6. Albert Einstein once famously said that the most important question anyone could ask himself was: "Is this a friendly universe?" How would you answer that question?

a. Yes.

b. Don't know.

c. No.

Q7. How would you describe your present situation in terms of having things to be grateful for in your life?

a. Very lucky! I have great relationships with family and friends. Like most people, I'd like to have more material things, but I feel great appreciation for the good things I have in my life.

b. I'm doing okay, but I'd be even more grateful if I had more!

c. It's hard to be grateful when I work so hard and have so little.

Q8. If there are dreams and goals that you have not yet achieved, what, in your opinion, has so far prevented you?

a. I haven't been 100 percent successful so far simply because I haven't fully focused my intent and made things happen for myself. It's not due to anyone else.

b. I would say it's partly due to my own beliefs and behaviors, which I am now trying to change, although some external factors have come between me and my goals.

c. I was prevented from reaching my goals because I have had so many setbacks in my life. Circumstances sometimes seem to conspire against me.

Q9. Do you consider yourself to be a lucky person?

a. Yes. Not necessarily in the sense of always winning stuff—but in the way things always seem to work out for the best for me.

b. Average.

c. Unlucky in a lot of ways. I've had many tough challenges in my life.

Q10. When you hear phrases such as, "You are a creator, you have the power to create" or "You are one with the great 'I am' of the universe." Which of these best describes your inner response?

a. Those lines are so true and resonate profoundly with me.

b. It's encouraging and uplifting, but I can't say I fully feel it or believe it.

c. That's all well and good, but I simply don't see how it relates to my practical day to day life.

3. Faith and Inspired Action

Q11. When you're faced with a difficult situation in which you're unsure of the right path forward or when going through an anxious period in your life where a lot is at stake, which of the following are you most likely to do?

a. I'd hand the situation over to God/my guardian angel/the universe and simply ask/pray for help. I find it relieves me of worry and things always seem to work themselves out for me.

b. It depends, typically I will look for options or perhaps talk to someone I trust or occasionally pray.

c. I would try to work things out for myself. I don't feel that prayer or asking the universe for help is going to achieve anything.

Q12. Answer this question on reflex: Would you be comfortable with someone telling you that they believe you are very talented (creative/logical/witty/sensitive/whatever you are) and that they want to pay you $500,000 per year to work for them simply using that talent?

a. Yes, why not? I think I'm worth it.

b. It's a nice thought—I know I am talented in some areas, but I don't know if I'm worth that much!

c. No, I don't believe I have anything to give worth that much.

Q13. When you think about actually living your ideal lifestyle and achieving your goals, how realistic do you feel you are being?

a. Very realistic. I feel that it's achievable and will come soon. I have had success in the past and I know I will again.

b. Well, I don't feel it's going to happen for me in the next few weeks or months, but I think it's realistic to assume that I will get there eventually.

c. It's a pipe dream for me. I cannot connect where I'm at right now to where I want to be—but I think it would be a good way to test the power of the Law of Attraction!

Q14. The Law of Attraction allows you to have, do, or be anything you want. How does that statement make you feel?

a. Really good. It's so simple when you stop fighting it and just believe.

b. I sometimes struggle with the faith side. But I'm actively trying to improve my faith by reading and meditating.

c. I don't think I could ever have the kind of blind faith implied in that statement. I'm a realist!

Q15. Regardless of your current job, do you feel that you know what your own unique talents are?

a. Yes, I make room for my real interests and talents in my life, and I hope someday to make a career from using them.

b. Yes, I'm aware that I possess various talents, although I don't think any of them translate into something I could make a living from.

c. Nothing stands out, and I have never really thought about it.

4. *Thought Control*

Q16. When driving a long journey or performing some repetitive task that frees your mind to process other thoughts, which of these most closely describes your pattern of thinking?

a. I concentrate a lot on progressing toward my goals. Whenever my mind is free I am usually thinking about my goals.

b. I do occasionally remember to focus on my goals, but it's hard to stop my mind from just drifting.

c. When I'm not forced to concentrate on something I just let my thoughts wander.

Q17. If thoughts are responsible for manifesting our reality, are you thinking mostly positive or negative thoughts?

a. Mostly positive thoughts.

b. Not sure.

c. Mostly negative.

Q18. We process about 12,000 thoughts each day. Do you remember what you were thinking about yesterday morning?

a. Yes. I know I would have spent some time in deliberately turning my thoughts toward achieving my goal.

b. Not sure. Obviously whatever I was working on would have required my thoughts to be focused. I can also recall other thoughts involving personal events and feelings.

c. No idea—whatever came into my head I guess!

Q19. Are you consciously carrying around resentment, hurt, or anger toward another person for something that happened in the past?

a. No. We've all been hurt and I have felt those feelings—but none are active right now. I am not wasting any time on anger or regrets.

b. Sometimes. I do have one or two hurts from the past that are not so easy to just forgive and forget—those feelings occasionally surface. But on the whole, I feel blessed that I have so many people around me that I love.

c. Yes. Sometimes when you get badly hurt it's almost impossible to forgive. I still get quite angry and/or emotional when I think of this person or event.

Q20. Do you consciously change your focus when you notice that you have started thinking something negative rather than just allowing the thought to carry on uninterrupted?

a. Yes. I often get some external trigger like a loud noise and realize I have just been allowing my mind to drift into negativity. As soon as I become aware of it, I immediately refocus my mind on something positive.

b. Sometimes. I generally try to stay positive, but I don't always notice my thought patterns.

c. No. I don't specifically control my thoughts in terms of stopping negative ones. I think about whatever comes naturally at the time.

5. Tools and Techniques

Q21. Do you meditate?

a. Yes, daily.

b. Yes, occasionally.

c. Never.

Q22. Do you practice visualization?

a. Yes, I always visualize my goals in great detail.

b. Occasionally. I find it a little difficult to master.

c. No. I don't set aside any time to visualize.

Q23. Do you use affirmations?

a. Yes, I repeat affirmations each day as part of my daily routine.

b. Sometimes. I do use affirmations, but I don't always remember to do it every day.

c. No, saying stuff out loud feels a bit silly and pointless to me.

Q24. Do you keep visual reminders of your goal somewhere prominent?

a. Yes.

b. Not exactly. I have made attempts to gather pictures, but I don't look at them as often as I should.

c. No.

Q25. Have you ever practiced repetitively writing out your goal?

a. Yes, I handwrite my goal quite often; it helps drive it deeper into my subconscious.

b. I have tried writing it down a few times, but it's hard work to keep on writing.

c. No, never.

Again, just taking the quiz will help you think about your current ways of creating your own reality. Remember, to see your results, go online and take the test at www.smart-attractor.com.

CHAPTER 3

An Attractor Factor Case Study

"We are largely what we have thought ourselves into being, the balance being represented by the character of the suggestions and thought of others, which have reached us either directly by verbal suggestions or telepathically by means of such thought waves. Our general mental attitude, however, determines the character of the thought waves received from others as well as the thoughts emanating from ourselves. We receive only such thoughts as are in harmony with the general mental attitude held by ourselves; the thoughts not in harmony affecting us very little, as they awaken no response in us."

—*Thought Vibration* by William Walker Atkinson (1906)

Before I walk you through the five steps in the formula, let me tell you a story about how these steps work. This will give you a reference point for understanding how to use these steps in your own life for anything you want. While the following story is about attracting a new car, remember that the principles will work for anything you want.

A car is only a symbol. I tell people that the spiritual and the material are one. They are two sides of the same coin. Anyone who says a material anything isn't spiritual is being self-righteous. The Divine created it all, including you, me, and really nice cars.

Sometime in early 2006, I picked up a copy of *Robb Report* magazine. It's a high-end magazine focusing on luxury items, from expensive watches to cars to wines to—well, anything that costs a lot.

In this one issue there was an article that listed the five best exotic sports cars of all time. I knew four of the cars, but not the fifth: a Panoz Esperante GTLM.

A what? I had never heard of a Panoz car before. I become curious. It's important to realize right here that I had a *curiosity* about the car, not a need. You can attract things faster if you aren't desperate for them. Now back to the story.

I studied the photo of the Panoz Esperante and felt the car was incredible. Spectacular. It's a barely street-legal race car. It's made by hand by a family outside of Atlanta, Georgia. The Panoz family. They only make a few cars a year. They are expensive and collectible.

I wanted one.

Note that I didn't *need* one. I didn't even begin my search for the car yet. I just figured I would attract it. Having been through this process before, I know that you don't have to worry about how you will attract something. What's far more important is that you know what you want. In my case, I wanted a Panoz Esperante of my own.

I let the intention go. I didn't worry about it, think about it, or in any way concern myself with it. From time to time I would poke around online and see if any Panoz cars were for sale. I also researched the company and learned what I could. Again, I wasn't desperate. I was simply curious.

Of course, I was taking some action. Not a lot. But some. My searching online was an action. My searching places like eBay was an action. I firmly believe that while most of your goals can come to you without a huge amount of action, you almost always have to do something. The car of your dreams doesn't usually just appear in your driveway. Somebody has to drive it there. And pay for it.

Almost a year went by before I actually saw a Panoz. One morning I got up, went to my computer, did my normal surfing and e-mail, and was surprised to see a Panoz listed for sale in San Antonio, Texas, not far from me. I called the dealership on the phone. (Note: I'm taking action again.) I asked about the car. The dealer was surprised I knew what a Panoz was, as most people don't. I was seriously mispronouncing the car's name at the time (it's pronounced *pay-nose*) but the salesman was polite in correcting me.

That same day—*the same day*—I went over to San Antonio to see the car. You might call it love at first sight. The chilipepper red convertible was a true head turner. The salesman opened the hood and let me see the Panoz company had named the car: Francine. She's a 2005 Panoz Esperante GTLM and she's a fiery redhead.

I drove her and loved the experience so much I was almost giddy. I had to go to lunch to settle down and then return to the dealership and drive Francine again. Some self-doubts crept in. I wondered, "Is this car right for me?" and "What about insurance?" and even "What would Nerissa think?" But I looked at each question and stayed with it until I answered it. To attract anything you need to first rid yourself of any stumbling blocks or negative beliefs.

When it came time to negotiate buying the car, I held my breath. I had been a used car salesman 30 years ago and hated it. I knew they could lie or at least mislead me. I was afraid. But I also knew that facing my fears is a key to my success. Fear is a block. It prevents manifestations. So I went in and faced my fear, which appeared in the form of the dealership owner, Rich Hovey.

This is where the story becomes magical. I knew a new Panoz costs about $130,000. Francine was barely used, with only 1,400 miles on her, and I knew the price wouldn't be much lower than if she were new.

But Rich told me an interesting story. He said the car was won by a local man in a lottery. Apparently he bought a $500 ticket to a fund-raiser and won the grand prize: Francine. But then he was presented with the tax bill for the car and he couldn't pay it. He wanted to sell the car, fast, and for almost anything he could get. Oh, and the taxes were due the following week.

I was the right guy at the right time. I negotiated a fair price—around $80,000—and drove home with the car.

I had attracted the Panoz car I said I would one year earlier.

Hopefully you see the key elements at play in this story: I set an intention, I was playful about it, I imagined what it would be like to have the car, I took action, I faced my fears and dissolved my limiting beliefs and I got the car.

This process works on anything you can name, of course, not just cars. So don't feel disconnected from the story just because you want to attract a house or a job or a spouse or anything else. The process is the same. The five steps are the same.

And now it's your turn to use them.

CHAPTER 4

The Truth about the Law of Attraction

"You don't know what Desire is. I tell you if a man wants a thing as much as the prisoner wants freedom, or as much as a strongly vital man wants life, then that man will be able to sweep away obstacles and impediments apparently immovable. The key to attainment is Desire, Confidence, and Will. This key will open many doors."

—*THOUGHT VIBRATION* BY WILLIAM WALKER ATKINSON (1906)

The other night I had dinner with a few friends on a wooden deck under the Texas stars. The conversation was about creating your own reality. We talked about Jane Roberts and the Seth material, including such books as *The Nature of Personal Reality*. Seth was one of the first to teach me that we create our own reality, as individuals and as groups, through our thoughts and feelings. Our inner self pulls the other to us, while helping to create life through us.

That led to conversation about the Law of Attraction. This is the law publicized in the mega-successful book and movie, *The Secret*, and in books of my own, such as *The Key*. The Law of Attraction has been around a lot longer, of course. William Walker Atkinson wrote about it in 1906 in his book, *Thought Vibration*. But others declare the law goes more than 2,000 years back, all the way to Jesus.

Philip Harris, in his book *Jesus Taught It, Too: The Early Roots of the Law of Attraction*, writes: "Jesus was by no means the first to introduce the concept of the Law of Attraction." He says the law had its earliest roots in ancient Egypt and Babylon.

What is the Law of Attraction? It's the law that states the energy you emit through your thoughts and feelings will attract corresponding circumstances. In short, think good thoughts and attract good things. There's more to it, of course, and I'll explain it in this book, but that's a simple explanation of this remarkable law.

Our deck conversation continued. Someone mentioned the law of gravity. Everyone has heard the story of Sir Isaac Newton having an apple fall on his head and from there formulating the law of gravitational pull or Universal Gravitation. The definition of this law is interesting:

"Every object in the Universe attracts every other object with a force directed along the line of centers for the two objects that is proportional to the product of their masses and inversely proportional to the square of the separation between the two objects."

You don't have to understand the definition to follow where I took the conversation with my friends on the deck.

"If Newton discovered gravity in 1687, what did people call it when they knocked over chairs or fell down *before* then?"

My point was this: Newton's discovery of gravity was simply an observation and labeling of something that had been working all along, right from the beginning. By writing about it in his treatise *Philosophiae Naturalis Principia Mathematica*, published in 1687, Newton helped us understand a law we could then use with awareness and intent. This law, and Newton's laws of motion, form the basis for modern engineering.

Knowing the Law of Attraction is similar. It's been working all along, just like gravity. It's been in your life since your birth, just like gravity. It's something you never think about, just like gravity, but now that you've been made aware of it, you can begin to construct a life of your dreams based on it.

What you want to do is work with *conscious awareness* of the Law of Attraction. This is similar to the world of engineering, which improved with Newton's discovery of the law of gravity.

Even if you don't regard the Law of Attraction as a true law, like those of scientific studies and physical realities, you can at least accept it as a *spiritual* law. Until more tests are done to prove the Law of Attraction is as valid and important as gravity, assuming it is a spiritual principle you can work with will take you miles ahead in achieving your dreams.

This book describes my Attractor Factor five-step formula for attracting whatever you desire. Its underlying premise is that the Law of Attraction is real. But you don't need to believe in the Law of Attraction to work these five steps any more than you need to believe in gravity to build a house. It's simply the hidden law that makes your construction—of a house or a life—possible.

With this in mind, let's get started.

CHAPTER 5

The Proof

Here is what some people are saying after reading the early editions of this book:

Thank you so much for this book that's changing my life. I am letting go of so much baggage, I can't believe I was able to walk down the street before.

The morning after I cleared myself of my fears of rejection and failure, Yanik Silver e-mailed me back that he would like to mentor or partner with me on my new Internet marketing membership site—and this is my first product! Two minutes after clearing my fear of leaving my baby with anyone else, the babysitter called. I had been trying to get a babysitter for two days. Thank you so much for sharing your experience with us that we can have better lives. You have given me the tools to make it happen.

Thank you.

—LIZ SHERWOOD

My name is Jackie Lind—actually now Jackie Rooney—and I wanted to share with you what your book, The Attractor Factor, *did for me. The first half of 2007 was in many ways one of the most difficult times in my life and the last half one of the best. I am a Canadian casting director. I had done okay at casting but was no where near where I wanted to be and struggling to pay bills. My expenses were higher than my fees. I was living with the love of my life and had been for seven years but for many reasons, one being financial, marriage was no where in sight. I mostly am a positive and happy person but depression and fear were coming at me fast and furious. No jobs in sight, tons of debt, forced to move out of our beautiful condo on the water to a basement suite, and struggling to support exes, I found myself sleeping and crying a lot.*

One day my love brought home your book, The Attractor Factor *and left it out on the table. I picked it up the next day and read the entire book. That day I started to believe that things could change . . . anyway, what did I have to lose? I started practicing the steps and slowly things started to come to me. I kept a list of all the things I wanted, and I would go back and delete them once I got them and started adding more to the list. I used your method to visualize winning an Emmy. How crazy is that since I was hardly working, living in a basement suite. Well, I got the nomination but my name was not on the ballot with the other two. I was devastated but continued visualizing and believing. The decision was overturned and my name was put on the ballot. I was going to the Emmys this year as a nominee. I then realized that I might not be able to go as we did not have enough money for a flight and hotel for myself never mind the love of my life. I again kept following the steps. My love had acquired air mileage points and had just enough to get me there and back. My best friend found out I was going alone, and she used her husband's points for her air fare and his points for our hotel and away we went. Just being there was magic. We did all the L. A. things. We went to the Universal Studios theme park where I saw Lucy's Emmy. I thought how great it would be if I actually did win. I even had a place set aside for it in my little place, just in case. Now, it was a longshot for a little prairie girl from Canada to win. But, the odd thing is, I did win the Emmy for 2007 Outstanding Casting for Broken Trail.*

I actually believed I could and would. I am still in my basement suite, with my Emmy, but life is good. I am busy, paying off debt, got married Dec. 14, and 2008 is going to be the greatest year ever thanks to you helping me to believe and never give up.

Thanks again.

—JACKIE ROONEY, AKA JACKIE LIND, C.S.A.

Hello! My name is Katie Seitz from Dayton, Ohio. I am 24 years old and in my second year of teaching sixth grade English in a suburban district. Last summer, I read The Secret, *watched the DVD, gave both to my friends and family, read* The Attractor Factor, *and just finished reading* The Key. *You are brilliant and I thank you for your work. I am still working on getting clear and attracting my dreams and desires with my subconscious. The real reason I have been wanting to contact you is to simply tell you a story about my students.*

As I mentioned, this summer was a transformative time for me after reading so much about the Law of Attraction. I felt inspired to subtly teach my students about your ideas. My real belief is that we should overtly teach the principles to children and dramatically transform the future, but of course the state does not mandate such standards. Anyway, I clung to a certain quote of yours in The Attractor Factor: *"Turn it into something good." I decided to make TIISG a fundamental rule in my classroom. I made huge posters for each letter of TIISG and wrote the words of the saying on each letter. They are posted on the front wall of my classroom and incorporated into my classroom philosophy. My students write about times in which they TIISG, or, rather, a time in which they could have TIISG. They love it! The word "TIISG" is now a verb that might as well be in my classroom dictionary!*

The other day, I was upset during school because I am overloaded and overwhelmed right now. I am doing way too much with my time (coaching extracurricular activities, teaching Pilates after school, doing dance choreography, and so forth). The students saw me upset, and began saying sympathetically, "Miss Seitz, how can you TIISG?" The smile that spread across my face erased my worry! I hope you feel like smiling too, knowing that you are impacting students in Beavercreek, Ohio, with the work you have done! Have a great week!

Sincerely,

KATIE SEITZ

Dear Joe,

I have watched The Secret *a half dozen times and also have you as a friend on myspace.com. I had heard about* The Attractor Factor *a few months ago and didn't know you were the author. Well, for my reward and refuge, I decided that I was going to get under the covers with your book and start reading. I'm halfway through it, and love it!*

I see how I am creating everything around me. As I recognize these things, it is so helpful because I have the ability to change them—through the power of thoughts, words, and feelings! I am so excited!!!

It also hit me that I have had this unconscious view about money. My parents struggled and worked really hard to get to where they are today, which is owning a successful business that has helped them become millionaires. My husband and I are always struggling financially.

Guess what I realized? It is because I have this mind-set that the harder I work the more deserving I will be of that money. My parents always told me that you had to bust your butt to become wealthy. And I bust my butt daily. Now that I see it, I'm thinking, hey, this does not have to be so hard. I am deserving.

I'm a mystery author, and through visualization and feeling it over the years, I was able to sell six books in nine months to

The Penguin Publishing Group. They now want two more books from me, and I have an intention to sell a family saga to Simon & Schuster, a thriller that I am collaborating on with another author to S&S, and a paranormal adventure series to a major house. I also intend my advances to be in the seven figures!

Last month I was wondering how I could get my Wine Lover's Mystery Series on QVC, because I know it would be a good fit for that audience.

I did not know how to get in touch with anyone at QVC or how to go about it. I let the idea go. Last week, a friend of mine e-mailed me saying that she had gone to a marketing seminar where the woman was talking about how to get on QVC and she said that right now they are looking for products created by women for women. She immediately thought of me, and I hadn't even discussed my thoughts on QVC with her. I hadn't even spoken to her in over a month. She sent me the link and a submission form. Ha! I've applied and now am intending it to happen, and I have let it go.

I want to convey how grateful I am to you for making this information available. My dad told me that it was about time someone started making the type of information contained in The Secret *and in your book available in a way that would appeal to the masses. Thank you!*

Cheers,

Michele Scott

Joe, my name is Chris Mitchell. Ever since I was 7 years old it has been my dream to help, educate, and inspire others. I have always wanted to change the world somehow. I'm a motivational success coach who helps people become wealthy by building their own home-based businesses. However, my entire life was a struggle (just like yours) growing up.

At the age of 7 years old, I told my struggling, single mom that someday I was going to become rich and famous, and when I did, I promised that I would take care of her. She smiled and said, "Thank you, sweetie". Well, two years later, when I was 9, my mom died of cancer. My abusive father then regained custody of me and my younger brother Andy.

My dad abused me both verbally and physically growing up. I told him my dreams just like I had told my mother, but he yelled at me and told me I was insane and living in a fantasy world. He kicked me out of the house when I was 16. From the time I was 16 to the age of 28, I lived (bounced around) in all of the following states: Ohio, Tennessee, California, New Jersey, Indiana, and Illinois. I have spent time in a dirty motel in the ghetto with roaches in the bathtub, and even had nights where the only place I had to sleep was in my beat-up automobile.

No matter what I went through, I continued to think positively, and refused to give up. Over several years, I had finally started to become successful. I had worked my way up and had just bought a brand-new red sports car and moved into my own place in sunny California. However, what took me years to achieve, was practically destroyed overnight.

In March of 2007, my girlfriend and I were driving my car on I-80 in Indiana on our way to Ohio. Though we were driving 20 mph under the speed limit, it didn't matter when we hit a patch of black ice. Within seconds, our lives were on the line. By the time my car stopped spinning, it was demolished, with me and my girlfriend inside. The impact of the crash had crushed my girlfriend to the point where she was lying on my lap with the passenger car door lying on top of her.

To make a long story short, we were rushed to the hospital in South Bend, Indiana. I refused treatment so the doctors and paramedics could spend all of their time with my girlfriend Melissa who was in much worse shape than I was. After hours of X-rays, MRIs, and CAT scans, we were told that Melissa had broken every bone in her pelvis and bones in her lower back. The doctors said it was a miracle that she wasn't paralyzed. She and I both had tons of cuts, scrapes, bruises, glass in our skin, and blood clots throughout our bodies.

The doctors told us that it would probably be at least a year before Melissa would walk again, and when she did start walking, it would be with a walker. She was only 23 years old at the time. Though I have always tried to be positive throughout my life, I'll be honest, this incident in our lives had me depressed.

Once we finally left the hospital, we moved in with Melissa's mother to try to recover and get our lives back on track. I left Melissa at home one day (she was knocked out on painkillers) and decided to go to a bookstore. A book practically jumped out at me. It was called The Attractor Factor *by Joe Vitale. I read a few pages and decided to buy the book. I went home and read the entire book within a few hours.*

I took out some paper and started writing just as you had recommended in the book. I immediately put the five steps into daily use. As I write this testimonial to you (November 30, 2007), Melissa and I are both 100 percent recovered from the accident. Not only is Melissa walking without a walker, cane, or any assistance whatsoever, she is also running, jumping, and doing regular kickboxing classes at the gym.

I have now attracted almost everything that I have wrote down and visualized since reading your book: I have a lovely high-rise condo in the beautiful city of Chicago, I dine at the most expensive hotels and restaurants, my business is EXPLODING with new growth and successful business partners, and, I even attracted meeting you at The Learning Annex a few weeks ago. (You can see the photo of us at my web site: www.itstimetogetrich.com.)

So, I just wanted to send you this testimonial and let you know how much I have learned and put to good use from your life-changing book The Attractor Factor. *I HIGHLY encourage every person reading this to go out and buy* The Attractor Factor *ASAP! It changed my life.*

It was great meeting you in person. You are an amazing guy. I wish you nothing but continued health, wealth, love, and happiness Joe. God bless you!

Sincerely,   CHRIS MITCHELL

While reading this book, I had an absolute breakthrough. For the first time in my life I gave myself permission to earn money! You know how we have those issues that hold us back until somehow we find the way to give them up? Even after all the affirmations for financial freedom I've done over the years, I didn't realize how much I was holding myself back with all kinds of money issues. This book SET ME FREE! and ignited in me a passion for life that I haven't had in years!

—JEAN M. BREEN, WISCONSIN RAPIDS, WISCONSIN

I have been a student of success since the age of 17, when I read the entirety of The Law of Success, all 1,500+ pages. Always learning, but never quite "making it." Spiritual Marketing *was the final link in my chain of knowledge, and has helped me achieve everything I set out to do.*

—PAUL HOUSE, MIDDLESEX, NORTH CAROLINA

As an advertising executive for more than 15 years, I often see much time and effort spent on the content and placement of ads. Joe Vitale's Spiritual Marketing *reveals a key secret to making ads work. Joe discusses how your energy is in everything from your*

business cards to your ads. This is what people respond to more than layout or color. Joe's book shows how your own personal belief in what you are advertising and the energy you put into what you create are what make ads successful.

—JOHN LIVESAY, LOS ANGELES

As a physician, psychiatrist and Internet marketing expert, I know how important—no, how absolutely crucial—it is to develop a "millionaire marketing" mind-set. Until you do this, any external attempts at marketing, such as writing sales copy, will fall flat. The author explains in great detail what is really needed to consistently adopt this winning psychology. And it is a lot easier than you might think. I highly recommend this book to anyone who is SERIOUS about marketing any product or service to anyone.

—STEPHEN GILMAN, M.D., NEW YORK CITY

I used to wake each morning feeling physically exhausted, emotionally drained, and mentally fatigued. Then I read Spiritual Marketing. *Joe's formula has helped me clear away issues of childhood mental/physical/sexual abuse, teen drug/alcohol dependency, lifelong poverty, and the deep-seated belief that I was destined to fail.*

I am no longer a slave to negative beliefs. Just by reading the book, I have been able to dispose of a TON of baggage which was weighing me down.

—A READER FROM FARMINGTON, ARIZONA

Joe Vitale has written an excellent, clear, succinct, and inspirational mini-guide and road map to manifesting your dreams. I have to admit that I am a prosperity book and tape junkie. After 15 years of reading, taking classes, and listening to tapes, it's clear that the true path to prosperity must be spiritually based. Joe distills the spiritual wisdom of many masters for achieving one's dreams and brings them to life lucidly, powerfully. By sharing some of the skeletons in his closet (like shoplifting to be able to eat) and showing us how he was ultimately able to create what he wanted by using a simple, straightforward, five-step program, he makes our own dreams seem much more accessible and possible! He speaks as a regular guy (rather than, say, as some super-duper, seemingly successful, motivational guru who achieved meteoric success in a way that most of us just know we couldn't possibly replicate) who shares miracles achieved by himself and other ordinary people using a simple, but life-changing plan. That is what makes this book so valuable. Joe truly speaks from his heart—his integrity and honesty ring throughout the text. I'm on my second reading of it—and I know this won't be my last reading of it.

—LAURA V. RODRIGUEZ, SILVER SPRING, MARYLAND

In the past 15 years I've read more than 150 books in the fields of spirituality, self-improvement, getting rich, and so on. Many of those books were very good and they helped me get on the right path to what I wanted to do with my life. But it wasn't until reading Spiritual Marketing *that I realized what was holding me back from living the life of my dreams.*

That missing key was in the chapter "Get Clear." I realized that my subconscious beliefs were holding me back. That I could not proceed with my visualizations until all of me was in agreement on going after my goal.

—ROGER HAESKE, SOUTH RIVER, NEW JERSEY

I live within 10 minutes of one of the world's largest metaphysical libraries, so I don't lack for anything to read. I've read Joe's book twice. I've sent people to Amazon.com to buy it, and I've purchased it to give away to friends and clients. I believe it is a blessing. Spiritual Marketing *is a must-read for anyone who wants to learn how to manifest what they desire in their lives. What sets Joe's book apart from so many that I've read is that he shows you how he found people who could heal, coach, and otherwise truly empower him to change his beliefs so that he was able change his outer reality.*

—Ann Harcus, USA

And here are some true stories of people who used the five steps you are about to learn to achieve miracles:

I first read Spiritual Marketing *with the ulterior motive of using it to gain prospects for my network marketing company, like one of my mentors had done.*

But as I read, I changed! I finally got it—after years of reading self-help books and taking seminar after seminar, I'd finally found something that was different. (And I had even unsuccessfully used affirmations at the beginning of one of my seminars to force it to be different!)

After reading Spiritual Marketing, *I was inspired to be the guinea pig on a teleconference with Mandy Evans, after which I quit the company I had just joined because at last I knew it was not in line with my values. Taking jobs like that had contributed to keeping me stuck, moving through 5 companies in the last 12 years, which left me open to the Universe for greater opportunities.*

When Joe released The Greatest Money-Making Secret in History!, *I was very excited and bought 10 copies just to get all the bonus goodies. I read the online PDF version that very day and was inspired to have a "Free Yard Sale." I gathered all the extra books I had collected and had considered selling on eBay, and GAVE them away to whomever wanted them at The Greatest Networker in the World web site, which is where I had first been introduced to Joe. The bulk of these books were brand-new* Network Marketing *book-and-tape sets, which sell for $45. But again, I was not completely without ulterior motive!*

When the first orders for books came in I realized I hadn't mentioned postage, and though money was tight I decided to pay for shipping too, even though some of the takers had offered to pay for the shipping. I purposely went to the drugstore where they have a postal center and gaming. I thought that I could use my good karma points with the gambling gods to win some money. I had planned exactly in my mind before I got there which machine, which denomination, which game, and what the result would be. I mailed my packages and went to play.

I chose everything according to my plan and with my first $20 I hit the Royal—$800! I had won before, even much higher amounts, but something about the way it had happened exactly how I had seen it in my mind was extra exciting, freaky, and the key to my present happiness in life . . . because the best thing that could have happened—something that you might think was the worst—occurred next.

Over the next six or so hours I lost all $800, plus whatever I had walked in with. Why is that good? Because I am a compulsive gambler. Even though I had logically argued that you couldn't use Spiritual Marketing *to win at gambling, that experience woke me up from my addicted thinking. A few days later, on June 15, 2003, I entered Gamblers Anonymous and have chosen to not place a bet since. (As a side note, joining GA fulfilled my affirmation, "I attract exceptional people to my reality who fully commit to partnering with me for our mutual benefit.") And according to my casino win/loss statements, which measure how much money you put through the machines, I was averaging $200,000 a year, plus time away from work, my husband, and a real life.*

So the coolest part of this all is that I am truly detached from whether or not my having written this essay gets me to the Summit. Part of who I am is that I waffle over decisions, which leaves it up to the Universe!

There's a huge amount more to this story, highlights of which are:

- *How I planned to partner with Joe and how it happened without my knowing it.*
- *Why* Adventures Within *is the last self-help book I'll ever have to read.*
- *Would Barnum have worn the tiara?*

But since I'm already over my 500 words, I'll have to tell you the rest in person at the Summit!

Be happy!

—Christy Hoffman

Sunday morning, May 23, 2004, I decided to read Spiritual Marketing *again. This is about the fifth time I have read it. Every time I read it, I discover something I'd not noticed before. Lately, I have not been enjoying the business I started eight years ago. I think it is time to move on to something I want to do more. I am not a maintainer. I am a creator.*

I considered keeping the business and letting someone else run it for me, but this did not feel right. After reviewing the five steps again, I made a list of my wants. I then made a "movie" of the day I sell the business. I went into my "dream" state, and played it over and over. I felt the freedom from the responsibility and the joy of having a Saturday off to spend with my husband. It was such a pleasant dream.

I was jolted back to the present by the phone ringing. I wondered who would be calling me so early on Sunday morning. It was a friend of mine. After we exchanged pleasantries, he said he would like to give my name to a friend of his who might be interested in buying my business. I said that would be fine. Five minutes after we hung up, the phone rang again. This time it was the guy who is interested in the business. We are going to meet sometime next week. I do not know if he will be the one to actually buy it, but I could have never thought of him, because I have never met him. WOW! That was fast!

I have been on this path for a long time, but the principles in the Spiritual Marketing *book are so simple to follow. The letting go is what makes it happen. I have miracles all the time, too, Joe. This is just the most recent one!*

—BECKY HUTCHENS

My dear friend Bill Hibbler wrote:

I'll never forget how much of a role Spiritual Marketing *played in my life. I'd ordered the book in August of 2001 but it wasn't until just after 9/11 that I began to do the exercises outlined in it.*

After nearly 25 years in the music business, I decided that it was time to try something new. I enjoyed teaching and also had a couple of book ideas, but needed to do something to keep money coming in while writing them.

I joined a friend of mine's limo service and started chauffeuring corporate executives to and from Houston's airports in a leased luxury sedan. It was quite a change to go from riding in the back of limos to driving one, but it did provide me with a steady income and lots of time to write using my laptop.

I developed a fascination with marketing, which led me to discover your Nightingale-Conant tape program, The Power of Outrageous Marketing. *I found many great ideas in those tapes, and* Turbocharge Your Writing, *a book included in the package, helped me immensely in writing my first book.*

The limo business wasn't doing well in 2001. The slowdown in the economy was hurting business and I'd racked up a huge amount of credit card debt. I was barely keeping my head above water and decided that the only way out was to sell my house, pay off my debts, and find a way to do writing and marketing full-time.

I devised a plan where I would drive seven days a week, putting as much cash together as possible. Then I'd put my house up for sale in the spring of 2002. Just as I was about to implement my plan, 9/11 hit.

I watched the news in horror, just like the rest of the world. Besides dealing with the tragedy itself, I was suddenly out of work. With flights grounded, we had no customers. Yet I still had a huge lease payment on my Lincoln as well as the expensive commercial insurance payments. There was no way to cover those bills. So I lost my job and my car and was in a whole lot of trouble.

I had excellent credit up to this point and probably had a dozen credit cards. Suddenly, my phone was ringing non-stop from creditors as my payment-due dates came and went. On top of that, I had a relationship that was ending badly, I suddenly had high blood sugar, and was having problems with my eyesight.

At this point, I became willing to try almost anything. I picked up Spiritual Marketing *and started working the five steps. I became clear on what I wanted to have in my life and put that in writing. I stated that I wanted to move to Wimberley, Texas, a relaxed, beautiful little town near Austin.*

I also asked for a healthy, positive, loving relationship with an attractive girl with wit and intelligence. I wanted to be in a place where I could continue to expand my knowledge of marketing and make a living from my writing. And I wanted to be debt-free and to have a new car that was paid for. It was a tall order, given my situation. Remember, I didn't have a job or even a car at this point.

I hit my knees that day and used the script in the book to ask for help. Within 48 hours, a friend I hadn't spoken to in some time phoned. I explained my situation. She told me that because she'd recently gotten a company car, I was welcome to borrow her personal car for as long as I needed it. She was happy to know the car would be in my locked garage every night rather than her apartment parking lot.

Now I had wheels. The next day, another friend called and offered me a temporary part-time job that would pay enough to keep me afloat for a while. I also had someone call me out of the blue and ask me if I was free to do some copywriting for a web site project.

I was absolutely floored by such immediate results. I followed the simple steps in Spiritual Marketing *and got exactly what I needed.*

That wasn't all. My physical situation changed as well. The new glasses I'd bought became totally unnecessary. I saw my blood sugar go from 245 to 165 in one month without medication. My doctor was shocked.

The next step was to put my house on the market but it was a bad time to sell. I was advised to wait at least until the spring buying season when, hopefully, the economy would recover a bit. I couldn't wait, though, and put my house on the market. Within a very short time, I not only sold it but got $25,000 more than I expected!

While all this was happening, I was getting a few copywriting jobs. One was for, of all things, a dating service in Russia. The company assigned one of their employees who was fluent in English as my liaison on the project.

Her name was Elena and there were immediate sparks between us. The more I got to know her, the more I fell for her. I'd had so many bad relationships that I'd almost given up hope of ever finding the right person but my Lena made all that a distant memory. She is everything I could possibly ask for and more. I've never met a person that is so loving and supportive.

Less than five months after 9/11, I moved to Wimberley. Wild deer roam the streets in my neighborhood. I live on a golf course with rivers and creeks all around. The community is filled with artists, musicians, and entrepreneurs.

I arrived in my brand-new Toyota Rav4, which I paid cash for. My office is exactly nine steps from my bedroom. It is stocked with all the latest computer gear and a huge marketing library. The credit card debt is long gone.

Internet marketing is now my full-time occupation. With more than a dozen web sites including RudlReport.com and Ecommerce-Confidential.com, I now get to help others achieve their dreams of making a living online, just like I have. And, best of all, Elena and I were married on September 8, 2002.

I now have a mastermind group of close friends that meets once a week to discuss business ideas and provide support. One of those dear friends is Joe Vitale, whose words led to the realization of so many of my dreams.

Looking back over the original wish list I wrote when doing Joe's five steps, the only things I haven't achieved are goals I decided I didn't want after all. I have my higher power to thank for that, but I probably would never have thought to ask for what I wanted had it not been for Spiritual Marketing. *The techniques in Joe's book definitely worked miracles for me.*

Now read about a car lover like myself, who created her new set of wheels:

There so many great things happening in my life since reading and applying your five-step proven formula.

Just to share one great BIG miracle that resulted from following your formula—in the summer of 2003, when your book came into my hands, I was at a place of disgust with my life and wanted desperately to change.

I had a dream car in my mind, and being a lover of Maximas I wanted the new 2004, blue, fully-loaded, black-leather, sun-roofed Nissan Maxima.

I immediately started to apply your steps: Wrote down what I wanted in detail, felt it, cleared it, and let go.

At the time my credit was not so hot and I didn't know how I might pay for my new car. But I didn't let that stop my dream. Every time I felt fear popping up its ugly head, I'd say the clearing prayer and thank God for my blessings and my new car.

Two months later my income increased, I got $5,000 off the price of the car, and I am cruising and sporting around in my new dream car with a BIG, BIG smile on my face, and the sun kisses me through the sunroof! Thank you, Joe Vitale, for sharing your story and results throughout your book, Spiritual Marketing!!!

—MISSI WORCESTER, WWW.THEHEALTHYSHOP.COM

This writer found the escalator to a publisher and bookstores:

My aim was to sell one or more of my books to a big publisher.

Step 1. Don't want—What I did not want was to have to send out lots of proposals and make it a struggle. Did not want to wait an eternity. Did not want to get lost in the shuffle at the publishers. Did not want it dropped after 30 days.

Step 2. Do want—What I did want was a publisher with integrity who could give the book the exposure it deserved in the bookstores. I wanted it to be easy, to just flow. I wanted a decent advance and some marketing behind it. I wanted someone who would stay with the book over time.

Step 3. Get clear—I wanted this because it's a great little book and I wanted it to be made more widely available. I wanted to help more people, sell more books, make more money, and have more fun. I wanted to be aligned with a prestige publisher. I wanted mass distribution.

Step 4. Feelings—I wanted to feel like a recognized author: successful, appreciated, excited at having a big publisher handling my books. I wanted to feel special, like I had "arrived."

Step 5. Let go as you take inspired action—My inspired actions included sending three faxes to publishers with a subtle challenge: "I've sold a bunch of books, but maybe a publisher like you could do more . . ."

The really, really cool thing was that in searching the Web for acquisition editors, I ran across a woman who had liked the book in 1996 when she was at another publisher (coincidence?). Her boss and I did not see eye-to-eye then, so it never happened. She had moved to a better publisher, and sold the book for me in-house. This process required absolutely no effort on my part unless you count the three faxes. It all happened in a blink. I met the publisher at BEA in New York, and we shook hands.

The new, enhanced, revised edition of Handbook to a Happier Life *was out less than 10 months later and on every bookshelf in the nation. A record in publishing circles. The German edition came out this year.*

Be well and God bless,

—JIM DONOVAN, AUTHOR & COACH, WWW.JIMDONOVAN.COM
AND WWW.THEBOOKCOACH.COM.

My journey began about two years ago when I read Spiritual
Marketing *for the first time. Your writing spoke very clearly to me,
and at times I did take the information and put it to good use.*

*About one year later, I eagerly started putting what I had learned
from your book into action. Since then, my life has taken off!*

*I am now at the point where I frequently skip Step One (Know
What You Don't Want) and jump right into Select What You Would
Like to Have, Do or Be.*

*The first year of "playing" with the five steps was exactly what
I needed. I learned better how to get clear, get into the feeling, and
most of all let go.*

*Within this last year I have found my true abundance. I now
create many incredible and exciting things in my life, including
a vacation to Hawaii, numerous workshops, meeting mentors in
person, and even partnering with some of them on projects. I've
created my own teleseminar series on abundance, and opportunities are literally appearing right before my eyes!*

*By getting clear and letting go I have opened myself to opportu-
nities and experiences that my ego could never have dreamed up.
Thank you, Joe. You've helped me to change my own life, and I am
eternally grateful to you. Your friend always,*

VELMA GALLANT
ABUNDANCE COACH, WWW.WELCOMECHANGES.COM

Here's a note from the other side of the world:

Mr. Joe,

*Actually I wanted to send you a thank-you letter for what you
have done to me, and how my life is taking a turn for the better (understatement), but you have asked us anyway about how*
Spiritual Marketing *has affected us.*

What Spiritual Marketing *has done for me is it has saved my life. I was going down pretty fast. Absolutely nothing was working in my favor. I was jobless for the last three years. The entire world was closing in on me. Everyone, including my parents and friends, had deserted me because I was not able to conform to the norms of society and provide for them the way they wanted. I believed that I was totally alone and on my own, and I had nowhere to go.*

In these desperate conditions I found the online version of Spiritual Marketing, *and life was never the same after that. Now I have a lot of job offers, my finances are strong. My future looks bright, and I am on my way to restoring my relationships with my family and friends.*

I am currently living in Karachi, Pakistan. Being in this part of the world is totally different. I lived in the United States for five and a half years, and graduated from the University of Kansas, so I can relate to that as well. But the biggest challenge for me is that life is a whole lot different here. There is so much negativity in society that it is not easy for one to remain positive and follow the five-step plan, especially the clearing part. I can see myself moving up, but I also have to struggle somewhat, due to the environment I am in. I am trying my best, though.

I also get a lot of help through the e-zines of Carol Tuttle and through TUT, which I also got to know from you. I also have read The Power of Your Subconscious Mind *by Dr. Joe Murphy. Also, Mr. Vitale, if you know someone over here in Karachi who can help me with this, I will really appreciate it. Actually, I am not aware of anyone who is practicing these concepts here in Karachi.*

I have plans to get as much stuff from you as possible since I am also interested in Internet marketing. I know your time is precious, but I also have to say what I wanted to. I cannot thank you enough for what you and your book have done for me and count-less others. Thank you for showing me "the other world."

—FAISAL IQBAL

This writer wanted—and got—something "amazing":

A few months back I went to see The Amazing Kreskin. I had seen him before and was impressed, but he had never called on me to read my thoughts.

That, to me, would be a convincer about the power of the mind. So this time, I set my intention beforehand that I was going to be picked, and he was going to convince me that this stuff works.

The drive was about an hour and a half long, so I planned extra time.

Well, on the way, there was a traffic accident that ate up more than my allotted time.

I was getting very nervous about making the show. I kept the intention first, even though my doubts were rushing in. When I arrived, the parking lot of the casino was packed. I tried valet parking and it had almost a half-hour wait.

I was now late.

I yelled a few times to relieve the tension, and kept my intention. I finally parked about a quarter mile away and ran to the show, which had started 10 minutes earlier.

I got the best seat that was still available. It was up front, which met another intention I had.

As I relaxed and got into the show, Kreskin asked us to think of three different things. Since I was at MrFire.com just before I left for the show, I pictured the web site with the flames and Joe's face, then I thought of my favorite colors and a snowman. I set my intentions, while keeping the images before my mind.

Within a short time, Kreskin blasted out, "Who is Mr. Fire?"

I stood up in front of 1,000 people, and he asked me if I was Mr. Fire. I said no. He wanted to know who he was, so I told him it was Joe Vitale's web site address. Then he asked why he was seeing blue and green, my favorite colors. Then he said he saw a snowman.

Wow, was I amazed!

After the show was over I met him and got a picture with him, another intention I had.

As Kreskin headed into the crowd of the casino, I was about 20 to 30 yards away, and I said to myself, I gotta try one more thing to totally convince me this is real.

I set my intention for him to turn around and wave to me. He was talking to someone while walking away, and then he just stopped and started to look around like someone was calling his name, and I was. In my head, I was yelling it. Finally, he turned right toward me and looked. We both started waving at the same time.

I am convinced this principle works, amazingly!!!!

Thanks,

Mark Ryan

This writer used the principles to make a difference in Istanbul:

Hi Joe,

Your www.IntentionalMeditationFoundation.com [explained in the last chapter of this book] is sheer genius!

When I read it I mentally ran through this checklist. It's one David Ogilvy devised:

1. Did it make me *gasp* when I first saw it? You bet!

2. Do I *wish* that I had thought of it myself? Yes, I do. On the other hand, I didn't, and I admire you for coming up with it!

3. Is it *unique*? It certainly IS a unique spin, and as Dan Kennedy says when someone declares they have a unique idea: "I've got five of them in the office." Well done!

4. Does it *fit* the strategy to perfection? Absolutely!

5. Could it be used for *30 years*? It will outlast both of us. It will change the world. It's changed me already!

So, I want to represent your idea here in Istanbul. Indeed, I want to start these groups wherever my feet touch the ground.

You've touched me, bless you!

And yes, indeed, I have already used the principles outlined in Spiritual Marketing *in the following ways:*

1. When my bank seemed impersonal, I used the principles to start a community of small-business customers, and got the bank to fund it!

2. When family therapy in Turkey was understood by only an elite few, while others were crying out for skills, I set up a recognized training for public service workers.

3. When a group of volunteers working with survivors of the 1999 earthquake "lost themselves" a few years down the line, I used the principles to help them tell their stories in a book published by the Turkish Psychological Association.

Details of all these accomplishments are available at www.quiet quality.com.

But they don't compare to your accomplishments.

Joe, in my home town there was a really nice man called Mr. Parker who delivered kerosene door to door. I think you once had a similar job, and look at you now.

Mr. Parker delivered oil for the whole of his life, and his business died with him.

You provide the oil for all of our heaters and will be blessed forever. Those Spiritual Marketing *principles are great, Joe. They are so much more than you or I. You articulate them clearly and lovingly so we all benefit.*

Please keep me posted on this one.

Truly yours,

STEPHEN BRAY

A people-pleaser sets her real self free, using my five-step process:

My biggest struggle has always been with pursuing my own goals instead of other people's plans for me. I yearned to live my own life, but I couldn't see how to achieve anything worthwhile.

Nevertheless, I worked through Joe's formula in Spiritual Marketing, *not expecting anything much. I love all of Joe Vitale's work, and believed he wouldn't give me anything that wasn't helpful. I did every exercise. The letting go part was easy. I had no time to pay much attention to what I wanted to do anyway. Then strange things began to happen. Choices came at me that I didn't want to miss, and so another struggle erupted . . . my will against other people's plans for my time and money.*

As Joe says, the hardest thing is to believe you don't have to do anything to figure out how to achieve your goals, so I committed to following his formula, faithfully, secretly. Another dream, another formula session! After a while, thinking like this became second nature to me. Does the formula work? Our family has created a very successful Internet business that helps many people with health issues. This is truly using my special talents in a very rewarding way!

Spiritual Marketing is practical. It helped me focus. It built up my confidence. Once I actually applied this formula and started to get my own results, it became one of my foundational tools. Now new projects are anticipated and welcomed, not feared or rejected.

Even now, when I know and believe without any doubt, I use the formula and my answer appears! Spiritual Marketing *helps you find and focus on your inner strengths. It is really fun to watch your life grow the way you want it to. Because of my success, I quickly committed to using it consistently in all areas of my life.*

Joe's many examples start your creative juices flowing. They give you ideas that might work in your own situation. Although the book is relatively short, the formula is repeated with each step. It is so much fun, KNOWING you will be successful! KNOWING you can achieve your dreams without a lot of effort. I knew there was more to me than just my physical being, but I had no idea how to find the REAL me. Here I am!

Joe, I know your book will change many more lives just like mine. Thank you for your courage and your formula.

—KARIN HENDERSON WWW.MENIERES-DISEASE.CA

Still skeptical? Listen to this story:

Situation/Background
There were two people whom I had lost touch with over the years who I had been thinking about. These two individuals did not know each other, but they were both old friends of mine. One was a guy I had gone to high school with, and the other was someone I met during my first experience with cancer in 1993. (He had the same type of lymphoma that I had, and he had apparently beaten the disease.) The last time that I had seen my high school friend was in 1993, at our 10-year high school reunion. Coincidentally, 1993 was also the last time I had seen my cancer survivor friend.

In late 1993, I moved to Austin, got married, and started working at Dell Computer Corporation. The winds of change had already begun blowing the three of us in different directions.

Fast-forward nine years to 2002. For whatever reason, I was spending a lot of time thinking about my old friends and sincerely wanting to reestablish contact with them. Thinking of myself as an experienced Internet detective, I used all available Web resources to track down these two guys. Despite my consistent efforts over a three-week period, I had absolutely no success. At first I was annoyed, then frustrated, and finally, I became a little worried. Whenever I meet disappointment, I know that my old friend "Mr. Fear" is not far behind.

I began to imagine all sorts of bad things had happened to my old friends. Perhaps my high school buddy had decided to accept another assignment in the Middle East and had met with some grisly fate in our post-9/11 world. Or perhaps my friend who was a cancer survivor had a recurrence of the disease and had succumbed to it. After all, I had my cancer come back to haunt me six years after the first incident, and we both had the same type of lymphoma. If I got cancer again and almost died the second time around, maybe he got it again and did die.

You can probably see where this is going. Stray thoughts left to graze on their own without the watchful eye of a shepherd invariably wander off in any number of directions, and sometimes fall off a cliff of fear. It wasn't long before I had reached the obvious conclusion that both of my friends were dead—one at the hands of terrorists in the Middle East, and the other as a result of a fatal recurrence of cancer. Of course, following that logic meant that I would soon be dead, too. Cancer was probably scheduling a third visit with me to finish the job. What a happy train of thought, huh?

Okay, so now it's late 2002, and I'm working in downtown Austin for the government. As I have little or no patience for traffic, I commute to and from work by bus. This provided the added benefit of giving me time to read books and listen to audio programs on the way to work and on the way home. One of those books was Spiritual Marketing.

I enjoyed the apparent simplicity of the five-step process. I was growing tired of my mental funk, and I decided to use the current gloomy scenario as a test drive of the Vitale method. In all honesty, I was just playing around. I didn't really take it seriously. I just followed the steps with no emotional attachment, partly because I was bored and partly because I wasn't sure it would work. Maybe that's why it did work—instantly.

I ran through the steps on the bus ride home.

The Process in Action

Step 1: *Know What You Don't Want*

That's easy. I don't want to think of both of my friends being dead.

Step 2: *Know What You Do Want*

I either want my old friends to get in touch with me or for me to find a way to locate and contact my old friends.

Step 3: *Get Clear*

My intention was simple and clear. I desired to be able to chat with my old friends as if we had never lost touch. I focused on that objective and erased all errant thoughts from my mind.

Step 4: *Feel Your Intention Already Achieved*

I imagined myself holding my cordless phone, pacing around my house as I always do on the phone, and talking with my two friends.

Step 5: *Let Go*

That was easy, too (this time). My bus had just arrived at the Park-and-Ride lot. I had no choice but to let go because I needed to focus my attention on driving home from the bus stop in rush-hour traffic. I completely forgot about the exercise during the 15-minute drive to my house.

The Results

As I pulled into my garage, my thoughts switched automatically to all of the things that I had to do that evening. I was about to go on my annual vacation and pilgrimage to Las Vegas, the Mecca of the western world. I had to get packed and prepare for my trip the next day. As I walked into my house, I wandered over to the answering machine. I had three messages. The first was from my mother. She indicated that she was on her way to Austin and would be arriving soon to house-sit and take care of the dogs.

The other two messages really shocked me. One was from my friend who was the cancer survivor, and the second was from my high school buddy. I was blown away. I had chased what I wanted for three weeks to no avail, and suddenly what I wanted had decided to chase me instead! Using an obscure technique that I had just read and then applied in a half-assed manner, two friends whom I had not heard from in nine years both *called me on the same day!*

I called my friend who is a fellow cancer veteran first. We exchanged contact information and made arrangements to get together the following month. It turns out that he had been living in Indonesia and was now back in Houston. While I was searching for him, he had also been searching for me. He did a Google search with my name, and stumbled upon several news articles describing the success of our latest project, Ticker Tape Toilet Paper. The articles mentioned that I was a former employee of Dell Computer in Austin, Texas. He then called directory assistance, got my number, and left the message.

As an added benefit, it turned out that he had left his former employer and was now a patent attorney, and I was looking for a new patent attorney. We have been doing business together ever since.

I then called my high school buddy. We traded cell phone numbers and swapped stories for a few minutes. He had been moving around a lot in recent years on different jobs, which is why I had no success in finding him with my Internet tools. The weird thing was that he mentioned that he was headed to Las Vegas that weekend and was staying at the Stardust Hotel. I replied that I was leaving for Las Vegas the next day and was staying at the Bellagio Hotel. Two guys who had not seen each other in nine years were going to be in a distant city at the same time. Pretty cool!

We made plans to meet for a drink one evening at one of the casinos that we both liked to frequent. And we did just that. It was great!

In conclusion, all I can say is that I was in awe of the process. Anyone who knows me will testify that I am a born skeptic. I am open-minded enough to try anything once, but if it doesn't deliver the promised benefits, you had better get out of my face because I won't be back for a second try.

This process is simple, but you have to have the discipline to use it. Even though I know it works, I must admit that I am sometimes too lazy or too egotistical to accept its gifts. That's my fault, not the fault of the process. It only works if you do.

—John Zappa

And that's just *some* of the proof that the Attractor Factor works.

Now let's get to work creating your own testimonial.

But first . . .

CHAPTER 6

What Are You Dismissing?

I had lunch with a dear friend the other day. Although I enjoyed the company and the food, I left feeling a little lower in energy.

When I thought about it, I realized my friend was brilliant at dismissing every book, concept, guru, self-help method, or healing approach he had read or heard about.

He was not directly negative or purposely critical. He sincerely wanted something that would work in his life. But he was unconsciously dismissing everything that came his way.

At one point I told him about a spiritual teacher I had studied with over two decades ago. I told him that people said, "Your teacher was obviously enlightened. He radiated it."

My friend cut in saying, "I'm sure there are people who saw that guru and didn't think he was any smarter than a paper bag."

Well, my friend is right.

But my friend is also unhappy.

I think there's a lesson here. When we dismiss people and ideas because the entire world doesn't agree with them, we get to be right. But we also get to stay empty inside. By dismissing what could work, we dismiss our own growth. We dismiss what's possible.

It doesn't matter if the book you read and love is loved by anyone else. It doesn't matter if the teacher you admire is admired by anyone else. It doesn't matter if the healing method that worked for you doesn't work for everyone else.

What matters is you. Your happiness. Your health. Your healing. Your well-being.

The truth is, no method works for everyone. No teacher is right for everyone. No book is going to inspire everyone.

It all comes from within. You are the first and final authority on your life.

Rather than dismissing what is possible so that you can be right, what can you accept so that you can grow?

Dismissing is often a way to deflect the messages. It's a self-defense mechanism. If you dismiss the book, idea, or method offered to you, you get to be right—and stay right where you are.

Dr. Richard Gillett, writing in his wonderful book, *Change Your Mind, Change Your World*, states, "Disapproval is, surprisingly, the most reliable indication of a hidden belief system. Quite often the only way disguised beliefs show themselves is through moments of emotional judgment or disapproval."

All the successful people I know have accepted new tools into their lives over the years, spent thousands of dollars on personal growth and self-study, and never regretted any of it.

The key is not dismissing, or disapproving, but *digesting*.

For example, Nerissa and I had dinner with friends recently. One friend was complaining about her job. From her perspective, there was no way out of the misery she felt at her place of work. Bad boss. Bad hours. Bad pay. You name it, it was bad.

Later, we were joined by other friends. As chance would have it, one of the new friends had connections where our complaining friend worked. He gave our unhappy friend a name, and said he could help her resolve her issues. He went on to say that this connection was a supervisor, head of many departments, and could probably resolve whatever was wrong.

I was stunned. So was Nerissa. We were seeing magic happen right before our eyes.

But what did our unhappy friend do with her new lead and new hope?

She dismissed it.

She didn't write down the name or the number, or show any signs that something wonderful had just occurred.

Do you see how this works?

Sometimes we can self-sabotage the things we say we want. We simply dismiss the good.

People often write and ask me what one single product can they get that will transform their lives. When I tell them I so loved Dr. Robert Anthony's material that I financed, recorded, and now market his *Beyond Positive Thinking* CD set, they are sold. They go to www.BeyondPositiveThinking.com and buy it. Or I may tell them about my latest audio-program, *The Missing Secret,* which explains the practical use of the Law of Attraction. And I tell them it is listed at www.nightingale.com.

Yet some people complain, "It costs $99." Ah, of course it costs money. And that's incredibly low for a studio-quality life-changing set of six audios. Are you going to pay it and get what you want, or are you going to dismiss the greatest self-help material of all time? Do you want the good you say you seek, or don't you?

Let me end this with another example.

Yesterday I received a letter in the mail about a new audio-program about dissolving illusions. I read the piece but dismissed it. I figured it was simply stuff I had already heard before and probably even recorded elsewhere myself.

Then today, I got another mailing. This time it was from a different source, but selling the exact same audio-program. I read it over closely. I thought, "This is interesting, but I bet there's little new in it." I then placed the mailing aside.

An hour or so later, as I was reviewing this very chapter you're reading right now, I suddenly realized that I was doing the very thing I am warning you not to do: I was dismissing an opportunity to learn.

I dug out the mailing, filled out the order form, and dropped it in the mail. The audios are on the way.

The point is not that you buy everything that comes your way but that you don't dismiss everything that comes your way. Sometimes a dismissal is a mask. It's your self-sabotage at work, keeping you where you're at. To grow, you must be open.

Again, you are the final authority on your life. Tune in to yourself and do what's right for you. And as you do this, be alert to those times when you may be dismissing the next gift to come your way.

Let your guard down, and let life in.

In the space below, write down things that may be trying to get your attention, which you may have been dismissing. This is simply to help you become aware of a pattern:

_____

_____

_____

_____

_____

_____

_____

_____

_____

_____

_____

> If we don't like what's happening to us in the world, all we have to do is change our consciousness—and the world out there changes for us!
>
> —LESTER LEVENSON, *KEYS TO THE ULTIMATE FREEDOM*, 1993

CHAPTER 7

How to Attract Money

"What do you do?" I asked.

I was standing in a line of 700 people in a hotel in Seattle, waiting to spend a day listening to an author and spiritual teacher.

"I do energy work," the woman beside me replied. "It's hard to explain. It's different for each person."

"Do you have a business card?"

"No," she said, slightly embarrassed.

I was shocked.

"Let me ask you a question," I began. "There are over 700 potential clients here for you. Why don't you at least have business cards?"

A woman beside her smiled and told her, "You were just hit by an angel."

I'm not an angel. But I was curious why this businesswoman was missing a huge marketing opportunity. As I talked to a few more of the 700 people at this event, I realized all of these people were in business for themselves. And they all needed help in marketing themselves.

That's when it dawned on me that I could write a concise handbook on spiritually based manifesting. No one else seemed better qualified. I'm the author of *The AMA Complete Guide to Small Business Advertising* for The American Marketing Association. I've advised PBS television and The Red Cross. And I have over 25 years of experience in metaphysics and spirituality, including a doctorate in metaphysical science. I've also interviewed many self-help spokespeople and have had some of them as my clients. Besides, I had already created and tested a secret five-step process for attracting anything you wanted.

I also knew that those 700 people at the seminar represented a still larger group of people who need help with their businesses, and with their lives. I further knew that they were all doing something inside themselves that was creating their outer results. In other words, their inner state of being was creating their business, or lack of it.

Put more simply, the woman who didn't have a business card had an inner insecurity about her business that showed up in her life by her not having business cards. Her Attractor Factor was attracting no business.

And taking this logic a step further in the direction I want to take you later in this book, if that woman were truly clear about her business, she might not even need business cards. Business would just come to her. Her inner spirit—her Attractor Factor—would do her marketing.

That's what this book will reveal. I've learned that we are human beings, not human doings. When you reach a clear inner state of being about your service to the world, the world will almost come to you. When you are clear about the car, person, house, job, or anything that you want, you will start to attract those things to you.

As one successful person said, "Angels now hand out my business cards."

Confused? That's okay. Therapist, author, and friend Mandy Evans says, "Confusion is that wonderful state of mind right before clarity."

Fundamentals of Prosperity

Maybe the following story will give you a glimpse of what I'm talking about and set the stage for what is to follow:

I once read a delightful old book from 1920 entitled *Fundamentals of Prosperity* by Roger Babson. He ended his book by asking the president of the Argentine Republic why South America, with all of its natural resources and wonders, was so far behind North America in terms of progress and marketing.

The president replied: "I have come to this conclusion. South America was settled by the Spanish who came to South America in search of gold, but North America was settled by the Pilgrim fathers who went there in search of God."

Where is your focus?

On money or on spirit?

On the goals you want or on the spirit that brings them?

Truth is, money is just a symbol. If you focus on the energy it represents, you will attract it.

How to Become a Millionaire

Years ago, Scrully Blotnick allegedly conducted a study of 1,500 people. They were put into two categories: Category A said they would pursue money first and do what they really wanted to do later. Over 1,245 people went into that group. The 255 people in Category B said they would seek their interests first, and trust that money would follow later.

What happened?

Twenty years later, there were 101 millionaires from the entire group. Only one came from group A. The remaining 100 millionaires all came from group B, the group that said they would pursue their passions first and let money come later. Right there is another clue about how to attract money.

Where is your focus—on money or passion?

Welcome to the Attractor Factor

In this book, I offer a new way for you to easily and effortlessly do almost anything you can imagine—increase your business, find your love, improve your health, attract more money, and so forth. It's based on timeless spiritual principles.

It will reveal how your inner state of being attracts and creates your outer results—and what to do about it so that you can have, do, or be whatever your heart desires. I call it the Attractor Factor. It is truly a spiritual formula for success that never fails.

Do the techniques work? The proof will be in the pudding. Try them and see. I can tell you about the successes I've had—and I do in this book—but nothing will be quite as convincing to you as using these simple ideas and seeing your own amazing results.

I could tell you that this method will help you manifest anything you want. You'll read about people who attracted cars and homes, healed themselves of cancer, created new relationships, and attracted more money. But I'm focusing on attracting wealth in business because there appears to be a serious lack of spirituality in business. And I'm going to let you discover the magic of marketing with spirit because nothing will be more powerful than your own firsthand experiences.

Pull up a chair. Get comfortable. Take a deep breath. Relax. Let's talk about how you can increase your wealth—and achieve anything else you may desire—through the magic power of the Attractor Factor.

It all begins with understanding that your life . . .

Spirit: That which is traditionally believed to be the vital principle or animating force within living beings.

Spiritual: Of, relating to, consisting of, or having the nature of spirit, not tangible or material.

—AMERICAN HERITAGE DICTIONARY
(BOSTON: HOUGHTON MIFFLIN, 1980).

CHAPTER 8

It Can Be Another Way

Before I became a marketing specialist and author, I was an inner-world journalist for over 10 years, writing for several leading-edge magazines. As a result, I've seen miracles with my own eyes. For example:

- I interviewed Meir Schneider, a man who was diagnosed as blind. He was given a certificate saying he was incurably blind, and yet today he sees, he reads, he writes, he drives a car—and he has helped thousands of people regain their vision, as well.

- I spent time with Barry and Suzi Kaufman at their Option Institute and saw and heard of miracles. Their own child was born autistic. They were told to give up on him. But they didn't. They worked with their son, loved him, nurtured him, accepted him—and healed him. Today he lives as an above-average, happy, successful adult.

- I've sat in dozens of workshops where I saw people heal their relationships with their lovers, their parents, their kids. I've interviewed gurus and mentors, talked to people who have had "incurable" problems dissolved, and I've experienced miracles firsthand in my own life. I've come to believe that nothing—*nothing!*—is impossible.

The Healer's Healer

For more than 10 years, I worked with Jonathan Jacobs, a man called "the healer's healer" because his track record for helping heal people is so stunning that doctors referred their own patients to him. I've seen Jonathan take people with everything from money problems to back injuries to cancer, and help heal them, often in a single session.

I've tasted this myself. For most of my life I struggled with money. When I lived in Dallas some 30 years ago, I was homeless and starving. I shoplifted to eat. And when I moved to Houston 25 years ago, I found it a frustrating nightmare to come up with $200 a month to live in a dump. It was hell. Yet I went through it for nearly 15 years. *Years!*

Then, after doing a few sessions with Jonathan, I somehow let go of my old beliefs about money, installed new ones, and now my finances are so amazingly different that I am often in awe that I have so much: new cars, new home, world travel, more clients than I can handle, and a constant stream of cash. I pay every bill that arrives, when it arrives, and I never experience lack. I attract money easily now. I'm basically debt free and entering the world of the affluent. And remember, I was once homeless!

What happened?

How can Meir cure the blind? The Kaufmans heal autism? Jonathan help people with any list of problems? How can I have money when for a decade I had next to nothing?

It begins with knowing that "It can be another way." That's what I want you to understand right now. That no matter what is happening in your life, no matter what you think will happen, it can be another way. The direction you appear to be headed can be altered. Very little is set in concrete.

In fact, as you'll see, everything in life seems to be plastic. You can mold it to fit what you want and where you want to go. Even right now, as you read these words, you can begin to play with new possibilities: What do you want to be, do, or have? Win the lotto? Why not? Increase your business? Why not? Heal something? Why not? Have more money now? Why not?

A friend of mine asked, "How do you know what is impossible?"

I replied, "How do you know what isn't?"

Shore Leave

I believe our planet is what was described in an original *Star Trek* television episode called "Shore Leave." When Kirk and his team land on a planet to check it out before sending the rest of the crew down for some much needed rest and relaxation, they begin to experience odd events. McCoy sees a huge white rabbit. Sulu sees an ancient samurai who chases him. Kirk sees an old lover and an old rival classmate. After experiencing the joys and sorrows of these events, it finally dawns on the crew (thanks to the logic of Spock, of course) that they are on a planet that reads their thoughts and creates what they think about.

I think Earth is that planet. What you hold in your mind with energy and focus will tend to be created in your reality. You'll attract it. It takes a little longer to experience results because we keep changing our minds. Imagine going to a restaurant and ordering chicken soup. But before it arrives, you change your order to wonton soup. And before that arrives, you change your order back to chicken soup. You'll sit there and complain, saying, "I can never get what I want!" when in reality you are the reason your soup is late!

Most of us do that every day. Our indecision makes attracting what we want nearly impossible. No wonder you end up feeling that you can't get what you want. Yet it doesn't have to be that way.

Consider what Frances Larimer Warner wrote in *Our Invisible Supply: Part One,* in 1907: "Spirit is substance which forms itself according to your demands, and must have a pattern from which to work. A pan of dough is as willing to be formed into bread as biscuit. It makes as little difference to Spirit what we demand."

That's the foundation of the five-step process I'll describe in this book: Knowing that life can be different for you and that life itself will support you in what you want. It's the Attractor Factor.

Here's a clue to how it works, written by Genevieve Behrend in her 1921 book, *Your Invisible Power*: "Try to remember that the picture you think, feel and see is reflected into the Universal Mind, and by the natural law of reciprocal action must return to you in either spiritual or physical form."

In the space below, write out a vision of how you would like your life to be. Pretend this book has a magic spell on it, giving everyone who holds it the power to attract whatever they can clearly name and openly accept. If you could have a new life, what would it look like? Write it down:

_____

_____

_____

_____

_____

_____

The activities we observe in the outer world are but typical of that which is taking place in man's inner world of thought and feeling. . . .

—CHARLES BRODIE PATTERSON, "THE LAW OF ATTRACTION," _MIND_ MAGAZINE, 1899

CHAPTER 9

A Shortcut to Attracting Whatever You Want

Let me tell you a little secret.

You don't need to practice the five steps in this book to manifest your desires or attract more wealth. Nope. There is an easier way. I'll tell you what it is if you promise not to spread this secret around.

Deal?

Here's the secret, what I call the shortcut to creating your life the way you want it: *Be happy now.*

That's it. If you can be happy right now, in this moment, you will have achieved whatever you want. Why? Because underneath everything you say you want is the desire for happiness. In 1917 Ralph Parlette wrote in his book, *The Big Business of Life,* "Whatever we do, we are doing it to be happy, whether we realize it or not."

You want a new car so you will be happy.

You want more money so you will be happy.

You want better health so you will be happy.

You want that loving or lusty relationship so you will be happy.

Happiness is your goal.

And here's another secret: You don't need to have anything else in order to be happy right now. You can choose to be happy.

I know that's a tough one to grasp. Just today, I received a call from a nurse caring for my best friend. The call was disturbing, to say the least. I was told my friend may need drug rehab. This news was causing me to go into a tailspin, right into unhappiness.

A few hours later, I went out for an acupuncture appointment. As I drove through the Texas country hills in the beautiful area where I now live, I realized that I could be happy anyway. My unhappiness wasn't going to help me, or my friend, or my driving. I could choose to be happy.

Does that sound like a wild thought? We're taught that outer circumstances dictate how we are to feel. What I've learned is that the outer is simply the illusion. Oh, it seems real enough. I agree. But what created that outer is *your* inner. And that's where the Attractor Factor comes into play.

As Paul Ellsworth wrote in his 1924 classic book, *The Mind Magnet*: "Consciousness is cause."

I'll explain this further right after this exercise . . .

In the space below, write down some things you are grateful for. Gratitude is a wonderful tool to appreciate the moment and activate the Attractor Factor. The more you feel grateful, the more you attract new moments to be even more grateful. What are you grateful for in this moment?

_____

_____

If you don't pay more now for a pair of shoes than you used to spend on a car, your prosperity consciousness needs work.

—RANDY GAGE, *101 KEYS TO YOUR PROSPERITY,*
WWW.MYPROSPERITYSECRETS.COM

CHAPTER 10

An Introduction to the Attractor Factor

Afriend and I were having lunch in my hometown, Niles, Ohio, one day. I was there visiting my parents. My friend wanted to know the key secret to manifesting your own reality and attracting more wealth.

I thought for a moment and then said: "The hardest concept for most people to grasp is that they are the sole reason they are experiencing whatever they have in their lives. They are totally responsible."

I could see my friend's head rear back.

"How is that possible!" he almost shouted. "I'm not responsible for a car accident I might get into, or for losing my job, or anything else that life deals my way."

I took a deep breath. This wasn't going to be easy to explain, but I wanted to give it my best shot.

"Spirituality is all about taking full responsibility for whatever occurs in your life," I said. "Good or bad, it has all come to you from you. Joseph Murphy used to say your life is an out-picturing of your inner pictures."

"I don't sit around picturing car accidents," my friend blurted out.

"Maybe not consciously," I said. "But do you watch the news?"

"Yes."

"Wouldn't you say the news is all about negative stuff—from accidents to murders to crises in countries we never heard of?"

"Yes, but—"

"Your mind is soaking up that programming," I explained. "And have you ever noticed how movies plant ideas in your mind?"

"What kinds of ideas?"

"Well, ever notice how big business is always the bad guy?"

"You mean like in movies like *Wall Street*?"

"Yes! Those movies teach you that money is bad, or that it corrupts, or that wealthy people are bad," I went on. "The point is, all of this is programming your mind to attract the very things you'd prefer not to experience."

My friend was quiet a minute.

"I think what you're saying," he began, "is that we are all robots or maybe machines."

"I gotta admit that's a pretty accurate explanation. Until we wake up, we attract things into our life unconsciously and then declare we didn't do it."

"I don't know about this," my friend mumbled. "I don't know. That means I chose to be in AA and to make a mess of my life."

"Well, it does mean that," I said. "And you did it for your own unconscious reasons. Maybe you wanted the challenge to make you stronger. Maybe you wanted the experience to help you understand life in certain ways. I don't know. *You* know, though, somewhere inside you."

"But what about all the people who come into my life and argue with me, or make our lives miserable?"

"My view is that everything in your life is an out-picturing of what is going on inside you."

"Huh?"

I smiled, but I knew these were not easy concepts to explain. I often have to reread my own books, or much of the success literature out there, to grasp the concept of unconscious manifestation or blind attraction.

"Look," I began. "I know a woman who has feminist sensibilities. Because she thinks men are out to rip her off, you can send her to any store by herself and if a man waits on her, she'll experience him being a chauvinist pig."

"Maybe the guy *is* a pig."

"He probably is, but send a woman without the belief that men are out to get her into the same store, and she'll either not get waited on by the guy, won't notice his personality, or will simply not experience what he might otherwise do."

"So you're saying we're creating it all—*all* of it?"

"It's like this," I began. "This very conversation is a cocreation. You wanted to hear someone explain the secrets of the universe. I wanted to articulate these secrets for my new book. We cocreated this."

My friend nodded but said, "I can see what you mean on something simple like this, but what if we were in an angry situation and we were fighting over these ideas?"

What could I say? I knew what he was asking. You probably are asking the same thing: What does it mean when people confront you or you have a fight with your relative or spouse or neighbor? You created that, too?

"You created all of it," I explained. "What you see is an out-picturing of what you believe inside yourself. I call it the Attractor Factor."

"I don't get it."

"Well, this very conversation is reflecting what I think about this spiritual approach to success."

"You created me?"

"I created this moment and our conversation," I said. "I needed it for my new book. I attracted you here so we could create this reality."

"Glad I could be of service to you," he grumbled. "Well, what about where I disagree with you? You create *that,* too?"

"That's a tough one to accept, but it's true. Your disbelief reflects areas in me where I don't believe everything I'm saying."

"This sounds pretty strange, Joe," he said. "If this is true, once you are clear about what you believe, then my own doubts will vanish?"

"Either that, or you simply won't air them to me."

"I gotta think about all this," he said.

"This is the Attractor Factor," I explained. "It means you are the source of the experiences you see. You cocreated them unconsciously to have experiences for your own reasons. The world is a mirror of you."

"Seems like I'd create a prettier world."

"Well, you can *now*," I said. "Now that you are becoming aware of your own inner power, you can begin to consciously create circumstances. You may not do it overnight, or master it in this lifetime, but you can begin it now."

"How?"

Ah, the question I had been waiting for!

"It all begins with the five-step formula I developed," I explained. "It's pretty easy, and you can even shorten the steps once you master them. But the five steps are where it all begins."

"You gonna tell me the five steps, or do I have to buy your book?"

"I'm going to tell you the steps right now," I replied, "and *then* you can go buy my book."

> Mind operates under its own conception of itself.
>
> —A.K. MOZUMDAR

CHAPTER 11

What's Your Prosperity IQ?

Before you dive into the next chapters, pause a moment. Take this quick little quiz by prosperity expert Randy Gage and see if you have been infected with "lack" and limitation programming. This can reflect where your current Attractor Factor is at work. You might want to make copies of this quiz first, so that you can share this with your friends and loved ones.

---

1. Do you secretly fear that if you became wealthy your family and friends might not like you anymore?
2. When you grew up, were you ever told things like, "We may not be rich, but at least we're honest!"?
3. Did your religious upbringing teach you that it is noble to sacrifice now, and that your reward will come in the afterlife?
4. Did you (or do you) feel guilty when you started to earn more than your parents did?
5. Were you raised to fit in and not do anything to stand out?
6. Did you grow up liking shows like *Dallas, Dynasty, Gilligan's Island, MASH,* and *The Beverly Hillbillies,* where rich people were always presented as unscrupulous and conniving, or pretentious and bumbling?
7. Do you have chronic health challenges that doctors can't seem to solve?
8. Did you ever get jealous of people with expensive clothes, cars, and houses—which may have led you to develop a subconscious "hate the rich" mentality?
9. On some level, do you think it is somehow noble, romantic, or spiritual to be poor?
10. Did you ever end a negative relationship—then immediately replace it with another one with a person just like the last one?

(continued)

(continued)

11. Have you sometimes used judgmental expressions like "poor as a church mouse," "filthy rich," or "obscenely wealthy"?

12. Have you ever made excuses for failure by saying things like "you have to have money to make money," "you have to know someone," or "you have to get in at the top"?

13. Do you relish being the underdog and fighting against the odds all the time?

14. Is it possible that you are experiencing health challenges, financial challenges, or business failures in order to evoke sympathy and attention from the people you are close to?

15. Are you in a stable relationship? Do you have enough money to meet your needs? Are you basically healthy? Despite all this, do you feel like life is passing you by?

How Did You Score?

Tally your results and enter the score below.

❏ Yes

❏ No

If you answered No to 13 to 15 questions: You have a very strong prosperity consciousness and can probably pass this quiz along to someone else.

If you answered Yes to three or more questions: You likely have some issues of worthiness on a subconscious level. You may be in a holding pattern, afraid to leave your comfort zone. You're probably not radically unhappy, but there is no passion and excitement in your life. You know something is missing, but you may not know what.

If you answered Yes to five or more questions: You are quite likely in a stagnancy cycle. You make small advances, but also experience setbacks, so that you are not really breaking through to the real success and happiness you desire and deserve.

If you answered Yes to seven or more questions: You are headed toward, or already experiencing, a definite downward track toward serious emotional, physical, and financial challenges. This is the kind of "victim cycle" Randy Gage was on when he lost everything when he was 30, before transforming his life and becoming a multimillionaire. It is imperative that you take immediate action to break the pattern and stop the failure cycle. This will involve uncovering the limiting beliefs you possess on a subconscious level, and radically reprogramming yourself with positive ones.

Now if you fall into one of the last three categories, Randy Gage's Prosperity Power Experience can definitely help you. Visit www .MyProsperitySecrets.com for help in prosperity thinking.

CHAPTER 12

Step One: The Springboard

Visit any bar and what will you hear? Gossip. Complaining. Bitterness. Negativity. Visit any lunchroom in any big company and what will you hear? Gossip. Complaining. Bitterness. Negativity.

Eavesdrop on any family gathering around dinnertime and what will you hear?

Gossip. Complaining. Bitterness. Negativity.

I could go on. The point is, the vast majority of humanity is stuck on this level of consciousness. It's the level of the media. It's the level of most conversations. It's the level of low energy. And this very same level keeps people exactly where they are.

Do I need to explain this one?

Most people I talk to every day know what they don't want:

"I don't want this backache."

"I don't want this headache."

"I don't want these bills."

"I don't want to struggle in my business."

You know the list. You have one of your own.

Unfortunately, that's where most of us leave it. The nature of our conversations, our newspaper reporting, our radio and television shows, and our popular talk shows surround us with ideas of what we don't want. It feels good to complain. We don't feel so alone. We feel heard. We feel relieved. We even sometimes get answers that make our problems lighter.

What we don't realize is we are activating the Attractor Factor in a negative way. When we say, "I don't want these bills," our focus is on—you guessed it—bills! The spirit of life will deliver whatever you focus on. So if you are talking about your bills, you'll get more bills. You'll attract it by spending energy on it.

Most people are on the level of fear. As Elinor Moody wrote in her 1923 book, *You Can Receive Whatsoever You Desire,* "Let us remember that fear is only wrongly directed faith. We are having faith in things we do NOT want, rather than in the things we desire."

Again, this is the level most people are on. It isn't bad, it just isn't very positive. And it probably isn't getting you the health, wealth, or happiness you want.

But we seldom take this process to Level Two. It's a rare person who will stop complaining, fighting, or fearing long enough to focus on the opposite of what they are experiencing. Yet Level Two begins to bring on the miracles and manifestations that we want. Knowing what you don't want is the springboard to your miracles. Knowing what you don't want is simply your current reality. And current reality can change.

Remove Negativity

One way to protect yourself from the negative influences of the world at large is to abstain from them. I remember reading how Mark Victor Hansen and Jack Canfield forbid any negativity in their offices. I love the idea. I don't watch the news or read the papers. After a while you begin to see how you are fed one-sided, negative news. None of it is designed to help my well-being.

But you also have to watch your friends. The people around you will share their views of the world with you. Sometimes it's not easy to separate their views from your view.

You want to step up from the world of outside cause and turn into the world of attraction based on energy. One way to do that is to remind yourself that the world in general is on the level of complaining.

You want to go up a level or two.

Beware the Five

Years ago I attended networking meetings. These were usually breakfast or lunch business meetings where people exchanged business cards and tried to help each other get new clients.

I spoke at many of these events. What I quickly noticed is that the same people seemed to be at the same meetings. One observant friend said, "It's the same people—and they're all starving!"

That's when I first learned about the concept of levels. That is, people tend to stay on the same level of business or social status. When they meet friends, it's usually in their circle of activity, whether church, work, school, or some club. As a result, they rarely get out of the level they are on.

That's not bad. You can stay on the level you are at and do well. But if you want more, or if you find yourself starving on the level you're on, you'll need to go up a level or two.

When I was speaking at these networking events, I was a notch above everyone in the room. This is not an ego thing. It's a social perception. I was seen as being at a slightly higher level than the audience simply by nature of being the speaker. I was the authority figure. As the teacher, I was elevated a slight degree above their level.

But that's not good enough. If you want to achieve big dreams in business, you need to step out of your circle or network of peers and associates. You need to go to a group with wider, stronger, richer connections.

You need to go up a level.

How do you do that?

In my case, my books brought me to the attention of other circles of people and higher levels of networks. For example, when I wrote *The AMA Complete Guide to Small Business Advertising* for the American Marketing Association back in 1995, I was immediately put on a new level. I was now the author of an important book for a prestigious organization.

This caused new people to contact me. All of these people had their own network of people. More often than not, these networks were at a higher level than anything I had ever touched before.

Here's another example: When I wrote my book on P. T. Barnum called *There's A Customer Born Every Minute*, for the American Management Association back in 1997, I managed to get the attention of famous tycoons like Donald Trump and Kenneth Feld. Clearly I had been introduced to a new level.

If you want to succeed in phenomenal ways today, you need to go up a level or two on the status scale of networks. The good news is e-mail makes this a snap to begin. Anyone alive can be reached through e-mail with some persistence and cleverness. That's how I first reached marketing superstar Jay Conrad Levinson, direct mail legend Joe Sugarman, and even the late gonzo daredevil Evel Knievel. I did it all by e-mail.

People write me all the time for favors. I'm now perceived as an expert, an authority, and an Internet marketing pioneer. They want to associate their name or product with me. I love to help people, so I usually at least give people a chance. But I never endorse anything without seeing, using, and loving what they have. This is important for me to maintain my level.

And now people write me from higher levels, too. For example, Dr. Robert Anthony is a man I studied 20 years ago. Last year, he wrote me after reading my book, *Spiritual Marketing*. Today, we're co-authors. I just produced and recorded his legendary audio-program, *Beyond Positive Thinking*. Two decades ago, I was way below his level. Today, we're partners!

Keep in mind that going up a level is different from thinking out of the box. You can be creative and still stay on your current level. Brainstorming with your neighbor is most likely different from brainstorming with, say, Richard Branson, the flamboyant owner of Virgin Records.

The point is this: *To achieve goals you've never achieved before, you may need to rise in levels and participate with new people on a new playing field.*

So the lesson in this section is to consider your current level, consider your goals, and consider what people outside of your network can help you achieve them. You may have to step out of your level (and comfort zone) to do it, but the step is well worth taking.

To look at this another way, the people closest to you will hold you down or help you up. As Randy Gage points out, the five people closest to you will influence your success. They will be either focused on Step One—the "I don't want this" stage—or they will be focused on Step Two—"What do you want?" The people around you will help you with your focus.

So, where do you want your focus to be?

Socrates' Advice

I love this story, attributed to Socrates, on how to handle negative people.

One day, a man rushed up to Socrates, saying, "I have some news to tell you!"

Socrates put up his hand to stop the excited man.

"First let me ask you three questions," Socrates said.

"Ah, er, okay," said the man.

"Is the news you are about to tell me something you personally know to be true?"

"Well, no," replied the man. "I heard it from a good source, though."

"Then let's go to the second question," Socrates said. "Is the news you want to tell me about someone you know personally?"

"Well, no," the man said. "But I think you know the person."

"I see," said Socrates. "Then let me ask you my final question. Is this news positive or negative?"

"Well, it's negative."

"Let me see," said the wise Socrates. "You want to tell me some news that you don't know personally to be true, about someone you don't know at all, and that is negative."

"Well, it sounds bad when you put it like that."

"I think I'll pass," Socrates said.

Where Are Your Thoughts?

Again, the Attractor Factor is always at work. It is spirit giving you what you focus on. Focus on lack, you get lack. Focus on your bad back, you get more of your bad back. So, for Step One, all you want to do is notice what you have been focusing on.

Where are your thoughts?

Where is your conversation?

Your answers will become the springboard to take you to the next step in this miracle making process.

Below, write down some of the things you typically complain about. These are your "don't wants" and they'll come in handy in the next step:

Man is a magnet, and every line and dot and detail of his experiences comes by his own attraction.

—ELIZABETH TOWNE, *THE LIFE POWER AND HOW TO USE IT,* 1906

CHAPTER 13

Step Two: Dare Something Worthy

Pull up a chair, and let me tell you a story or two. This will set the stage for Step Two in this miraculous formula for making your dreams come true.

Exceed You

When I was a teenager one of my heroes was the late Floyd Patterson. Floyd was Heavyweight Boxing Champion of the world—twice. He was also the youngest man in history to win the title.

He was a nice guy in an often bad business. He wrote his autobiography and titled it something intriguing, *Victory Over Myself*. I love the title because of the ideal it conveys. Instead of trying to beat the world, just try to improve yourself. Runners call it "exceeding your personal best." In other words, if you aren't happy with yourself, find a way to be victorious over yourself.

There is no competition. There is no enemy. There is only the desire to improve *yourself*. As you improve, the world improves.

Floyd Patterson knew this. And he became one of the most famous and lovable boxing champions of the world.

I met Floyd when I was maybe 16 years old. It was right after a bout in Cleveland, Ohio. I managed to crawl over bleachers, jump a rail, and stand in the path where Floyd would be headed back to his training room. He looked at me with this gentle, kind smile. I reached up and patted his massive shoulder as I congratulated him on his win that night.

I never forgot it. Floyd was in boxing because that was the job that took him out of poverty. But he knew the only real opponents in the world were the things in himself he didn't like. He worked to have victory over himself. Floyd succeeded.

Ask yourself, "What do you want to improve in yourself?"

Write it here:

_____

_____

_____

_____

_____

_____

Peace Pilgrim

Peace Pilgrim may have been the Mother Teresa or the Gandhi of the United States of America. This kind woman spent 28 years of her life walking for peace. She dropped her real name. She owned nothing but the clothes on her back. She only ate or slept whenever someone along her path gave her food or shelter.

She walked over 25,000 miles for peace. She walked in total trust that what she was doing was making a profound impact on the world. She was interviewed by the media, seen on television, heard on radio, and read about in the newspapers.

Yet she was simply following her own calling. She dared to do something worthy.

She wrote, "The most important part of prayer is what we feel, not what we say. We spend a great deal of time telling God what we think should be done, and not enough time waiting in the stillness for God to tell us what to do."

Peace Pilgrim died in 1981. But her spirit lives on. Her life and words can be found online at www.peacepilgrim.net/pphome.htm.

She was and continues to be an inspiration to millions of people.

Now I'll ask you to ask yourself, "How does Peace Pilgrim inspire me?"

Or "What is the nudge within you urging you to do?"

Write it here:

_____

_____

_____

_____

_____

_____

Be a Trillionaire

As you'll see in this chapter, knowing what you want—knowing your calling, your goal, your ideal, your challenge, your dream—is the next step to attracting your desires.

Most people have no idea what they want. Or if they do, they think small. I want you to think bigger than you've ever thought before. I want you to *Aude aliquid dignum,* or *Dare something worthy.*

For example, why not become a trillionaire? According to my friend Brad Hager, CEO of *Millionaire* magazine, there are 22 trillion dollars of personal wealth floating around in the world. Yet there are—so far—no trillionaires.

Why not choose to be the world's first trillionaire? (Actually, that's *my* goal. But you can pursue it, too.)

One thing you'll learn in this book is that your mind can be directed to find answers for you. When you ask questions—such as "How can I become the world's first trillionaire?"—your mind begins a search-and-find mission. Your question directs it to find a solution.

Step Two in our Attractor Factor process involves choosing what you want, and doing it in such a way that you activate your mind to complete the job for you.

Let me explain.

What Do You Want?

If you realize you can have anything, be anything, or do anything, then the question becomes: What do you want?

Here's the secret: *The trick is in turning every one of your complaints around to something you DO want.* Start focusing on where you want to go, not on where you were or where you are.

"I don't want this headache" becomes "*I want a clear head.*"

"I don't want this backache" becomes "*I want a strong back.*"

"I don't want these bills" becomes *"I want more than enough money for everything I desire."*

"I don't want to struggle in my business" becomes *"I want business to come to me easily and effortlessly."*

There's an art to rewriting what you don't want into what you do want. All I do is write the opposite of my complaint. Turn the sentence around 180 degrees. If I say, "I'm tired of being interrupted when I write," the opposite would be, "I want to write in a place that is safe, quiet, and without interruptions."

You're probably wondering what this has to do with anything. Why write these sentences if they won't help you pay the bills or heal your problems or anything else?

Good question. The answer: *Refocusing on what you do want will take you in the direction of what you want.*

As Deepak Chopra wrote in his book, *The Spontaneous Fulfillment of Desire,* "All we really need is clarity of intent. Then if we can get the ego out of the way, the intentions fulfill themselves."

Take the complaints you wrote in the last chapter and turn them into statements of intent:

_____

_____

_____

_____

_____

_____

_____

_____

_____

_____

_____

_____

_____

_____

_____

The Magic of Intention

My friend Kent Cummins, master magician, great speaker, and co-author of _The Magic of Change,_ knows about the power of intention in business.

He ran a sandwich shop business (the SamWitch shops) in Austin, Texas, for 15 years. One day, he decided to run a radio ad offering free beans with any Po-Boy (encouraging customers to purchase the larger-size sandwich). Don't ask him why he thought beans would be a draw. All he remembers is that the business had found a source for some very tasty beans.

They stocked up on beans. They placed an ad with a popular local radio station. And the next day when the SamWitch shop opened for business, there were so many customers he had to turn some away. Business exploded. He couldn't keep up with the orders.

But here's the odd thing. When Kent called the radio station to thank them for running his ad, he was shocked to hear, "We were going to call you and apologize. We never ran the ad."

How did Kent get so much business from an ad that never ran?

"It's all in your intention," he told me over dinner. "I intended for new business, and that was the signal that attracted people. Apparently, the intention was more important than the actual ad!"

That's not the only time Kent has experienced the power of knowing what you want in business. Recently, he decided to implement a publicity campaign for his summer camp, "The Kent Cummins Magic Camp." He read books. Attended a seminar. Drafted a plan. His intent was to get publicity. But he got busy with operational details and never actually implemented the plan. He forgot to do it.

It didn't matter. One of the former camper parents turned out to be a writer for the Austin *American-Statesman* newspaper. He called Kent and asked for permission to write an op-ed piece for the editorial page. A stunning story about their counselor training program ran within weeks of the idea. One of the local TV stations called and asked Kent to appear on its morning show to promote the camp as an interesting idea for viewers. Kent appeared, demonstrated some magic, and answered questions about the camp.

Kent then discovered that The Magic Camp had been nominated for recognition by BIG Austin, a city-sponsored nonprofit organization for small business. To his surprise, he won the Most Creative Small Business in Austin for 2004, recognition that included some $4,000 worth of prizes.

The Business Success Center had already asked him to speak on entrepreneurship. He would speak at the Lakeway Breakfast Club about the camp. *Austin Family* magazine notified him that The Magic Camp had been designated in a readers' poll as the Best Specialty Camp in Austin.

Finally, Kent discovered that one of his counselors had sent in a magic trick from the camp to *The Tonight Show with Jay Leno*, and they used the piece and paid the camper $100.

Not bad results for a publicity campaign that was never implemented!

Kent calls it "the *magic* of intention."

As you'll see throughout this book, the clearer you are about what you want, the easier it is to simply attract it into your life.

For example . . .

How I Raised $22,500 in One Day

One day, I pulled up beside a truck delivering new cars. One of the cars on the flatbed made my heart leap and my blood dance. I had never had a piece of machinery turn me on before. This one did. I fell in love.

It was a BMW Z3. A roadster. A luxury sports car. One of the sexiest cars ever known to man and made by gods. Okay, maybe I'm overplaying it. But the point is, this car spoke to me. I wanted it. And wanted it bad.

I also knew BMWs are pricey. So the first thing I did was try to win one. I entered two contests where Z3s were the big prizes. I knew I would win. I was destined to have that car. But I didn't win. Alas. So much for the laws of chance. It was time to create my future by attracting it.

So I decided I would just buy the car and that I would pay cash for it. I had just completed an e-book on how to create miracles, called *Spiritual Marketing,* and I figured I would prove to myself that I could create a Z3. I used my own five-step method to get the sexiest car of my hottest dreams.

I began by setting an intention for getting that car. Oprah once said, "Intention rules the Earth." I know it. My car's license plate holder says, "I am the power of intention." Once you declare that something will be so, you send a signal into the universe that begins to move that something to you, and you to it. Call it Real Magic. Call it the Attractor Factor. I call it one of the most powerful steps in the manifestation process. From that step alone, miracles can happen.

After I set my intention to have that car, I then acted on the hunches that bubbled up within me and the opportunities that came my way. To be more exact, here's what happened.

One day, it occurred to me to offer a seminar on the subject of my new book. I could rent a hotel. Write a sales letter. Invite everyone I knew on my online and off-line list to it. I could make a killing in a weekend. That's the ticket!

But then it occurred to me that I don't like to market seminars, that I didn't know if it would sell, that postage and printing to promote it would cost a fortune, and that I'm not such a big fan of speaking in public, anyway.

And here's where the shift occurred:

I began to play with the idea that I could hold the seminar online. I would simply announce an e-class to my e-mail list. It would cost me zip. If no one signed up, so what?

But—BUT!—if they *did* sign up, I could teach the entire class by e-mail. Every week, I would send out a lesson. I would give assignments. They would complete them and e-mail them back. I would then comment on their homework. It would all be nice and neat, easy and convenient. Sounded good to me.

I decided to teach five weeks of classes, mainly because there were five chapters in the original book. I would send out one chapter a week as a lesson. I would add assignments to each one to make it more of a legit course.

Then I wondered, "What do I charge?"

I spent a lot of time on this question. Most people give away their e-classes, if they teach them at all. A few charge low fees. But I wanted a BMW Z3. They cost $30,000 to $40,000 each.

Yikes!

Well, I decided I wanted 15 people in my class. That was an arbitrary number. I just figured if 15 people actually did their homework over a five-week period, I would have my hands full reviewing it. So, like everything else in the developing of this first e-class, I simply made up the class size.

I then divided 15 by how much I wanted to raise for my Z3. If 15 people paid me $2,000 each, I'd have enough to pay for the car in cash. But two grand a person seemed a bit high. So I settled for $1,500 a person.

I then issued a sales pitch/invitation to sign up for the class to my e-mail list. I had about 800 good names on my list at that time. I had no idea if anyone would bite. I even feared I would be flamed to death. But I decided to take the risk. I decided I could survive whatever occurred. Besides, what if this crazy idea actually worked? I sent the letter to my list.

What happened?

Sixteen of them immediately signed up for the class.

Talk about easy money! I made $24,000 in one day.

The class was easy to do, too. The students loved the lessons, my assignments, and my feedback. Only one person immediately asked to bow out, saying the e-class wasn't for him. So I ended up with 15 people after all. I made $22,500. I was happy.

But I didn't stop there. A few weeks later, I announced another e-class. This one on how to write, publish, and promote your own e-book. I just followed the same model that already worked: I issued an invite to my e-mail list, I went after 15 people, I charged $1,500 per person for a five-week class. I got 12 paying customers. I made $18,000.

At this point I had been thinking about writing a sequel to my best-selling e-book, *Hypnotic Writing*. But I didn't want to write it and just hope it would sell. I wanted to be *paid* to write it.

So I created yet another e-class. This one would be on *Advanced Hypnotic Writing*. It would be three weeks long, rather than five, because I wanted to take it easy this time around. (I was getting lazy.) I still charged $1,500 and I still went after 15 people. I then announced the class to my e-mail list.

Here's where something wild happened:

Almost 18 people immediately signed up for the class. But when I asked them to pay the $1,500 fee, every single one of them said they thought the class was free! I was stunned. I reread my invite. It clearly said there was a hefty fee. All I can figure is that people skimmed the letter, got excited, and just shot back e-mails to enroll in the class. Or maybe they read the word "fee" as "free." Go figure.

But that's not the only odd thing that happened with this class: I had trouble filling it from my own e-list. So I went and asked a person with a giant e-mail list if he would promote my class to his people. He would—for 50 percent of the pie. Yowsa! That was a lot, but I wanted to get paid to write my sequel to *Hypnotic Writing*, and I'd still end up with good money, anyway. So I agreed.

Well, 20 people signed up. And the really odd thing is that no one—no one!—did their assignments. So I got their money (half of it, anyway: $15,000), I got paid to write my *Advanced Hypnotic Writing* e-book, and I had no homework to review or grade.

What a cool business!

Most recently, I announced yet another e-class. I was about to buy a large country estate and wanted more money fast. This new class is on my new proprietary marketing formula, called Guaranteed Outcome Marketing. I raised the price on this five-week e-class to signal its value. I asked for $2,500 a person. Since I normally charge $50,000 to create a

Guaranteed Outcome Marketing strategy for someone, asking for only $2,500 to teach someone how to do it seemed very fair.

I lowered the class size because I wanted to be sure to give each student personal attention. I promoted this class to only my own e-mail list. I got five students. Which meant I raised $12,500. Not bad for a month's work. And yes, I bought the country estate. I'm writing this section from it.

I went on and taught my method for teaching classes by e-mail to several people. Copywriter and Internet marketer Yanik Silver has made over $90,000 following my method. Executive coach Paul Lemberg has made over $100,000. And Tom Pauley, author of *I'm Rich Beyond My Wildest Dreams, I Am, I Am, I Am,* has made over $250,000—so far. And in each case, I made as much as 50 percent of what they made for helping them promote their e-classes online.

And all of this began because I implemented Step Two in the Attractor Factor method!

The moral here? There are several:

1. *Intention rules.* You can float with the circumstances life brings you, or you can create your own direction and your own circumstances. It begins with a decision. What do you want? Decide. Choose. Declare. My motto is "Dare something worthy." This is the power of Step Two in the Attractor Factor formula.

2. *Break the model.* Just because others are selling their services for a song doesn't mean you have to, as well. Respect yourself. What are you worth? Most people devalue themselves and their skills. Obviously you need to offer true value, but you don't have to give it away. If you are clear about money being a tool for good, you should be able to charge whatever the market will bear.

3. *Go for something other than money.* Wanting my Z3 caused my mind to stretch in new ways to raise the money needed to get the car. If I were just going after money for money's sake, I might

not think so boldly in my ideas or my pricing. What do you *really* want? Keep in mind, too, that the wealthier you are, the more people you can help. Money helps solve problems. If you want to make a difference in the world, get rich.

4. *You can do this, too.* Just look at what you know that others would pay you to learn. Then turn it into an e-class, complete with lessons and assignments. After the class is over, you might even compile the material into a book. Or a CD. Or? Think big! What would you teach if you had no fears? You can attract wealth when you are fearless. Your wealth may be hiding right behind the very thing you are reluctant to do.

5. *The spiritual is not separate from the material.* Since I've focused on money in this example, it may be easy to declare my focus was only on the dollar. Not so. I used spiritual principles—as will be explained in this very book—to attract wealth. Once you realize that the spiritual and material are two sides of the same coin, you are free to have happiness as well as cash. As it says on the dollar bill in your pocket, "In God we trust." Do you trust?

Finally, yes, I attracted my BMW Z3 into my garage. I bought it off the showroom floor. It's a 1999 Montreal Blue stunning piece of rolling beauty. Since BMW no longer makes that model, it's a collectible, too. I've had it for years now. I've never had so much fun in my life driving. In fact, I think I'll aim it up and down some Texas country roads right now.

The Number One Thing People Do Wrong

I admit it. I'm frustrated. I'm tired of getting e-mails from people who write, "I can't do what you did because—" or "I can't attract wealth into my life because—"

Just fill in the blank with whatever excuse you can think of. People say they can't write as many books as I have because they don't have the time, or they're too old, or too young, or too married, or too single. People say they can't make their book a best seller as I did because their book is different, or they're different, or the timing is different. People say they can't ask celebrities for endorsements as I did because they feel insignificant, or insulting, or imposing.

The list of excuses is endless. Here are actual ones I've received:

"You're more famous than me. I could never write people and ask for their help, as they wouldn't give me the time of day."

I started asking people for help, advice, input, suggestions and direction when I was a teenager. I have letters from FBI king J. Edgar Hoover, boxing legend Jack Dempsey, and master magician John Mulholland. I was certainly unknown then. Yet people always helped me. I've managed to connect with Evel Kneivel, Donald Trump, Jimmy Carter, best-selling authors, and more—and I did it before anyone knew my name. I simply *asked* for their help. They were kind and replied.

"You have a large network of people to ask for things."

Yes, I do. *Now.* But I didn't when I first started. I developed my network by building relationships. I reached out to people, helped them, they helped me, and trust was formed. Because I've nurtured my relationships online for almost 10 years now, a bond is set. When I announce that I want contributions for a new book, my network responds. When they want something, I respond. I was able to compile all the information for one of my marketing books, *The E-Code: 47 Surprising Secrets for Making Money Online Almost Instantly,* in less than seven days—all because I asked my network for help.

"You have a big mailing list so you can sell things faster."

I went online with no mailing list. *None.* I didn't even recognize the importance of having my own list until the day I offered my first e-class to my then tiny list and made $22,500 in one day. Then I woke up. I've been working on building my e-mail list ever since. Anyone can do it. And while you're waiting to do it, you can always partner with people who already have mailing lists. How? Just *ask*. One day, some person in Norway wrote me. He wanted to know if I would help him sell his new software. I liked his program and agreed. He didn't have a list. I did. He had software. I liked it. I did a mailing and split the profits with him. It was a win-win.

"You are more talented as a copywriter so you can sell better than me."

I learned to be a copywriter by investing time, money, and effort into studying the greats and getting out there and doing it. My first sales letters were garbage. I still write and rewrite to make my letters as hypnotic as I can. I wasn't born writing, reading, or even walking. I learned it all. Can't you?

"I don't have anything to offer free to get people to buy what I am selling."

There are a million things for free online. You can find thousands—thousands!—of free e-books online. Just grab a few and offer them as your incentives to get people to buy your product or service. Anyone can do this. Just look around online. The fruit is there for the picking. I've seen people take classics of literature—now in the public domain and available as e-books—and offer them as incentives for prospects to buy their product. It works. How do you find them? *Search.*

"I can't teach an e-class like you because I have no credentials."

Your credentials are you. They are your life experiences more than anything else. Few today care about whether you have a degree or any other credential. They care if you can deliver on whatever you promise. My life mate, Nerissa, is about to teach an online video editing class. Anything you can teach off-line can be taught online.

With video, audio, graphics, text, and chat rooms, you can have a virtual classroom on *anything* you can imagine. Why not?

"I can't make money selling my stuff on the Internet."

Look around. The Internet is so big and vast, and even incomprehensible, that truly anything can be sold online. I've seen people sell tumble weeds and buggy whips, greeting cards and computer-generated art. Anything sold off-line can be sold online. Go look at eBay. People sell cars, used clothes, dirt, used wedding dresses, and even snow there. I once sold an "Elvis Mermaid" on eBay. (You can see a picture of it at www.mrfire.com) Are there really any limits to what can be sold online?

"I missed the right time to sell my idea."

Really? Just look at the title of one of my books: *There's a Customer Born Every Minute*. A new crowd of prospects appears every single day. You can sell virtually anything at virtually any time if you think of what people want and cater to them. Sometimes you have to think of other uses for the same product, or other audiences than what you originally had in mind. But the best time to sell what you have is now. What are you waiting for?

"You live in America, and I live in Mexico, and selling doesn't work here."

Give me a break. Friends of mine always go to Mexico (and other countries said to be behind us), and they come home with truck loads of things they bought. Besides that, with the Internet, where you live is almost meaningless. Take your product and go online. Then, you're not selling to just your neighbors, but to the entire planet. Think *big*.

The list goes on and on.

To me, excuses are the number one thing people do wrong—online and off. While all of these excuses seem legit to the person saying them, they are virtually all hogwash.

Excuses are beliefs. If you buy into them, you're stuck. If you believe instead that there's always a way around whatever the excuse is, then you'll move forward. My philosophy is "There is *always* a way."

So let me try to help you here.

First, what are your excuses?

When I began this section by asking you to answer the question, "I can't do what you did because—", what did you say? How did you complete the sentence? Those are some of your excuses. Write them here:

_____

_____

_____

_____

_____

Second, ask yourself if there's any way on earth to get around your excuses. In other words, are the excuses you stated real or imagined? Have you tried to get past any of them? Has anyone else, ever, gotten past the same excuses? Write your answers here:

_____

_____

_____

_____

_____

_____

Finally, what would you do if you had no excuses? Write your answer here:

_____

_____

_____

Whatever your answer, that's a clue to your biggest goal.
Leave your excuses behind, and you will begin to attract wealth.
Leave your excuses behind, and you can achieve success, too.
Leave your excuses behind, and your life will begin to soar.
If you don't act now, why not?
Whatever your answer, *that's* an excuse.
Are you going to let it stop you?

Who Directs Your Life?

You see, we seem to create our lives out of our perceptions. If we focus on lack, we get more lack. If we focus on riches, we get more riches. If we focus on excuses, we attract more blocks. Our perception becomes a magnet that pulls us in the direction of where we want to go.

If you don't consciously select where you want to go, you go where your unconscious wants you to go. To paraphrase the famous

Swiss psychologist Carl Jung, "Until you make the unconscious conscious, it will direct your life, and you will call it fate."

In that regard, most of us are on autopilot. We simply haven't realized that we can take the controls. Knowing what you want helps you aim your life in the direction you want to take it.

But there is a little more to it . . .

For What Purpose?

I just had lunch with a delightful friend of mine. She had a session with Jonathan Jacobs last week, and she was still glowing. Her eyes were large and alive, full of passion for life. She reminded me that even though you may think you know what you want, you may have to probe deeper to discover what you really want.

She had gone to see Jonathan with the intention of creating a successful business for herself. Jonathan asked, "For what purpose?" After dodging the question for a while, she realized that she wanted a successful business "to prove I am a worthwhile person."

I remember saying I wanted to write books that were colossal best sellers. Jonathan asked me that same famous question, "For what purpose?" At first, I squirmed and said things like "I deserve it," or "I want the money," or "My books are good enough for it." But the real reason, the underlying motivating factor, was that I wanted best-selling books "so people would love and admire me." When I said it, I felt a shift within myself. I knew I had reached the real thing I wanted. My goal, my intention, was to feel love.

Most people live their entire lives being driven by an unconscious, unacknowledged need for something. The politician may have been a child who never got enough attention. The business woman may have been a youngster who didn't feel equal to her peers. The best-selling author may still be trying to prove he's smart, or lovable, or admirable.

Freedom and power come from knowing what you want without being a prisoner to what you want.

But there's another reason for knowing and stating your intention. When you declare it, you begin to discover all the things standing in the way of its happening. You may say you want to pay off your house so you are free of those big payments, but suddenly here come all of the objections: "I don't make enough money to pay off my house!" or "No one ever does that!" to "What will my parents think?"

You know what I mean. It's easy to come up with objections. The trick is to dissolve those objections until you are clear inside. When you are clear, manifesting whatever you want will be easier.

Let me explain . . .

How You Create Reality

A woman went to see Jonathan because she was going to have a cancer operation on Monday. She saw him on Friday. She was terrified of the operation and wanted to get rid of her fears. Jonathan helped her release all of her fears, and two hours later, when she sat up on his table, she felt healed. But she still went through the operation. On Monday, when the doctors opened her up, they could not find any cancer. It was gone.

What happened?

Again, our beliefs are powerful. The woman believed she could remove the beliefs that were causing her fear, and she did. But she didn't know that the fear was what created the cancer. When she removed the fear, the cancer left. It no longer had a home in her body. She had taken conscious control of her life by choosing to see Jonathan and take care of her negative beliefs. She knew her life could be another way.

Beliefs are how we create reality. I'm not sure how to explain this to you in a way that makes sense. You've probably noticed that people seem to have recurring problems. Did you ever wonder why it was the same problem for each person? The person with money problems always has money problems. The person with relationship problems always has relationship problems. It's as though each person specializes in a disorder.

Beliefs, unconscious or not, are creating those events. Until the beliefs that create the events are released, the events will continue to reoccur. I know a man who has been married seven times. He hasn't gotten it right yet. He will continue to marry and divorce and marry until he removes the underlying beliefs that cause the events to happen. And while he continues to marry and divorce, he will blame other people for his problems, and maybe even blame fate, or God. But as you read earlier, "Until you make the unconscious conscious, it will direct your life and you will call it fate."

What Are Your Beliefs?

Look at your life. What you have are the direct results of your beliefs. Not happy? In debt? Poor marriage? Not successful? Bad health? There are beliefs that are creating those experiences for you. In a very real sense, some part of you wants what you have—problems and all.

I remember motivational guru Tony Robbins talking about a schizophrenic woman who had diabetes when she was one personality and was healthy when she was another personality. Beliefs make up personality. The woman with diabetes had beliefs that created the diabetes. It's obvious that if you change the beliefs, you change the situation.

How do you change the beliefs? It starts with selecting what you want for your life. As soon as you select what you want to be, do, or have, you'll discover beliefs in the way of it. They'll surface. They'll be your excuses. That swings back to what I was talking about earlier, that you can then restate your complaints so that they become goals or intentions for you.

So, what do you want?

What would make your heart sing?

What would make you dance in the streets?

What would make you smile right now thinking about it?

What would you do if you knew you could not fail?

What would you want—if you could have anything?

Write your answers here:

_____

_____

_____

_____

_____

_____

Ask and You Shall Receive

I picked up *Ask and You Shall Receive*, a book by physicist Pierre Morency. It's a quick read but a stimulating one. Pierre says you must ask for what you want. Asking gives you focus and directs the energy of the universe to help manifest it with you. The cover of the book asks, "What did you ask for when you got up this morning?"

I love the question and am now asking it every morning when I awaken. It's now my breakfast. Another question in the book can help you find your passion. Morency asks:

"What would you do if you possessed all the money in the world? What would you do if you could make money appear by simply snapping your fingers? What would you do once you owned 12 houses, made 14 exotic trips, and bought 28 luxury cars?"

That's the kind of question my mentors ask in my Miracles Coaching program.

How would you answer it?

Your answer is a major clue to your calling. Write it down here:

_____

_____

_____

_____

_____

_____

_____

Can You Really Have Everything?

What are the limits to our desires?

I'm not sure there are any. You could argue for physical or scientific limitations, but I think those are limits based on current research. At one point it was understood that no human could run the four-minute mile. Now many can do it. At one point, we knew lead would sink in water. Now we build ships out of it. At one point, no one believed we could get to the moon. Been there, done that. At one point, people assumed the disabled could not participate in sports. Now we have the Special Olympics.

The list goes on. Again, I'm not sure anything is impossible. I'm not sure you can't have it all. Certainly, the goals, intentions, and wishes of the average person reading this book are within reach. You may not know *how* to achieve something, but you know the dream is attainable, somehow, some way.

As I write this, Hollywood actors, actresses, directors, and investors want me to have my own weekly television show. It would be called *Expect Miracles*. The idea is that when you expect miracles, you attract miracles. Each week I will find someone who did the impossible or cured the incurable. As you view these real stories, you begin to realize that nothing is impossible. You literally can have, do, or be whatever you can imagine.

The only thing you need to be aware of is what the Buddhists call "hungry ghosts." These are desires that run you, rather than you running them. A desire for new shoes when you have many pair and don't need more might be a hungry ghost. A desire for more property when you have plenty might be a hungry ghost. Desire for more food when you just ate might be a hungry ghost, too.

"The hungry ghosts are driven by intense neurotic craving," writes Dominic Houlder in *Mindfulness and Money.* "Neurotic, because the craving they experience is often the displaced desire for something else—something they are not consciously aware of."

I am not trying to stop you from desiring anything. Desire is good. It is what motivates you to get up, to live, to work, to grow, to love. It's built into your human system. You can use desire to transcend desire. But you also have to watch the mind. It can be like a wild monkey, telling you to get this and now that and never letting you have any peace.

You want to watch the hungry ghosts. You want to honor the desires welling up from deep within you, the wishes that are from your core. When you come from that place, nothing is impossible, and you can have anything you can imagine. At that point, you are aligned with the universe itself. In many ways, the universe's desires will be your desires.

The point is, you can attract virtually anything you want. But the question remains, do you want your goals like a spoiled child in a candy store or a wild monkey drunk on power, or do your desires come from the essence of who you are?

I know a woman who used the five steps in this book to win money in Las Vegas. The rush was wonderful. The accomplishment was wonderful. But she then misused the money and ended up in Gambler's Anonymous. She now pays attention to the hungry ghosts inside her and only uses the five-step Attractor Formula to do good in the world.

I once used the Attractor Formula to win money in the Texas lotto. I found it took a lot of energy to win a little money and that the accomplishment was empty. Now, I focus on joyfully creating books, courses, and audio recordings that bring me residual income while helping people. I also have a Miracles coaching program and an executive mentoring program. I make a great deal of money and feel wonderful about it. I'm following my calling. I'm making a difference. And I'm attracting wealth.

What good do *you* want to do for yourself and others?

Close Your Eyes

About 20 years ago I attended a seminar by Stuart Wilde, author of *The Trick to Money Is Having Some* and many other books. I had interviewed Stuart over breakfast, found him fascinating, and he invited me to his event. One exercise in it stood out and is relevant to this second step in the Attractor Factor formula.

Stuart led us through a remarkable imagery experience. We were asked to outline our own bodies in a ray of white light. "Use a finger or a beam," Wilde suggested. "Trace your body with the white light."

I found myself centering remarkably fast. I felt myself relax into the here and now. All tensions slipped out of my body. I let go. I felt present like never before.

"Now make a beam of light from the top of your head to the floor in front of your feet."

I did. I could see it like a walkway for ants. For some reason, I thought of the joke about two mental patients who want to escape their prison. One says he'll turn on the flash light and the other can escape by walking on the ray of light. The other said, "You think I'm crazy? I'll get half way out, and you'll turn the light off!"

Wilde now urged us to create a mental image of ourselves and shrink it down.

"Now have that image walk down the ray of light, from the top of your head to the floor," Wilde instructed.

I did what I was told. "Little Joe" walked down my mental beam and got to the floor. I watched in my mind as this midget image of me walked around my shoes and looked around the room.

"Just observe what your image does," Wilde said.

My little guy seemed a bit confused. He decided he didn't know where to go or what to do, so he just sat on the end of my shoe and watched Stuart Wilde with me.

After a few minutes Wilde had us bring the guy back up the light, grow to full size, and then merge with our bodies.

"What was that like for you?" Wilde asked everyone.

A tall man stood and said, "It was confusing. My miniature image didn't know what to do."

"Do *you* know what you want to do?" Wilde asked.

"Well, ah, I think so."

"Someone else?" Wilde asked.

"My shrunken me had fun. She ran around and looked for coins on the floor!"

"Great!" Wilde said, "Anyone else?"

I stood up.

"My little one just sat on my shoes and did nothing," I said.

"Why nothing?" Wilde asked.

"I guess he wanted to know *what* to do."

"Are you caught up in right and wrong, Joe?" Wilde asked me. "If your image didn't know what to do, maybe he was afraid to make a move unless he knew what the right move would be. Is that how you live your life?"

"I dunno," I said.

"Think about it," Wilde said. "Anyone else?"

Turns out that this little imagery technique was revealing. Whatever the little person did at the end of the beam—or didn't do—revealed something about how we act in our day-to-day lives. We all learned something about ourselves from this unique experience. After that moment, some 20 years ago, I started to pay more attention to my own desires.

You might use this imagery exercise to see what your little self will do. And then ask yourself if you are being honest about what you really want in your life. As you'll see in this next section, you *always* know what you want. But you may not always admit it.

What does the person within you want? Write it here:

_____

_____

_____

_____

_____

_____

_____

_____

What If You Still Don't Know?

Some people tell me, "I don't know what I want."

I know those people. I used to be one of them. When I asked Dr. Robert Anthony, author of many best-selling books and the great audio course, *Beyond Positive Thinking,* "What do you say to people who claim they have no idea what they want?" He replied: "I tell them they are lying."

And he's right.

You know what you want. You know it right now. If you are one of the few who say you don't know what you want, you are lying to yourself. Somewhere inside of you, right below what you are willing to admit, are your desires. You simply haven't spoken them.

Dr. Robert Anthony told me, "Everyone knows what they want. They are simply afraid to admit it. Once they admit it, they have to own up to the fact that they don't have it. They have to begin to take action to get what they want, or they have to make excuses for not trying. Both may be uncomfortable. To stay safe, people lie."

You have the chance to achieve your desires. This book is designed to give you a spiritual formula for success that never fails. The five steps in the Attractor Factor are already proven to work. With this information on your side, why not admit what you really want?

Isn't it time?

What do you really want?

_____

_____

_____

_____

_____

_____

Think Like God

Many years ago, I gave a talk called, "How to Think Like God." In it, I told the stories of how people have been cured of blindness, or healed of autism, or achieved great wealth where none seemed possible.

I then urged the audience to take off their blinders, remove their inner mental limits, and to think as if they had superhuman or even supergodly powers. This was a very empowering experience. People loved it. It released their restraints so that they could think bigger than they ever thought before. God wouldn't worry, doubt, bicker, delay, stall, or think small. After all, what *would* you do if you had all the powers of God?

No matter how you view God, you probably admit that your concept is a being with enormous power and no limits. Well, if you thought like that God, what would you want for yourself? What would you want for the world?

Start Here

Use the space below to write what you want to be, do, or have. A study by author Brian Tracy revealed that people who simply wrote down their wants and put the list away, discovered a year later that 80 percent of what they wrote came to be. Write down your wants!

_____

_____

_____

_____

_____

_____

_____

_____

_____

_____

_____

_____

_____

_____

_____

_____

_____

_____

_____

Did you write down many goals?

Sometimes, people feel greedy when they start to ask for what they want. They feel they are taking from others. The best way around that limiting belief is to be sure you also want others to have success, too.

In other words, if you want a new house but don't want your neighbor to have one, you're stuck in ego, and that's greed. But if you want a new house and think everyone ought to have one, then you are in tune with the creative spirit, and you'll pull or be led to that new house. You'll attract it.

You see, there really isn't any shortage in the world. The universe is bigger than our egos and can supply more than we can demand. Our job is to simply and honestly ask for what we want, without wanting to harm or control another person. Never ask for a specific person or for a specific person to do something. Allow the universe, the power in everything, to arrange the right person, place, and time. Your job is to state your intention.

The desire in you is coming to you from your inner spirit. In the space provided, honor your inner spirit by writing down what you really want to have, do, or be:

_____

_____

_____

_____

_____

_____

_____

_____

_____

_____

_____

_____

_____

_____

Now, what would be even better than what you selected?

In other words, you may have written down, "I want $50,000 in the bank by the holiday." Well, what would be better than that? Wouldn't you prefer $100,000? The idea is to stretch yourself a little while still being honest with yourself about your desires.

Write down what would be even better than what you have already stated you want:

_____

_____

_____

_____

_____

_____

_____

_____

_____

_____

_____

_____

_____

_____

Now write down *one* goal or intention, something that you would really like to have, do, or be.

Focus brings power. Look over your lists and see what goal or goals jump out at you. Which goal or intention has the most energy, or charge, on it? A goal should scare you a little and excite you a lot.

And keep in mind that you can always combine goals. There's nothing wrong with stating something like, "I want to weigh 120 pounds, own a brand new Corvette, and have $50,000 in the bank, by this coming Christmas."

In the space below, write down the most powerful intention you can:

_____

_____

_____

_____

_____

_____

_____

_____

_____

_____

_____

Here's the next step:

Write your intention as if you *already* have it.

In other words, "I want to weigh 120 pounds, own a brand new Corvette, and have $50,000 in the bank, by this coming Christmas," becomes "I now weigh 120 pounds, own a brand new Corvette, and have $50,000 in the bank!

"If you want an alternative that may feel better to you, consider the approach Dr. Robert Anthony advises in his audio-program, *Beyond Positive Thinking.* He says it may be more powerful to write, "I now *choose* to weigh 120 pounds, own a brand new Corvette, and have $50,000 in the bank!"

Do that now. Just rewrite your goal into present tense, pretending that you already have what you want, and using the word "choose" if you so desire.

_____

_____

_____

_____

_____

_____

_____

_____

_____

_____

_____

Before we go on, add one more line to your request. Add the phrase "this or something better."

"This or something better" is the loophole that allows you to get out of your ego. If you insist on getting whatever you desire, you are coming from pure ego. As you'll see in Step Five, letting go is an important element to success. The real secret to getting whatever you want is to *want without need*. This will become clear later. For now, add the freeing line, "This or something better" to your stated goal.

Do that here:

_____

_____

_____

_____

_____

_____

_____

_____

_____

Divine Intentions

I spent last Saturday with a small group of wonderful people from all over the world who just completed my year long Miracles Coaching Certification Program. The day was upbeat and buzzing with energy. But at lunch one person asked me a question that may be on your mind, too.

> "In the movie *The Secret* and in your book *The Attractor Factor* you said you believe in intentions, but in your book *Zero Limits* you say you no longer believe in them. What do you do now?"

I can see where that could confuse people.

In my new Nightingale-Conant audio-program, *The Missing Secret,* I explain my approach to life in a way that clears the air. I'll try to recap it here:

Today I realize that most intentions are limitations.

Intentions come from your ego and can actually limit what is possible for you to receive. Intentions are wonderful when you are first awakening to your own power. It's thrilling to set goals and achieve them. But there's an easier, better, more magical, and even miraculous way to go through life. I explain this in *Zero Limits*, where I say there are three stages of awakening.

Stage One:

In the first stage you are a victim. We're all born into it and most of us stay there. With coaching or the right books or the right movies, you one day break free.

Stage Two:

In the next stage you realize you have more power than you ever thought before. In this stage intentions are fun and exciting and useful. You aim your life where you want it to go. It's exhilarating to manifest things like new cars or a new house or anything else you can imagine. But there's a stage after that.

Stage Three:

In the third stage you realize you have choice but you don't have control. You realize you don't have *all* power. This is where you surrender. This is where you can receive inspiration from something greater than your ego awareness.

I was filmed for two more movies last week. One of them is all about letting go to inspiration. For me, I want inspiration. When it comes, *that* becomes my new intention. But the intention comes from inspiration not from limitation. The intention comes from the Divine not my pipsqueak ego.

In short, when I receive an inspiration to do something, *it* becomes my intention.

So I still believe in intentions, not those of the ego but those of the Divine.

Intentions Are for Wimps

When I set an intention to do something like, say, write a book, I use my conscious will and my energy and get it done. But when I *allow* an inspiration to become my new intention, and combine my energy with it, than I often create something astonishingly unexpected like, say, my own television show.

Inspiration might also direct me to write another book, of course, but the point is, inspiration will often *surprise me* with something bigger and bolder than I ever imagined before.

As P.T. Barnum said, "Not my will, but thine, be done."

When you follow inspiration, you get to say (like the Blues Brothers), "I'm on a mission from God."

How do you know an intention from an inspiration?

Usually by how it feels.

When I was on Donny Deutsch's CNBC television show *The Big Idea* November 19, 2007, I told him and his audience that the directive to do anything needs to come from your heart, or your gut, not your mind. When you follow that, you follow your divine path.

It's different for each person, of course. You may be inspired to enroll in Miracles Coaching or Executive Mentoring to better understand my marketing and metaphysical methods; somebody else may not. I still use coaches today, and think everyone needs to. We all have beliefs and limitations to release.

For example, inspiration nudged me into creating my own TV show, called *Expect Miracles*. But my ego was resisting it. It was stretching my self-image limits. For that reason, I needed Miracles Coaching to help me get and stay clear. As long as I stay clear, miracles happen.

I'm now clear and ready for this TV show to be a megasuccess. And now the investors, actors, directors, editors, and writers are coming to me. Why? How? Because I cleared the blocks *within me*, with the help of my coaches, to allow it all to happen.

So let's go deeper. You have a goal or intention that is coming from deep within you. It may scare you. It may excite you. It may confuse you. But trust that the goal is a desire from the Divine. Whatever it is, even if you aren't sure how to attract it, write it here:

_____

_____

_____

_____

_____

_____

_____

Now, before you complete this process, let's be sure this goal or intention is right for you. There is a way to test your intention. I'll explain that procedure next.

You'll love this one!

Let Your Body Speak Its Mind

Most people who do muscle testing do it wrong. I'll explain what it is and then teach you the right way to do it.

Muscle testing, or behavioral kinesiology, is a way to ask your body questions. In short, if your body goes weak when you ask something, that something isn't good for you. If your body stays strong, that something is right for you.

You may have seen this done before. Usually, one person stands, arm stretched out from their side, as another person stands in front of them. The testing person puts one hand on the other's shoulder and the other hand on the outstretched arm. While the person with the arm stretched out thinks of something, the other pushes down on the arm. If the arm goes down, the subject was thinking of something that weakened him. If the arm stays strong, the person was thinking of something that was positive for him.

That's a simplistic explanation of an involved process. But you get the idea. People like Dr. David Hawkins have written numerous popular books, such as *Power vs. Force,* about their work testing a long list of everything from people to theories to time periods in history. All of it is fascinating reading. It has caused a movement in which best-selling authors such as Wayne Dyer tout the benefits of the muscle test.

But again, testing is often done wrong. People can smile and throw off a test. They test products by holding them, when they have to hold them over their solar plexus to get an accurate answer. They push too hard, or with their whole hand, and any number of other things. If you do muscle testing right, you can find out if your goals are right for you. If you don't, you'll deceive yourself and pursue a path that is not for you.

So, how do you do muscle testing right?

The Right Way to Test

First, both people have to be clear.

That is, both people involved have to be centered, calm, and open. You can see right here that this is a potential trouble spot. Few people are centered, calm, and clear. Anyone testing you better be, or they will unconsciously influence the test. The way to get clear is easy:

- You can drink a large glass of water.
- You can tap your chest, over your thymus (upper heart area) a few times.
- You can tap the underside of your left hand (the karate chop area) as you say, "I deeply love, accept, and forgive myself."

All of these methods clear you so that you will be able to get an accurate answer. Both people involved in a muscle test need to do this.

Second, you need to do a control test. In other words, if you are being tested, the person about to press down on your arm needs to ask you a neutral question; something like, " Is your name Joe?" (if your name is Joe) is a valid test. Obviously, you should test strong. If you don't, go back and do some clearing.

Third, the person doing the pressing down needs to use only two fingers, and gently but firmly give one quick push down. This is not a test of strength. This is not a contest.

The Solo Testing Method

There is also a way to test yourself by yourself. I wrote about this method in my e-book, *Hypnotic Marketing.* Here's how you do it:

The best one-person testing method I discovered works like this:

Hold out your left hand, with your fingers spread apart, as if you were going to hold a softball or large grapefruit.

Now, take the thumb and index finger of your right hand and touch the thumb and pinkie of your left hand.

Are you with me? You should have your left hand wide open and your right thumb on your left thumb and your right index finger on your left pinkie. Got it?

Now all you do is try to squeeze the left thumb and left pinkie together as you try to resist.

Go ahead and do that now.

You should have found it easy to resist.

Now think of something negative (Hitler works every time) and try to resist as you also try to squeeze.

Your thumb and pinkie should have weakened.

Now think of something loving (your favorite pet should work) as you resist your own squeezing.

Your thumb and pinkie should remain strong and apart.

See how this works?

I know all of this must seem wild to you. But hey, no one is looking, and I won't tell. So let's keep going.

Test Your Goal

You now have the basics for doing a muscle test. What you will do next is test your written goal. It should make you strong. If it doesn't, consider rewriting it and testing it again. You want it to be right for you. A muscle test is one way to find out if it is a match for you. If it is, it will be easier to attract.

Write your goal here, and then muscle test it:

_____

_____

_____

_____

_____

If you need to rewrite your goal, do so here:

_____

_____

_____

_____

_____

_____

_____

Carry Your Intention

You might now write the above goal on a card and put it in your pocket or purse. By doing so, you will be unconsciously reminding yourself of your intention. Your own mind will then help nudge you in the direction of making your goal a reality.

So relax. You have just planted a seed in your mind. The rest of this book will tell you how to water it, give it sunshine, clear out any weeds, and let it grow.

Prepare to attract your miracles!

Prosperity is the ability to do what you want to do at the instant you want to do it.
RAYMOND CHARLES BARKER, *TREAT YOURSELF TO LIFE*, 1954

CHAPTER 14

Step Three: The Missing Secret

I was on a teleseminar with a marketing friend of mine. We were telling our listeners how important it was to watch out for self-sabotage in their lives. We were pretty impressed with ourselves as we told them that their unconscious beliefs would create their reality, that if they didn't get clear, they could manifest failure.

Halfway through the call we introduced our surprise guest for the evening. He was a famous self-help guru from another country. The guru came on and began by dismissing what my partner and I had just covered.

"Can I take this to a new level?" he asked.

"Well, of course," we told him. "You're the guru."

"You don't need to unearth your past or change your unconscious," he began. "All you have to do is focus on what you want and stay focused on it in each moment."

I totally agreed with him, but also wondered how he expected people to stay in the moment—the greatest spiritual challenge of all time. But I kept quiet and let our guest tout his beliefs.

"I used to be a therapist and quickly saw that it was a waste of time to go into someone's past looking for the cause of whatever they were getting," he explained. "All you have to do is pay attention to your feelings. If it feels good, go in that direction. If it doesn't feel good, stop."

I agreed with all of what our guru guest was saying, but I had to wonder if he was only seeing part of the big picture. I began to feel that he was making the same mistake every other goal-setting, self-help, self-improvement, new-age, guru type was making. So I had to ask a few questions.

"What if a person sets a goal, watches his feelings in each moment, and still doesn't get the result he wanted?"

"Then that individual has a conflict with his subconscious mind," he answered. "He needs to back off from his goal and go for something more believable."

"Then we're right back to needing to unearth beliefs and get clear," I said.

"Well, you don't really need to do that. Just know your intention, follow your feelings, and adjust in each moment."

Our guru friend missed the point. And from what I can see, so have virtually all of the current spokespeople when it comes to how to manifest whatever you want.

What is that point?

Let me explain with a story . . .

Watch Spot

Spot was a stray dog I claimed as my own when I was in college. But he used to run off and tear up the neighbor's garden, run across the street and make drivers slam on their brakes, and just make a nuisance of himself. So I put him on a short leash. But I felt guilty for keeping this wonderful friend on a three-foot leash. I bought a longer leash, six feet of freedom, and put it on Spot. I then walked six feet away and called Spot to me. He ran—three feet. He wouldn't go an inch beyond the length of the old leash. I had to walk over to Spot, put my arm around him, and walk him out the full six feet of new leash. From then on, he used all of that leash.

I think each of us has a limit we've placed on our freedom. We need a "miracles coach" to help us see that in reality we have no limits. Jonathan Jacobs does that with his clients. But he does it in a way that may seem pretty strange to you. Hang on to your seat and let me see if I can explain it to you . . .

Touching the Sky

The first time I had a session with Jonathan I didn't know what to expect. I thought the man was a little strange because he couldn't articulate what he did. But I'd been a curious journalist for many years, so I jumped in and did a session with him.

"What's your intention for this session?" Jonathan asked.

"What do you mean?"

"You can have anything you want. What do you want to focus on?"

I thought it over for a moment and then spoke.

"I want clarity on the book I am writing about Bruce Barton."

"What kind of clarity?"

"I want to know what I'm supposed to do next," I said.

"Okay. Let's go upstairs."

Jonathan had me lie down on his massage table. He gently guided me to breathe in different colors.

"Breathe the color red through the top of your head and imagine it going through your body and out of your feet."

We went through numerous colors.

"What other color do you need to breathe in?" he asked.

I said gray. He then asked me to breathe in that color. After several minutes of my breathing deeply and relaxing on his massage table, Jonathan put his hand over my heart and said, "Open this up."

While I didn't consciously do anything, I felt a rush of electricity and energy shoot through me, almost blinding me. There was a strong white light surging through my body, blasting into my head, somehow illuminating the inside of my skull.

Suddenly, I felt in the presence of angels, spirits, guides. I don't know how to explain it. But it was real. I felt it. I sensed it. I knew they were there. And these beings somehow worked on me, altering my beliefs, helping me realize I had more "leash" than I thought.

I'm not sure how long I was in that altered state. Twenty minutes? An hour? I don't know. When I finally sat up on the table, I noticed that Jonathan had a tear rolling down his cheek. When the energy started to blast through me, he moved aside to let it do its work. But the beauty and miracle of what he was seeing touched him. He was crying.

As my head cleared and I got my bearings, I realized I knew the next step for my book project. I was to go to Wisconsin and continue my research by looking at the private papers of Bruce Barton at the historical museum. I had gotten my intention.

And that's not all.

Shortly after that first session with Jonathan, I began to notice other changes in my outer life. The book I had been working on began to take direction, and became *The Seven Lost Secrets of Success.* I found a publisher for it. I found the money to complete my research. I bought a new car. I bought a new house. My income soared.

How? Why?

I had invited the other side to help me, and it did.

The Wise Choice

As I write these words, I'm very aware that you may think I've lost my mind. After all, here I am—an adult, an author, a fairly well-known speaker and marketing specialist who advises business executives about their work—talking about spirits.

But I also know that you know what I mean. Even the most atheistic among us has been touched by the miraculous, the uncanny, or the unexplainable. Although no one knows what awaits on the other side of this life, we all tend to believe something intelligent is there.

Maybe it's worth mentioning that the book that helped me the most here was *What Can a Man Believe?* by Bruce Barton. In it he explained that there was little proof for heaven after earth, but that it was far wiser to believe than not believe.

In other words, while I can't prove that angels and guides are standing ready to help you, isn't it a much more delicious and comforting and magical thought to believe in them than to not believe in them? There's no concrete evidence to support them or deny them. But when you can use the belief in them to create miracles, wouldn't you be wise to do so?

That Mysterious Something

Yesterday a friend of mine called and said she wanted to believe in guides and angels and teachers from the spiritual side of life, but a part of her doubted they existed.

"That's okay," I said. "I have my doubts, too."

"You do?"

"Sure," I said. "If I had to go into a court of law and prove I had spirit guides, they would laugh me out of the courthouse. There's no proof for them, but also there's no proof against them."

And then I remembered something I had read in a recent issue of *Reader's Digest,* where Larry Dossey talked about prayer. He said praying helped people recover from illness. In many cases, they recovered from what doctors had said were incurable illnesses. What these successful patients did was pray. Even the patients admitted they didn't know if the prayers were answered, but it was the belief in the praying and the act of praying that helped them, anyway. Again, as Barton pointed out, it is wiser to believe than not to believe. Believing helps create miracles.

Barton wrote the following passage in 1927, in *What Can a Man Believe?* I've always loved it, as it seems to stir the very something he talks about within me. See what it does for you:

> In every human being, whether emperor or cowboy, prince or pauper, philosopher or slave, there is a mysterious something which he neither understands nor controls. It may lie dormant for so long as to be almost forgotten; it may be so repressed that the man supposes it is dead. But one night he is alone in the desert under the starry sky; one day he stands with bowed head and damp eyes beside an open grave; or there comes an hour when he clings with desperate instinct to the wet rail of a storm-tossed boat, and suddenly out of the forgotten depths of his being this mysterious something leaps forth. It over-reaches habit; it pushes aside reason, and with a voice that will not be denied it cries out its questionings and its prayer.

So let's assume you don't have access to a healer like Jonathan (though you can reach other healers and mentors by e-mailing the people in the back of this book or by visiting www.miraclescoaching .com). What can you do?

Easy. Focus on what you want, and make one of your intentions finding someone to help you clear yourself of old beliefs so that you can create the life you want. Help exists. State your intention to the world, and allow it to come to you.

I feel it's important to have support from a mentor. It's too easy to fall back into the old way of thinking, to feel sorry for ourselves, and play the role of victim. The vast majority of your current friends probably won't support your desire to create miracles. This is why I created my Miracles Coaching program. I've personally trained coaches to help you get clear so you can easily and quickly attract miracles.

When I first started seeing Jonathan, I would visit him once a month. He and I quickly saw that we needed to stay in touch at least once a week. Jonathan and I made a pact that said, "Whenever I'm not clear, I am to call him." Then, whenever I let something in life throw me for a tailspin, I would call him.

Another woman recently asked me what it meant to "get clear" with my beliefs. I thought about it for a while before I could answer. The image that came to me was of a football team. If one of those players is hurting, upset, feeling neglected, angry because the coach overlooked him earlier or his girlfriend dumped him, that one player can jeopardize or sabotage the entire team's success.

You are like the whole football team. If all parts of you, all of the beliefs inside of you, are in alignment, no problem. You'll attract your wealth. But if any part of you, any belief in you, doesn't support your intention, it will jeopardize or sabotage you. That's why you may have had lousy luck at love, romance, money, or health. Some part of you doesn't want it. We need to heal that part. When you do, you are clear.

And when you are clear, you are free to attract anything you can imagine.

The Most Important Step

As far as I'm concerned, this is the most important step in the entire Attractor Factor formula. When you are clear, there's nothing in the way of you attracting whatever you want or something even better.

But what does "clear" mean? I wrote an entire book to offer cleaning and clearing methods in *The Key*. I also recorded an entire audio-program on the subject as well, called *The Missing Secret*. Those methods are all designed to create an alignment between your conscious and unconscious mind.

Let me explain with the following "The Universe" diagram.

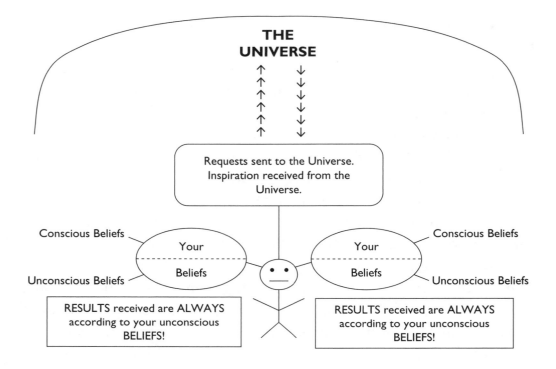

What the image shows is that energy is coming to and through you from the Divine, but it hits a "filtering" system. That filter is in your unconscious. It is made up of your beliefs. If, for example, you say you want to attract wealth, but deep inside your mind you believe "money is bad" or "rich people are evil," then you will actually stop yourself from attracting wealth.

This is true whenever you are trying to attract something but feeling frustrated by your results. The Universe/God/Divine is trying to help you, but it is limited by your own unconscious beliefs. Clear up those limiting beliefs and you can have, do, or be virtually anything you can imagine. The limits are yours.

It was in his work *Project for a Scientific Psychology* written in 1895 that Freud first laid down the radical (at the time) idea that thinking is intrinsically unconscious. We are effectively conscious icebergs with most of our thoughts occurring below the water line, out of conscious perception.

The fact that this idea is no longer considered radical is testament to the last few decades of research, which have shown the importance of unconscious processes. We now have abundant evidence for the unconscious in the operation of memory, affect, attitudes, and motivation.

What this means is that what you consciously think isn't anywhere near as important as what your unconscious mind thinks. Both are tools for you to use, but one is in your awareness and the other isn't. If the below awareness part of you doesn't want what you want to attract, you won't attract it, or if you do, you won't keep it.

Getting clear means your conscious and unconscious mind are in alignment. This third step in the Attractor Factor is all about realigning your inner selves so all of you wants the same thing.

Your New Year's Resolutions

My favorite example is when you state a resolution on New Year's eve. You consciously say things like, "I intend to work out three times a week," or "I intend to date more," or "I intend to stop smoking."

But what happened the next day or the next week?

Most likely you forgot your resolutions.

But why? You stated what you wanted. You had the best of intentions. Why didn't you follow through? Why did you stop doing what you knew would be good for you?

Basically, you had *counterintentions* within you. These are beliefs in your unconscious that don't want what you say you would like to attract. For example, you might say, "I want to be slim," but in your deeper mind you hold the belief, "If I'm thin, people will harm me," or "If I'm slim, people will want to have sex with me."

Again, you must be clear to attract and achieve what you want.

Are You Clear Right Now?

How do you know if you are clear right now?

Think of something that you want to have, do, or be.

Why don't you have it yet? Write your answer here:

_____

_____

_____

_____

If your answer is something negative, you aren't clear. If you say anything except an honest, "I know it's on the way to me," you probably aren't clear inside with what you want.

Another question to ask yourself is, "What does it mean that you don't yet have what you want?" Write your answer here:

_____

_____

_____

_____

Your answer to that question will reveal your beliefs. For example, if you say, "I have to do such and such first," then you have a belief that you have to do something before you can have what you want.

If you say, "My soul doesn't want me to have this," then you are stating your own beliefs about what you think your soul wants for you.

If you say, "I don't know how to get what I want," then you are revealing a belief that says you have to know how to get what you want before you can have it.

The truth is, nothing means anything in and of itself. You and I apply meaning to events and call it truth. But our meaning reveals our beliefs. Sometimes those beliefs serve us, and sometimes they don't.

I've also learned that the meaning you give an event is the belief that caused it. This is huge. When you declare, "This always happens to me," you actually just found the belief that caused the event. The belief came first.

How to Locate Your Beliefs

Your beliefs aren't that hard to find.

First, understand what a belief is. According to Bruce Di Marsico, creator of The Option Method, a brilliant tool for exploring beliefs, "A belief is assuming something to be true, to be a fact. A belief is not caused, it is created by choice. A belief *about* a thing's existence is not the same as its existence."

In other words, a shirt is not a belief. It's a fact. It's an existence. But saying a shirt is good for you personally, or not, is a belief.

Self-help author Mandy Evans, an Option Method practitioner, says certain beliefs can lead to a very bad day. *Beliefs cause stress, not your business or life situations.* It's your perception of events that cause how you feel.

"There's what happened to you in your life, and then there's what you decide it meant," Mandy told me over lunch one day. She's the author of *Travelling Free: How to Recover from the Past by Changing Your Beliefs.*

"Change your conclusions or your beliefs about the events in your past," she explained, "and you can change the way you live your life today. Certain beliefs can really trip us up."

Beliefs shape the way we feel, think, and act, Mandy says. She's an expert in personal belief systems. But you often can't change those inner systems until you know what they are. She offers a list of "The Top 20 Self-Defeating Beliefs" in *Travelling Free,* her second book, as a way to begin exploring them.

"As you look at each belief, ask yourself if you believe it," she suggests. "If you do, then ask yourself why you believe it. Gently explore your own reasons for buying into any self-limiting belief."

Here are 10 of her top 20 limiting beliefs.

1. I'm not good enough to be loved.
2. No matter what I do, I should be doing something else.
3. If it hasn't happened yet, it never will.
4. If you knew what I'm really like, you wouldn't want me.
5. I don't know what I want.
6. I upset people.
7. Sex is dirty and nasty; save it for the one you love.
8. Better stop wanting; if you get your hopes up, you'll get hurt.
9. If I fail, I should feel bad for a long time and be really scared to try again.
10. I should have worked this out by now.

Those are all beliefs. Sometimes you need another person to point out your beliefs. When my friend Linda and I had breakfast one day, and I hired her to help me with some promotion, she said, "I'm afraid some of my friends will be jealous of me."

"That's a belief," I said.

Linda's eyes widened and her face lit up.

"It is?" she asked.

It had never occurred to her that her fear was a belief—a belief she could let go of. She needed another person to shine a light on the belief.

Here's another example of what I mean.

How to Get a New Car

The following happened many years ago, but I remember it well . . .

I needed a car *bad*. The one I was driving was an old clunker that could only move if you pushed it. Okay, it wasn't that bad. But whenever the car broke down, I broke down. Paying the repair bills was killing me.

And never knowing if the car would get me where I was going was stressing me out. I needed help. I called Jonathan because of my fear of car salespeople. (I had been one once and knew of their tactics.) I told Jonathan what I wanted.

He said, "What you really want is often under what you say you want . . . What would having this new car do for you?"

Huh?

Jonathan went on to explain that what we want may be a feeling rather than a product. Focus on the feeling, and it will help me get what I really want. What would I feel if I had a new car?

What a mind stopper! I developed a brain squeezing headache just thinking about it. I got off the phone, and my head began to throb as if it had been hit with a sledgehammer. Although I almost never take medicine, I ate a handful of aspirin like it was popcorn. It didn't help.

I went to see Jonathan in person. Sitting in the presence of his accepting energy, letting my pain "speak" to me, I suddenly saw the ache between my eyes as a huge black ball of tightly woven thread. Mentally, a thread would loosen, and I'd hear a belief:

"You can't afford a new car."

I let it go and another belief would unravel:

"What would your dad say about this car?"

And then another thread/belief would slide out: "How will you afford it?"

And then another . . . and another . . . and another . . .

As these beliefs slowly came apart and left, the black ball of pain got smaller. And smaller. Within 20 minutes, the headache was completely gone! I was healed. I was clear. I was happy.

Now get this:

Although I didn't think it was really possible, I followed my intuition and immediately went to the car dealership I felt led to visit. Consciously, I knew there was no way I could get a new car. (I had *never* had a new car in my entire life, and my credit was lousy.) But I let go. I trusted.

I went to the car dealership, and the gentleman there let me look around. I told him what I wanted, and he said he had one car that fit the description. We walked out back, and he was right. It was perfect. It was gold and beautiful and new. I said, "Does it have a cassette player?" He looked and nodded. "Well," I said, "let's do the hard part. Let's see if I can buy it."

We filled out forms, and he asked me to place a deposit. I didn't. I wasn't confident enough to think I would get the car, so I put nothing down on it. I then left. I drove to a friend's outside of the city, and we played music all day, him strumming his guitar and me blowing on my harmonica. Later in the afternoon, I decided to call the dealership.

"You qualify," said the salesperson.

I was stunned.

"I do? Are you looking at *my* paperwork?" I asked. "I'm Joe Vitale."

He laughed and assured me he was. He then asked me when I wanted to pick up my car. I went and picked up the car, in delighted shock that it was mine. Although I had no idea how I would make the payments, I did. In fact, I mailed my checks in early.

And that's not all.

As soon as I decided to get the new car, my life went into an upward spiral of magical coincidences.

Suddenly, the money I needed appeared. Clients began to call. Classes sold out. I was invited to speak to groups I had never heard of. And two publishers gave me book offers on the very same day.

In some real way, my allowing the car in my life sent a message to the universe that I was *trusting*. Instead of worrying and wondering how I'd pay the bills, I leaped off the mountaintop of fear and—to my surprise—I didn't fall.

I soared.

But I had to get clear inside before any of this could happen. Had I gone to buy a new car when I was still carrying limiting beliefs about what I could have afforded, my beliefs would have sabotaged my purchase. I would have attracted not paying for the car to support the beliefs I had at the time. The first thing that had to happen was clearing the beliefs.

And for the record, I went on to buy *four new cars* from that same dealership over the next decade, and today I drive even fancier cars.

Clearing beliefs can really pay off!

Money beyond Belief

What do you tell yourself when you look at your business and see it isn't yet where you want it to be?

Do you blame it on the economy? Your salespeople? Your marketing? On your own ability to accomplish anything?

Whatever your answer, *that* is a belief. Common ones include:

- "I must work hard for the money I earn."
- "I need more money than I can generate."
- "I feel helpless in changing my financial picture."
- "I think my salespeople are loafing."
- "I don't handle money and wealth well."

What you want to do is replace negative beliefs with positive ones, such as:

- "Money is a natural manifestation of the universe."
- "It's good to be rich."
- "I don't have to work hard for my money."
- "I am destined for great wealth."
- "My staff earns money for me."
- "I handle money and wealth well."

You see, most of the beliefs you have were given to you when you were a child. You simply absorbed them. Now, you are becoming awakened. You have a choice. You can choose to let go of the beliefs you don't want, and you can choose to replace the beliefs with ones that better serve you.

Other beliefs come from our culture itself. I was sitting in a movie theatre just today, explaining to a friend how we can consciously choose new beliefs, when over the speakers came the song, "It Ain't Easy." It kept repeating the same words, "It ain't easy. It ain't easy. It ain't easy." That song was followed by the Rolling Stones classic, "You Can't Always Get What You Want." My friend and I started laughing, realizing the cultural brainwashing at work. Unfortunately, no one else in the theatre seemed to realize they were being programmed with limiting beliefs.

I remember that I used to have the belief, "The more I spend, the less I have." Seems logical, doesn't it? If you spend your money, you will have less of it. But I decided to change that belief. Instead, I accepted the new belief, "The more money I spend, the more money I receive." Now, I know I'll receive money whenever I write a check. Why? Because I choose to believe that.

You can do this, too. As you become aware of the beliefs you have about wealth, ask yourself if you want to continue believing them, or if you would prefer new beliefs. Then, consciously choose the belief you prefer. You may have to do this a few times at first, but the end result will be attracting the results you prefer.

Some people say you are lying to yourself when you declare an intention that isn't true yet. My counterargument is that you are *already* lying to yourself. Saying, "I'm always broke!" is a lie. It's a belief that causes your current reality. It seems like the truth but it's just a statement infused with energy that you choose to believe is real. As long as you keep it, it *will* be real. You'll continue to attract situations to prove it to you. But the belief is what is causing the attraction, and that belief is a lie.

Tell yourself a lie you prefer. Instead of saying, "I keep having problems with my tenants or my landlord!" change it to "I am at peace with my tenants or my landlord." At first the new intention will feel uncomfortable, but only because it's new. As you sit with it, and let it become part of you, you will begin to notice it reshaping your reality. It will soon be your reality.

Isn't that a wonderful feeling—to know that you can now create your life the way you want it to be?

What new beliefs would you like to install? Write them here:

_____

_____

_____

_____

_____

_____

_____

_____

_____

_____

_____

_____

_____

_____

_____

Remote Clearing

Clearing beliefs can be an easy process. The easiest time I ever had was when I wanted to overcome my sinus allergies.

I had suffered terrible sinus infections and sinus headaches for years while I lived in Houston. I can't begin to describe how miserable they made me feel. I took herbs. I had acupuncture treatments. I wore air purifiers. Everything helped, but nothing worked permanently.

Then one day, I asked my dear friend Kathy Bolden, a remote healer, if she would try to help me. While having dinner, I looked her in the eyes, slammed my fist on the table, and said, "I don't want relief. I want healing. I want this thing *gone.*"

My intensity shook her. But she also realized how sincere I was and how much pain I had been in. She said she would try to help.

And she did. She went home, got quiet, and used her skills to clear my body. I was not present as she did this. I wasn't even aware that she did anything. But within a few days I noticed that I could breathe again. I called her and asked what she had done.

"You had some negative energy in you, and I scared it off," she said.

Apparently, she was able to use her remote healing skills to clear my beliefs and my energy from a distance. Talk about making things easy for me!

Releasing the Past

Here's another example of clearing beliefs. This one still amazes me, because it happened to my late ex-wife, and I saw the dramatic change.

Marian never learned to drive a car. I was her chauffeur for more than 15 years. I'm not complaining. That's just the way it was.

But after seeing my changes with my work with Jonathan and other healers, Marian wondered if she could get clear about driving. She booked a session with Jonathan. Within one hour, she was clear.

What happened? Marian remembered being a little girl and being in the back seat of her mom's car as her mom learned how to drive. Her mom was naturally nervous. Marian picked up on that energy and locked onto it. While Marian went on to grow up, the little girl who sat in the back seat of her mom's car remained alive in her. As an adult, that little girl kept Marian from driving.

Under Jonathan's guidance, Marian was able to remember that experience and release it. She realized it was an old memory, and it no longer served her. She let it go. Her energy was now clear.

And Marian continued to drive her own cars—new ones, to boot—and she loved it. I remember one night there was a terrible storm in Houston with lots of flooding. I was worried about my wife and how she would handle the weather. When she got home late that night, I ran to the garage to greet her.

What I saw amazed me. Marian was smiling ear to ear. Her face was beaming. She rolled down her window and said, "I had an adventure!"

Even being stuck in traffic is something Marian felt grateful for. She simply sat there and listened to music.

And one day we went to lunch in separate cars. After it, I was behind her at a stop light. I saw her moving her lips and tapping her fingers on the steering wheel. I wondered if she were getting impatient. Then I pulled up closer and realized she was singing and tapping her fingers to the music!

Talk about a transformation!

Later, Marian was in a bad car accident. She was hit by a van, and hit hard enough to break the back axle on her car. Despite the shock of it all, Marian was fine, although her car wasn't.

Now here's the juicy part: Two days later, Marian was ready to rent a car and start driving again. I couldn't believe it. I told her I was proud of her, that many people are too nervous to drive so soon after an accident.

Marian just looked at me, smiled, and said, "Why? Driving is too much fun not to do it!"

Free Your Past

Jonathan has a saying, "It's all energy." What he means is that we are energy systems. If we are clear, the energy moves in one direction. If we aren't clear, the energy moves in several directions, and without full power.

Caroline Myss, a medical intuitive and author of *Anatomy of the Spirit,* talks about being "plugged into" the past. If there was a situation in your life where you were hurt, abused, or left anything unfinished, you are probably still carrying around that unfinished business. You are still plugged into that old event. That means a part of your energy is still back there, reliving and probably recreating the old event.

I know this is tough to understand. But let's use another example from Myss. Think of the energy you get each day as cash. You wake up in the morning with $500 available for the day. But you are still mad because your spouse said something mean to you last night. That's going to cost you. You are spending $50 to keep that energy alive in you.

And say you are still upset because a friend owes you money from five years ago. Now you are spending $100 to keep that memory alive.

And let's assume you were abused as a child. You are spending another $100 to keep that memory in you. You woke up with $500 to spend, but before you get out of bed you have spent half of it on old memories.

When you try to attract something today, you won't have all of your energy available to make it happen. When you get clear of the old events, hurts, memories and beliefs, you will have more energy to attract what you want now. And the more energy you have now, the more you will get.

You will end up like the supermodel who once said, "I don't wake up for less than $10,000 a day."

Your Results

Another saying Jonathan has is, "The energy you give out is the results you get."

Yes, he's great at coming up with mind benders like that. But I think he means that the beliefs you have create the results you get.

If you are unconsciously sending out vibes that attract lousy conditions, you will experience lousy conditions.

If you find yourself recreating similar events—like my friend who has been married seven times so far—you know you are stuck in an energy pattern that will continue to create those events until it gets dissolved.

My dear friend Karol Truman, author of the great book *Feelings Buried Alive Never Die . . .*, put it this way:

"It's the continual suppression of unresolved feelings and emotions that cause the problems we experience in our lives."

I can hear you now: "How can I get out of this pattern?"

One of the fundamental principles of Jonathan Jacobs' work is that everything is energy. It's not a new idea. Stuart Wilde writes about it in his books. Joseph Murphy refers to it in his works. Bob Proctor talks about it in his seminars. Scientists are discovering it, as well. Nothing exists but energy formed into things we then name, like tables, chairs, houses, cars, people.

The thing is, you and I are different from tables, chairs, houses, and cars because we are spiritual. That's the miracle of our lives!

As Bob Proctor once told me, "Although everything is energy, the difference between people and objects is that we are spiritual. That means we have the means to alter and influence other energies. We can change the energy of a table, chair, house, car, or even other people."

Taken a step further, it means we are all connected. If we're nothing but energy and we're all one, then what you do affects me, and what I do affects you, even if we're miles or even continents apart.

Got it?

Oh.

Well, neither did I, at first.

So let's look at a couple of stories that may help.

How to Change People

One day, a client of mine hired me to be his marketing wizard. He gave me a lot of money, and I hired some folks to help me. All went well. Months passed. Then one day, the bomb dropped.

My client suddenly sent me a letter saying I had lied to him. It was two pages of pain for me to read. It got pretty confusing, and it made me dizzy, confused, and shocked. I had meetings with my staff, and I even called my client. I couldn't figure out why this was happening. I sent the client a two-page letter explaining my position. The next day I got another two-page letter from him, almost as shocking. Finally, I went to Jonathan.

"The key word is trust," Jonathan pointed out. "You keep saying he didn't trust you. Let's look at how that applies to you. Where in your own life aren't you trusting?"

This is typical of Jonathan. He'll have you look at your own life to see how what you are complaining about is relevant. In a way, you use your experiences as mirrors. You use the outer to see what you are doing inside. (Stay with me on this.)

I thought and said, "Well, I've never done marketing like this before. He's hired me to direct his entire marketing campaign and expects me to lead his staff to victory. I guess I don't trust that I can do it."

"And that's what your client is picking up on an energy level. That's the signal you are sending out."

"What do we do?"

"Are you willing to release the fear and feel the trust?"

"Yes."

And that's about all it took. I felt a shift inside me, and I felt that I knew I could trust myself to do the job. I let go and breathed a sigh of relief. I feel it happened so easily because most of me was already clear with the problem. I didn't have a lot of work to do in clearing old beliefs. Now here comes the good part.

I went home and called my client. He answered and sounded remarkably at peace. I told him I was going to do a great job for him.

"I know you are," he said, stunning me. "I decided a little while ago to just trust the man I hired to do his job."

"You decided a little while ago? When?"

Yes, he had decided to trust me about the time Jonathan and I looked at the trust issue in me. Once it was clear in me, my client felt it. Once I sent out a different signal, my client picked it up.

Coincidence? Then let me tell you another story . . .

Where Money Comes From

Another client of mine went on to great fame and fortune. He's a 25-year-old stockbroker who wrote a book on wealth. I knew it would be a success before he did. I acted as his literary agent and marketing consultant and went to work to find a publisher for his book. As it worked out, he left me and went to an agent in Dallas, thereby cutting me out of the $45,000 in profits I would have earned from his $300,000 advance. But he's a very honorable guy and said he would pay me some money when he got his big advance.

Days passed.

Weeks passed.

Months passed.

Nothing.

I wrote him a few kind notes. I sent him copies of my articles to share my own successes. I called him a few times and left messages.

Still nothing.

I asked Jonathan about it. He suggested I write a letter to the client and state my feelings, state what I want, and forgive him. I went home and did that. It felt very good.

But still nothing.

I went to Jonathan and said I did what he told me but still no reply.

"What does that mean?" he asked.

"It means he hasn't contacted me yet."

"And?"

"And it means he may rip me off."

"There it is," Jonathan announced.

"Where what is?" I asked.

"It's the fear of being ripped off that is blocking your energy. That's the belief in your way."

"How do I let go of that?"

"Feel that feeling of being ripped off."

I closed my eyes and did so.

"Let it take you back to the other times when you may have been in experiences where you decided on beliefs about money and people."

I recalled being taken by a Dallas company for money I had nearly died to earn. I had felt cheated. I held a grudge against that company for nearly eight years. I breathed into that feeling and felt a shift inside. I opened my eyes and smiled.

"The money he owes you doesn't have to come from him," Jonathan explained. "The universe is prosperous and can give you money in a wide variety of ways. Release the need for him to pay you and you allow the money to come."

Accepting that concept is a biggie. It means totally letting go of any and all grudges against people. It means trusting that you will get what you want, as long as you aren't attached to how it comes to you.

I felt like the release was there. I felt lighter and clearer. And when I got home there was a message from—my client!

After six months of nothing, suddenly a call! He was very polite, very friendly, and said he was mailing me a four-figure check. He did, too, as I received it the next day. I feel that only a fool would call that experience a coincidence. The connection is too obvious, and happens to me too often to blow over as mere chance.

As Jonathan says, it's all energy, and we're all connected. Clean the energy pathways, and you can have, do, or be anything you want.

What Runs Your Life

If you feel that you have cleaned your energy circuits and are free from the past and yet you aren't attracting money or miracles or anything else, then you haven't cleaned your energy circuits or gotten free from the past.

This happened to me a few years ago. After doing several sessions with Jonathan by phone, I realized that my income wasn't increasing. My bills were being paid, and money was arriving just in the nick of time to pay them, but it was too close for my comfort. I began to get worried. Not a good sign. My worry was evidence that I had some unfinished business to clear up. I wanted to contact Jonathan, but he was not available.

Then one day Bill Ferguson offered to give me one of his sessions. Bill is a former divorce attorney who has created a way to help people release the key core issue that sabotages their lives. He's been on *Oprah*, and he's written several books, including *Heal the Hurt that Sabotages Your life*. I was helping Bill with his publicity, and he wanted me to experience what he does. When he said I could have a session with him, I accepted. Especially because it was free. Now that I have had it, I would have been willing to pay anything for it.

"People are starving to learn how to find peace," Bill told me when I went to his Houston suite. "But they keep looking outside of themselves and blaming people or circumstances for how they feel. That's not how life works."

He asked me to think about a recent event that pushed my button. That was a snap. I had just fired a client of mine who didn't agree with my ideas on how to promote his business. I was insulted and angry.

"Note that how you felt had nothing to do with the other person. All the person did was reactivate your hurt by pushing the right button. Once you disconnect the hurt, your hot button for emotional pain won't be there.

"Every one of us has a hurt from the past that runs our life," Bill added. "For one person, the hurt is failure. For another, it's the hurt of feeling worthless, not good enough, not worth loving, or some other form of not feeling okay with who they are."

He added that avoiding these feelings creates emotional pain.

"Until a person releases the core issue, it will continue to operate," Bill told me. "You could be 90 years old and still recreating painful experiences because of a core belief you accepted when you were six."

Although many psychotherapists believe people have unresolved past issues, few claim they can be healed quickly. Bill developed a new technology that helps people release their emotional pain—and in less than two hours. You might say he has created a way to achieve "push button healing."

"Pick another event where you were upset," Bill told me. I did. Again, it was easy. While I hadn't thought about it before, I suddenly began to see a pattern. Almost every time I was upset with someone, it was because I felt insulted.

"What does it mean that you feel insulted?" Bill probed.

After a moment, I realized it meant that I didn't feel good enough. I must not be good enough, went my logic, because these people don't like what I am doing and I end up being insulted.

Now Bill started to rub my nose in it.

"How's it feel to not be good enough?" he asked.

I was getting depressed. I looked into Bill's boyish face, wondering if he really wanted me to feel this bad. He did.

"Until you can fully feel the hurt that's been buried alive inside you, it will continue to operate and sabotage your life."

Whew. By now I was feeling like life itself wasn't worth living.

"If you are truly feeling the key issue for you, you should be feeling like life isn't worth living."

"I'm there, Bill. I'm there," I said, slowly.

"Good!" Bill declared. "So how's it feel to be not good enough?"

"Like the worst feeling I've ever felt."

"Can you accept that you really aren't good enough?"

I struggled with that one. While I could look at my life and clearly find evidence that I was good enough, I had to admit that I wasn't good enough in all areas. And I had to further admit that this belief that I wasn't good enough was unconsciously causing me to be upset with clients and friends. I had been losing many opportunities. Even money.

"Yes, I can admit it."

Something shifted right there. I somehow felt lighter. More relaxed. Free. Where before I felt tense and angry, now I felt relaxed and calm. Even happy. It was as if some giant electrical wiring had been disconnected and I suddenly looked at life differently.

Bill and I did some additional work before I left. But after the session, I noticed major differences. Nothing seemed to irritate me the way it used to. The next day, I had a client argue about an ad I wrote for him, and this time I didn't fly off the handle. I calmly stated my case. And I noticed that I looked at each moment with love and optimism. And I saw that I wasn't afraid to do things that I used to not do at all, like play the guitar in front of friends or perform magic over dinner. Before, I didn't feel good enough. And I also noticed that money started to roll in. One morning a few days after my work with

Bill, a woman faxed me that she was sending me a check for several thousand dollars to begin promoting her business.

What had happened?

Now that the core belief was disconnected, I had opened the energy centers in me to allow the abundance of the universe to flow my way.

And flow it did.

The Science of Getting Rich

In Wayne Dyer's book, *Manifest Your Destiny,* he says if you aren't manifesting what you want, there probably is an absence of love somewhere in your inner world.

That's another way of discovering where you may not be clear inside. Think of how you feel about the people involved in what you want to create. If there is a negative "charge" or uncomfortable feeling about someone, you aren't clear with that person.

Forgiveness is the best way I know for getting clear by yourself. And the best way to become forgiving is to feel gratitude. I'll talk more about gratitude a little later, but for now know that if you focus on what you like about people, you will feel grateful, and then you will begin to forgive, and then you will get clear.

And when you get clear, you can have, do, or be whatever you want.

Here's one more easy way for you to get clear, and it's something you can do on your own. I learned it from my friend Bob Proctor, at one of his famous Science of Getting Rich seminars.

Take two sheets of paper.

On the first sheet, describe the negative condition you are in. Describe the picture of the situation as it is now, and really feel the emotions associated with it. This probably won't feel great. But you want to get into that feeling, because the more you feel it, the more you will release it. In other words, whatever emotion you suppress will sooner or later need to be expressed. While it's suppressed, it's clogging up your inner vibration. Release it, and you free your energy to go out and attract what you want. Let your feelings come to the surface as you describe this situation or condition that you don't want. You can write it here if you like:

_____

_____

_____

_____

_____

_____

_____

Now put that first sheet aside.

Take the second sheet, and begin to write out how you want the situation or condition to be. Get into the joyful feeling associated with having or doing or being the thing you desire. Really immerse yourself in this good energy. Describe the situation the way you want it to be, and paint this wonderful picture so completely that you can feel it as you write it. Just as you wanted to experience the negative emotion so that you could release it, you now want to experience the positive emotion so you can create a new picture to anchor in your subconscious. The more you can fall in love with this new image and these new feelings, the faster you will manifest them. You can write it here if you like:

_____

_____

_____

_____

_____

_____

_____

Now take the first sheet, look it over, and burn it.

Take the second sheet, fold it up, and carry it with you for a week.

You're done. You probably just cleared yourself of your negative block. And if it should ever resurface, just do the exercise again.

See? It's easy!

Patterns

Have you ever noticed a reoccurring theme in someone's life? Maybe even yours?

It's the same issue again and again, maybe with different characters playing it out, but it's always the same problem at heart.

Why is it always *the same* problem?

For example, for most of my life I had problems with money. I was homeless for a while, lived in virtual poverty for years, declared bankruptcy once, went to court and was fined for bad checks I had written, was constantly in debt and always desperate for money. I had that same problem for most of my adult life.

Beliefs like these fueled it—though I was unconscious of them at the time – *I don't deserve money, money is bad, money is not spiritual, rich people are greedy, I'll never succeed, I'm not good enough, business is bad, there's not enough,* and so on.

So the life pattern of having money problems surfaced again and again, with my car breaking down, accidents, illness, and unforeseen emergencies.

I had the same problem with losing weight. I spent most of my life, from childhood on, fighting obesity. The operating beliefs behind that reoccurring problem—again, most of which were unconscious to me—were *diets don't work, I hate exercise, healthy foods taste like crap, my DNA is wrong, I'm destined to be fat, fat people are safe, fat people are happier, nobody likes me anyway,* and so forth.

I had the best of good intentions for wanting to be healthy and wealthy, but the unconscious counterintentions stopped them from being manifested. And that pattern continued until I unraveled the beliefs and broke free.

This is true for all of us.

Even you.

If you look at your life with an objective eye (knowing that is not fully possible but go with me on this), you'll see patterns. Maybe it's always a relationship issue . . . or health issue . . . or money issue . . . or work issue. . . . or—you name it.

For example, I discovered a pattern in myself that I had been unaware of until last weekend. Three people I know (or thought I knew), one of whom has been a dear family friend for over a decade, came out with a book slamming *The Secret*, with me in it, and none of them shared the book with me, or even told me when it came out. I had to stumble upon it *six months* after the fact.

I was more upset that none of these *friends* had the decency to share their project with me, than that they wrote it.* I was sick for several days. I was literally ill. I had a fever, weakness, aching joints, and coughing fits.

Why?

Everytime something happens, there is meaning behind it. When you stop and reflect, you can decode the operating beliefs that brought it about. In my case I caught a bug, and that bug was named *betrayal.*

As I looked back, I saw that betrayal had been a pattern in my life, just as money issues and obesity once were. Because of hidden operating beliefs, the pattern came into reality one more time. When you get to the end of this book, you'll know the nightmarish betrayal I went through with Jonathan. I'm no stranger to it.

Obviously, I had attracted my experience. But this isn't about betrayal, it's about patterns. *Your* patterns. And mine.

But here's the good news: Once you learn the lesson from the pattern, you no longer need the pattern. You can actually stop the patterns!

I've done it with money. I've learned that the more money I make, the more I can help myself and my world. Whether it's a Panoz exotic sports car or a $15,000 therapy machine for a child I don't know, I'm now able to make the choice and write the check. It's a beautiful place to be.

I've done it with obesity. I've lost 80 pounds and been in seven fitness contests. The obesity pattern is history, too.

Now that I'm aware of the old betrayal pattern, I can let it go, as well. Sometimes all you need is the awareness that you attracted what you got due to your beliefs. Sometimes you have to sit down and consciously search and find your beliefs, and then choose to let them go as you insert new ones in their place. And sometimes you have to hire a Miracles Coach to help you climb out of the mental quicksand.

The point, again, is that you and I are cocreating our reality with our beliefs. If you've got a reoccurring pattern in your life, it's not your fault and it's not anyone else's fault. It's simply mental software. It's a program. You can rewrite it. That's how you begin new, healthier, happier patterns.

And you can begin it right now.

Write down your recurring patterns:

_____

_____

_____

_____

_____

_____

_____

_____

Now write down what you think the pattern means:

_____

_____

_____

_____

_____

_____

_____

Now write down the pattern you would prefer to have:

_____

_____

_____

_____

_____

_____

The Work

Byron Katie, author of _Loving What Is,_ has a remarkable clearing method called "The Work." It's basically a simple questioning process. You take a statement that is bothering you and "work" on it.

For example, "My boss infuriates me" (which could be "My spouse infuriates me," or "My neighbors infuriate me," or "That blogger infuriates me,") could be the statement you focus on. It could also be, "Not attracting what I want makes me frustrated!"

You now ask these questions:

"Is it true?"
"Can you absolutely know that it's true?"
"How do you react when you believe that thought?"
"Who would you be without that thought?"

There's a bonus technique to do after you answer those questions, too.

You take the original troublesome statement—"My boss infuriates me"—and turn it around, to be more personal, such as *"I infuriate me."*

Note how that feels.

This procedure is a powerful way for exploring what troubles you. At heart, they are just thoughts. There are many books and audios by and about Byron. A good place to start is www.thework.com. While in Canada, I picked up a copy of her book, *Question Your Thinking, Change the World.* It's a collection of quotes from Byron. Here's one:

"There's no suffering in the world; there's only a story that would lead you to believe it. There's no suffering in the world that's real."

Chew on *that.* And then use her process on something that is bothering you, to help you get clear about it. Here's a worksheet to help you:

"Is it true?" _____

"Can you absolutely know that it's true?" _____

"How do you react when you believe that thought?"

_____

_____

_____

"Who would you be without that thought?"

_____

_____

_____

And then "turn it around" and make the thought about you.

_____

_____

_____

How does that feel?

_____

_____

_____

The Mustard Seed

Years ago, I gave a talk about spirituality at a business conference. At one point, I told the audience that I carry a souvenir coin with a mustard seed in it. The coin has a saying engraved on it reading, "If you have faith as small as a mustard seed, nothing shall be impossible for you."

I then asked the crowd, "Have you ever thought about a mustard seed?"

I paused and then added, "A mustard seed has no doubts. It doesn't second-guess its goal. It doesn't worry, wonder, or fret. It is clear."

This is the essence of this step in the Attractor Factor. You want to be clear within yourself—no doubts—so you can attract the very thing you say you want.

As Ernest Holmes wrote in *Creative Mind and Success*, "You can attract only that which you first mentally become and feel yourself to be in reality, without any doubting."

But how do you get clear of the deep-seated and even unconscious doubts?

Karmic Surgery

Dr. Marcus Gitterle is an emergency room physician and antiaging specialist. We met after he read one of my books, loved it, and e-mailed me, saying he lived in the same small town I do. We had lunch and became quick friends.

One day, he told me about a way to do "karmic surgery." This was news to me, and made me aware of a new tool that was almost magical. It could help you release any troubling problem, or heal any condition, or achieve any intention, and do it without your doing anything. In fact, others did it for you.

Marc explained it like this: "Just as you have a problem and go into the surgery, the problem is taken out while you are asleep. When you awaken, the problem is no longer there. You might be told to rest more, to drink more fluids, but in essence you are now free of the problem. All you did was agree to let others remove it for you."

What Marc is talking about are *yagyas,* or *yagnas.* These are known in the East and little known in the West. They are not surgery, but instead a way to have spiritual masters perform rituals on your behalf, with the intent of achieving your intention.

I know this may sound strange. But *yagyas* have a long history. A *yagya* is a religious or spiritual ceremony performed by a Hindu priest in order to alleviate karmic difficulties. Basically, a *yagya* is the chanting of specific Vedic mantras (sounds) by professionally trained and dedicated Vedic Pandits. This is generally the most preferred method to dissolve a crisis situation or a dangerous, life-threatening one. But you can also use *yagyas* to get clear, so you can have, do, or be whatever you want.

Rather than continue trying to explain what a *yagya* is, let me instead give you a testimonial on how one influenced my best friend.

Saved from Death

My best friend of two decades was on her deathbed a year ago. After being in a near-fatal car accident, having both knees replaced, her back broken, suffering from depression, then becoming suicidal and anorexic due to medications she never should have accepted, she was taken by ambulance to the hospital, where she lay unconscious and dying.

We had already tried everything. She had gone to healers, doctors, therapists, and psychiatrists. I hired home health care for her. She prayed, meditated, listened to tapes. I asked 500 friends of mine to pray for her and send her healing energy. Nothing was breaking her free. I feared I would lose my best friend of 25 years.

In desperation, I arranged for a month-long *yagya* to be done for her. Within two days, she woke up in the hospital, sat up, and stood up. The day before, she could not move or even turn over in bed! Now she was ready to go home. The hospital was stunned. The doctors couldn't explain it. They kept her for further testing and observation.

She just got better and better. A week later, this same woman who was near dead was released from the hospital. She is now walking, talking, smiling, driving, and very glad to be alive. I saw her yesterday. I thought I might never see her again. This is a genuine miracle.

And that's the power of a *yagya*.

Some people argue that a *yagna* uses the placebo effect to help you get better. The placebo works because you belief it will work. That's interesting in itself as it proves belief is powerful. But in this example, my friend in the hospital didn't know I had arranged a *yagna* for her. It was impossible for her to benefit from a placebo effect because she had no idea anything was happening!

Another example is when my father was ill with prostate problems. He had gone to several doctors but the result was the same: he was bleeding and he was in pain. I finally arranged for a *yagna* to be performed for him. Keep in mind my father had no idea this was being done. He's an old school ex-Marine and not very open minded about alternative methods of healing. So this healing was done in stealth mode.

Yet a month or so later he said he didn't have prostate problems anymore. That was more than two years ago, and he's still fine today!

Publishing Miracle

Dr. Gitterle does *yagyas* for himself, wife, and son. I have done them several times for myself. Let me give you an example.

As you know by now, this book you are holding is based on a popular little work I released a few years ago called, *Spiritual Marketing*. I knew the book contained a powerful five-step process for manifesting your heart's desires, and I knew it from all the people who e-mailed me every day, telling me their miraculous stories.

What frustrated me was the fact that the book was basically available only online. I knew that it needed to reach a wider audience. So I set the intention to find a strong publisher, with distribution abilities, and the power to get my book out there into the world.

To help make that intention happen more quickly, I arranged for a *yagya*. I went to www.yagna.by-choice.com and asked for a *yagya* to be done on my behalf. I didn't know how this would work, or if it would. But I trusted. I took action.

Within a few weeks, I received an e-mail from a senior editor at Wiley—who is now the publisher of this very book!

Now stop and think about this. My original book, titled *Spiritual Marketing*, had been a number one best-seller at Amazon *twice*. Its success had been written about in the *New York Times*. The e-book version of the book had been downloaded an estimated *one million* times. The e-book had been translated into *seven* languages. Thousands of people wrote me about it. The best agent in the country shipped the book to major publishers for two years.

Yet—*nothing*!

Nothing ever happened to bring the book to a global audience until I arranged for a *yagya* to be performed to help my intention, and to clear me of any inner blocks preventing my goal from manifesting.

This is karmic surgery. A *yagya* is a way to clear you of any current blocks—whether those blocks are from this lifetime or another—so you can go on to attract whatever you want.

Talk about effortless healing!

"I Love You"

I'd be doing you a disservice if I didn't tell you the following story. It's a short version of what is in my book, *Zero Limits*. Since this is so powerful, I have to include it for you.

A few years ago I heard about a therapist in Hawaii who cured a complete ward of criminally insane patients—without ever seeing any of them. The psychologist would study an inmate's chart and then look within himself to see how he created that person's illness. As he improved himself, the patient improved.

When I first heard this story, I thought it was an urban legend. How could anyone heal anyone else by healing himself? How could even the best self-improvement master cure the criminally insane? It didn't make any sense. It wasn't logical, so I dismissed the story.

However, I heard it again a year later. I heard that the therapist had used a Hawaiian healing process called *ho'oponopono*. I had never heard of it, yet I couldn't let it leave my mind. If the story was at all true, I had to know more.

I had always understood "total responsibility" to mean that I am responsible for what I think and do. Beyond that, it's out of my hands. I think that most people think of total responsibility that way. We're responsible for what we do, not what anyone else does. The Hawaiian therapist who healed those mentally ill people would teach me an advanced new perspective about total responsibility.

His name is Dr. Ihaleakala Hew Len. We probably spent an hour talking on our first phone call. I asked him to tell me the complete story of his work as a therapist. He explained that he worked at Hawaii State Hospital for four years. That ward where they kept the criminally insane was dangerous. Psychologists quit on a monthly basis. The staff called in sick a lot or simply quit. People would walk through that ward with their backs against the wall, afraid of being attacked by patients. It was not a pleasant place to live, work, or visit.

Dr. Len told me that he never saw patients. He agreed to have an office and to review their files. While he looked at those files, he would work on himself. As he worked on himself, patients began to heal.

"After a few months, patients that had to be shackled were being allowed to walk freely," he told me. "Others who had to be heavily medicated were getting off their medications. And those who had no chance of ever being released were being freed."

I was in awe.

"Not only that," he went on, "but the staff began to enjoy coming to work. Absenteeism and turnover disappeared. We ended up with more staff than we needed because patients were being released, and all the staff was showing up to work. Today, that ward is closed."

This is where I had to ask the million dollar question: "What were you doing within yourself that caused those people to change?"

"I was simply healing the part of me that created them," he said.

I didn't understand.

Dr. Len explained that total responsibility for your life means that everything in your life—simply because it is in your life—is your responsibility. In a literal sense the entire world is your creation.

Whew. This is tough to swallow. Being responsible for what I say or do is one thing. Being responsible for what everyone in my life says or does is quite another. Yet, the truth is this: If you take complete responsibility for your life, then everything you see, hear, taste, touch, or in any way experience is your responsibility because it is in your life.

This means that terrorist activity, the president, the economy—anything you experience and don't like—is up for you to heal. They don't exist, in a manner of speaking, except as projections from inside you. The problem isn't with them, it's with you, and to change them, you have to change you.

I know this is tough to grasp, let alone accept or actually live. Blame is far easier than total responsibility, but as I spoke with Dr. Len, I began to realize that healing for him and in self identity *ho'oponopono* means loving yourself. If you want to improve your life, you have to heal your life. If you want to cure anyone—even a mentally ill criminal—you do it by healing you.

I asked Dr. Len how he went about healing himself. What was he doing, exactly, when he looked at those patients' files?

"I just kept saying, 'I'm sorry' and 'I love you' over and over again," he explained.

That's it?

That's it.

Turns out that loving yourself is the greatest way to improve yourself, and as you improve yourself, you improve your world. Let me give you a quick example of how this works. One day, someone sent me an e-mail that upset me. In the past I would have handled it by working on my emotional hot buttons or by trying to reason with the person who sent the nasty message. This time, I decided to try Dr. Len's method. I kept silently saying, "I'm sorry" and "I love you," I didn't say it to anyone in particular. I was simply evoking the spirit of love to heal within me what was creating the outer circumstance.

Within an hour I got an e-mail from the same person. He apologized for his previous message. Keep in mind that I didn't take any outward action to get that apology. I didn't even write him back. Yet, by saying, "I love you," I somehow healed within me what was creating him.

I later attended a workshop run by Dr. Len. He's now 70 years old, considered a grandfatherly shaman and is somewhat reclusive. He praised my books, including the early edition of this book, *The Attractor Factor.* He told me that as I improve myself, my books vibration will raise, and everyone will feel it when they read it. In short, as I improve, my readers will improve.

"What about the books that are already sold and out there?" I asked.

"They aren't out there," he explained, once again blowing my mind with his mystic wisdom. "They are still in you."

In short, there is no out there.

It would take a whole book to explain this advanced technique with the depth it deserves, and that's why I wrote *Zero Limits.*

Suffice it to say that whenever you want to improve anything in your life, there's only one place to look: inside you.

"When you look, do it with love."

Just start saying "I love you" inside yourself to everything and everyone. It helps to address this to your connection to the Divine. But it's easy and it's free! In fact, I'm saying "I love you" as I write these words. Can you feel the love?

The Script

Finally, let me give you one more method for clearing yourself. This one doesn't cost any money, doesn't take more than a minute to do, doesn't hurt at all, and is guaranteed to work every time.

Interested?

The method involves a simple script that you say out loud to release a belief or a feeling you no longer want, and to replace it with something you prefer. I learned it from my friend Karol Truman, author of the truly amazing book, *Feelings Buried Alive Never Die.* . . .

I'll give you the Script in a moment. First, understand that this powerful tool is so simple, it's easy to dismiss. All you're asked to do is say a couple paragraphs of words. That's it!

Yet what the Script does is reprogram your basic DNA structure. It speaks to your spirit and asks it to help you get clear on the most fundamental levels of your being.

I don't want to complicate things here by trying to explain how this process works. My job is to give you the tools and show you how to use them. After all, you don't need to know how a fax machine works in order to send or receive a fax. All you do is insert the paper, and it does the rest.

The Script works the same way. All you do is say it, inserting in the appropriate place what you are feeling at the time that you want to clear, and inserting in the appropriate place what you prefer to feel. This will make more sense once you know the words in the Script, so here they are:

Spirit, please locate the origin of my feeling/thought of feeling negative about (insert the feeling or belief you want to release here) _____

_____.

Take each and every level, layer, area, and aspect of my being to this origin. Analyze and resolve it perfectly, with God's truth.

Come forward in time, healing every incident based upon the foundation of the first, according to God's will; until I'm at the present, filled with light and truth, God's peace and love, forgiveness of myself for my incorrect perceptions, forgiveness of every person, place, circumstance, and event which contributed to this feeling/thought.

With total forgiveness and unconditional love I delete the old from my DNA, release it, and let it go now! I feel (insert the way you want to feel here) _____!! I allow every physical, mental, emotional, and spiritual problem, and inappropriate behavior based on the old feelings to quickly disappear.

Thank you, Spirit, for coming to my aid and helping me attain the full measure of my creation. Thank you, thank you, thank you! I love you and praise God from whom all blessings flow.

Simple, isn't it? Now, if you don't believe the Script will work for you, use the Script on that belief.

In other words, insert "Help me release my doubt about the power of this Script," in the first open spot in the Script. That's where you insert the belief or feeling you desire releasing.

In the second spot in the Script, insert the belief you prefer, which might be, "I now understand that any belief can be changed in just a moment, even with such a simple tool as this Script."

Just before going to press with this book, Karol told me she had a new and improved version of the Script. She said this was even more powerful than the previous one. Here it is:

Spirit/Super-Conscious, please locate the origin of my feeling(s)/ thought(s) of _____. Take each and every level, layer, area, and aspect of my Being to this origin. Analyze and resolve it perfectly with God's truth. Come through all generations of time and eternity, healing every incident and its appendages based on the origin. Please do it according to God's will until I'm at the present—filled with light and truth, God's peace and love, forgiveness of myself for my incorrect perceptions, forgiveness of every person, place, circumstance, and event which contributed to this/these feeling(s)/thought(s).

With total forgiveness and unconditional love, I allow every physical, mental, emotional, and spiritual problem, and inappropriate behavior based on the negative origin recorded in my DNA, to transform.

I choose Being _____.

I feel _____.

I am _____.

(Basically, use the same appropriate positive feeling/s for each blank line, to replace the negative feeling/s.)

It is done. It is healed. It is accomplished now! Thank you, Spirit, for coming to my aid and helping me attain the full measure of my creation.

Thank you, thank you, thank you! I love you and praise God from whom all blessings flow.

Again, either Script is powerful. Read Karol's wonderful book for a detailed explanation of it. Meanwhile, use the Script whenever you feel the need to get clear.

It works—almost like magic!

And once you are clear, you can truly attract virtually anything you can imagine!

Isn't this a fun, exciting, even exhilarating way to live?

> We learn the lessons in life we are to learn two ways: either through obedience to natural laws or through suffering the consequences of not observing those laws. . . . None of us consciously create the suffering we experience.
> —KAROL TRUMAN, *FEELINGS BURIED ALIVE NEVER DIE* . . ., 1998

CHAPTER 15

Step Four: Nevillize Your Goal

One of my favorite spiritual authors is Neville Goddard. He wrote such classics as *Out of This World* and *The Law and the Promise*. He was a charming character who seemed to have access to a world most of us don't see. He taught people how to use their "imaginal" mind, add feeling, and create results. He once said in a lecture:

"I urge you to use your imagination lovingly on behalf of everyone, and believe in the reality of your imaginal acts. If you have a friend who would like to be gainfully employed, listen carefully until you hear his voice tell you of his new position. Feel his hand clasp yours. See the smile on his lips. Use every sense you can possibly bring to bear into the imaginal scene. Persist until you feel the thrill of reality, then drop it and let that scene fulfill itself on the outside."

You may have noticed that Neville didn't say just focus on the image of your friend getting a job. He also advised you to *hear* your friend's voice. And to *feel* your friend touch you. And to feel the thrill of reality of the scene having taken place.

Neville's great contribution to the science of attracting your own reality was the idea that you must first feel the thing you want as if you already had it. I call this Nevillizing your goal.

In one old book I have by Neville, he signed it with the phrase "Assume the feeling of the wish fulfilled." That's the key. That's the secret. You have to learn how to "Nevillize Your Goal" by assuming the feeling of the wish fulfilled.

How? Begin right now by answering the question, "What do I want to have, do, or be?" Write it down:

_____

_____

_____

_____

Now, get into the feeling of having already accomplished it. In other words, if your goal is to make $200,000 in sales this year, what does that *feel* like when you consider *already having achieved it*? You assume the feeling of that intention already fulfilled. What would it feel like to have what you want right now?

_____

_____

_____

_____

What Neville was suggesting is that you must feel whatever it is you want to attract. You might see it in your mind, but until you *feel it as already complete,* you will be missing a key step in the attraction process. This is a step missing from virtually all self-help books. This is the step missing in most hypnosis, visualization, and other mind-expanding programs.

This is Step Four in the Attractor Factor.

The Real Reason the Titanic Sank

I've repeatedly used Neville's method in my own life, to help me on the Larry King television show, to help me prepare for a presentation where I spoke after Tony Robbins and before Donald Trump, to help me write books like the one you are reading right now.

Before I explain the method to you in detail, let me offer a small slice from Neville on how powerful scripting your future with feeling can be:

"Fourteen years *before* the frightful sinking of the Titanic, an Englishman by the name of Walter Lord wrote a book entitled, *A Night to Remember*. In it, he conceived a fabulous Atlantic ocean liner called the Futility.

"She was 800-feet long, triple-screw and carried 3,000 passengers. Believed to be unsinkable, the liner carried only a few lifeboats. Then one night, Mr. Lord filled her to the brim with the rich and complacent and sunk her on an iceberg in the Atlantic.

"The Titanic was built by the White Star Line. She was 800-feet long, triple-screw and capable of carrying 3,000 passengers. Because she was believed to be unsinkable her lifeboats were few.

"Completed 14 years after the fictitious Futility was imagined, the Titanic sailed out of Southampton on her maiden voyage filled to capacity with the wealth of Europe. Five days later, this glorious ship struck an iceberg and sank on a cold April night."

Neville goes on to point out that the work of fiction may in fact have created the disaster. The novel "scripted" the event. Neville goes on to say the following:

"I do not know the motive behind Mr. Lord's book, but I do know that the identical ship was built 14 years later and that it carried the same kind of a passenger list and went down in the same manner as the fictional ship.

"I tell you, there is no fiction. Tomorrow's world is today's fiction, just as today's world is the fiction of yesteryear. One man dreamed of talking to someone across space using only a wire, another of hearing music being played across the land in their own living room, another desired light without the use of a candle. These desires have all come true, but when they were first conceived they were all fictional, all unreal products of the imagination."

This may seem preposterous or actually insane at first glance. How can a novel written 14 years earlier create a disaster in real life? But Neville is revealing the power of a focused mind. When you write something filled with passion, and you script out all the details so it appears to have actually happened, then you are programming it *to* happen. Neville goes on to say the following:

"Stop reflecting life around you and begin to select the thoughts you choose to plant in your wonderful mind and imagination. Single out that aspect of reality to which you want to respond, be it success, health, dignity, or nobility. Make it something wonderful where you contribute to the good of society, the community, and the world.

"Feel the thrill of witnessing these from within and you have planted your seed. You need not labor to produce your seeds, for they are already finished, waiting for you to encounter them in your community. Plant your seeds and let others think they are bringing them into being."

Keep the above in mind as you keep reading . . .

Emotion Has Power

Marketing specialists know that people don't act for logical reasons, but for emotional ones. Emotion has power. Emotion also has the power to create what you want. Find within yourself what it will feel like to have, be, or do the thing you want, and you will begin to manifest the thing you want. The energy in the emotion will work to pull you toward the thing you want while also pulling the thing you want toward you.

I know, I know. I'm getting philosophical again. But I'm writing about spiritual concepts, which few people can relate to. It's easy to see why. We are taught from the crib to pay attention to reality, to obey the laws of man, to worship books and leaders. While that can help our society run smoother (actually, it hasn't worked, but that's another book), it limits you. Belief in leaders, rules, and outside authorities limits you from creating the life you want.

I once told a friend that a belief in a guru can limit her own power to manifest what she wanted. (You'll see how true this was for me when you read the upcoming chapter "The Shocking True Story of Jonathan.") When you give your power away to anyone, you are spending your own energy in their direction.

If you want to attract wealth and anything else, you need to own your own power. You need to own your own energy. You can ask everyone what they think about any of your goals, but in the end, you have to decide. You are the best authority on you. As my friend Mandy Evans often asks, "After you read all the books and hear all the lectures, how do you know what to do for you?" In short, you have to own your energy and decide for yourself.

This energy is a key ingredient in the Attractor Factor.

A Powerful Energy

One of the most powerful energies you can ever experience is gratitude. Feel gratefulness for anything, and you shift your entire outlook. Feel thankful for your life, your lungs, your home, this book; it doesn't matter. Once you feel grateful, you are in an energy that can create miracles.

Jonathan taught me this. I remember going to see him when I was broke and depressed. One of the first things he did was guide me into realizing that I had plenty in my life. When you compare your own life to that of people living in third world countries, you quickly see that you are living like a king or queen. You probably have food, water, and shelter, as well as a refrigerator, a television, a radio, and probably a computer. Millions of people don't. Realize you are blessed with enormous abundance right now, feel grateful for it, and you will attract even more abundance.

What are you grateful for?

_____

_____

_____

_____

_____

_____

_____

Curing Illness

My friend Jonathan Morningstar (a completely different Jonathan) once cured himself of a terrible illness with a simple one-line statement of gratitude.

Jonathan got double pneumonia. Nothing seemed to help him. Then, he felt inspired to write down one simple but potent sentence that he repeated every hour, recorded on audiotape and played back to himself, and wrote on signs that he hung around his home. He made this one-liner part of his very being.

And within 24 hours, Jonathan was healed. What was the one line he used?

"Thank you, God, for all the blessings I have and for all the blessings I am receiving."

I'm not a scientist, so I won't pretend to explain how this works. Somehow, your energy sends off signals that attract more of what you are sending off. Change your signals, and you will change your results. Change your energy, and you will change what you experience. "The energy you give out is the results you get."

That's the Attractor Factor.

Again, gratitude can shift everything. Just start feeling sincerely grateful for what you have. Look at your hands, or this book, or your pet, anything you feel love and gratitude for. Dwell on that feeling. That's the energy that can help you manifest whatever you want.

In the space below, write down something or someone you are grateful for. I know you did this exercise earlier, but you can't do it enough. Again, gratitude is a powerful and free tool for engaging the Attractor Factor:

_____

_____

_____

_____

_____

_____

_____

_____

_____

Imagine the Outcome

Another energy you want to experience is the energy that comes from imagining what it will feel like to have, be, or do the thing you want. This can be fun.

Imagine how good it will be to have what you want, to be what you want, to do what you dream. Feel the electrifying feelings that come with the images. These feelings can create the life you want. They can manifest it for you. Somehow, those feelings lead you, guide you, direct you to do the things that will make the events.

The great German thinker Goethe may have said it best when he wrote the following inspiring message:

> Until one is committed, there is hesitancy,
> the chance to draw back, always ineffectiveness.
>
> Concerning all acts of initiative there is one
> elementary truth,
> the ignorance of which kills
> countless ideas and endless plans:
> That the moment one definitely commits oneself,
> then providence moves, too.
>
> All sorts of things occur to help one
> that would never otherwise have occurred.
> A whole stream of events issues from the decision,
> raising in one's favor all manner of
> unforeseen incidents and meetings and

material assistance which no man
could have dreamed would come his way.

Whatever you can do or
dream you can, begin it!
Boldness has genius, power,
and magic in it.

The Camera

I was in Seattle once to see friends. One night, I turned on the television and caught the ending of a fascinating Larry King interview with the famous actor and singer, Andy Griffith. Andy was talking about one of his first motion pictures. He said something unknowingly relevant to the Attractor Factor process when he talked about a director who told him: "The camera is just a machine. It picks up what you give it. All you have to do is think something, and feel it, and the camera will record it."

They then cut to a scene from the movie Griffith was referring to, when he was to look at a woman with a heart full of lust. You could tell from the actor's eyes that he was projecting thoughts that were pretty hot. Larry King later said, "It was one of the most X-rated looks in movie history."

The universe is like the movie camera. Think something, and feel something, and the universe will pick it up and project it. The advice Andy Griffith was given as a young actor is advice I want to give to you: *When you know what you want, all you really have to do is think it and feel it.* That's it. The universe—the spirit of all that exists—will pick up your signal and project it.

Take a few moments and write out a detailed scene of the vision you want, writing it as if it has already passed and you are celebrating your victory. You are Nevillizing your goal. Get into the feeling of accomplishment.

Catching Fire

This is powerful stuff. When Jonathan Jacobs and I practiced this, our energy levels shot skyward. We had so much energy surging through us that the very electrical outlets in our homes burst into flames.

This is the truth! When I lived in the dump I could barely afford to pay rent for, the electrical system there fried. It cost the landlord over $7,000 to repair it.

When Jonathan was first experimenting with energy, the fuse box in his garage caught on fire. Although this isn't why they call me "Mr. Fire!" it does demonstrate that when you make changes internally, you'll see changes externally. Jonathan had to have a new fuse box put in. My landlord replaced the entire electrical system in the house. But as my energy increased, I also had to move into a bigger home with better wiring.

Again, *what you embrace in your inner world creates what you experience in your outer reality.*

Your Inner Becomes Outer

Jonathan and I were having lunch at a favorite Chinese restaurant one day, when I noticed there was hardly anyone in the place. The owners looked worried. They were huddled around their cash register and talking. Usually, they came over to us, smiled, talked, and treated us like royalty. It was clear something was wrong. I mentioned this to Jonathan, saying, "They seem concerned about money."

Jonathan replied, "That's why they're concerned."

At first, my mind screeched to a halt. But then I started laughing. Jonathan asked me what was so funny. I explained as best I could.

"Were you a Zen master in a past life or something?" I began. "What you just said was one of those unanswerable mind stretchers that Zen masters come up with."

"What do you mean?"

"I said those people look worried about money, and you said that's why they're worried about money. To the outside world, that makes no sense."

"But it's the truth," Jonathan explained. "Their concern for money was something already in them that got manifested. Now they notice it in the outer world. They manifested their belief."

He then went on to tell me about a man he had worked with who ran an Indian restaurant and was failing at it. Business was lousy. He did a session with Jonathan and realized he didn't want to run a restaurant at all. Once he was clear, he let go of the restaurant and sold it. As a result, people started going to it under its new owner.

"Once you take care of the inner, it will show results in the outer," says Jonathan.

Cut through Pain

Another time he told me, "When you get the lessons, you don't need the experiences."

As bizarre as all of that dialogue might seem to you, it's been the truth in my experience as well.

One time a company hired me to help promote one of their Dallas seminars. I advised them on what to do, and then I got angry when I saw that they did the opposite. They were, in essence, screwing up their own success.

I talked to Jonathan about it. He asked me what I got out of this. In other words, what was the benefit to me? Assuming a part of me did create the company doing everything wrong, how would it serve me? I thought about it and had the answer.

"Their screwup takes the pressure to succeed off of me," I said. "They hired me to help them make the seminar a success. I wasn't sure I could do it. By their not listening to me, they have almost guaranteed that the seminar will fail. When it does, I can point my finger at them and say, 'You did it, not me.'"

It keeps coming back to what we are doing and feeling inside plays a giant hand in what we end up experiencing.

No matter what the situation you are in, some part of you helped create it.

Get in touch with it, release the old beliefs and energy, and you can move toward creating what would serve you better and bring you more joy. One of the best ways to do just that is to focus on what you want, on how it would feel to have it, be it, do it. In this way, you can begin to attract it to you.

Write Your Future

One wonderful technique to help you in this area is called scripting.

I first heard of this method from my longtime friends Jerry and Esther Hicks. I later learned that Neville had taught it decades earlier. The concept is deceptively simple.

Just imagine that you *already* have what you want and write out a scene that describes it. Describe it in such detail that you can feel it. Pretend you are a movie director, and write a script for what you want to experience. Really get into it as you write it. Feel it. Sense it. Experience it.

I have a notebook full of scripts. Every one I have written has come into reality. Again, when you think it and feel it, it comes to be.

Why not take a few minutes and write your own script right now, and right here? Get some paper if you don't want to write in this book, but now is a good time to create your future.

Neville's advice may help you here. This is from his book, *Immortal Man,* and it works for both men and women.

"First, have a dream, and by a dream I mean a daydream, a gloriously wonderful daydream. Then ask yourself, 'What would it be like if it were true that I am now the man I am dreaming I would like to be. What would it be like?' Then catch the mood of the wish fulfilled and drench yourself with that feeling."

Now, choose what you want to experience. Whatever it is, write up a description of it, as if it *already* happened. Instead of writing, "I want a customer to call me with a big order," you write, "A brand new customer just called and ordered $5,000 worth of product from me. I feel fantastic! The call came a few minutes ago. I'm still smiling about it, as the customer was a delight to work with. The customer even gave me his credit card and I'm running it right now."

You get the idea. Pretend the day is done and you're recording the experience of what you want to have happen in your journal, after it happened. Be detailed. Be joyful. Enjoy the process. Describe it the way you want it, just after the fact. And do it right now!

_____

_____

_____

_____

_____

_____

_____

_____

_____

_____

_____

_____

_____

_____

_____

Why Not?

If you didn't write a script right now, why not?

You create your next moments out of *this* moment. What you do right now is the energy you send out that attracts what you get later. That's the Attractor Factor, remember. When you write a script, being sure to do it with emotion, you create a powerful "thought form," or ball of energy, that goes out into the world to make your script come true.

This is too important to pass over. We are all connected on an energy level. In 1943, Lucius Humphrey wrote in his rare little book, *On the Beam*: "While we think of ourselves as individuals, we are not cut off from the whole. We are *separate* beings but not *separated* beings."

Because we are all connected on this behind-the-scene energy level, we can put requests into the universe at large and, if we're not too attached to the outcome and we are open to receiving the outcome we request, we *will* receive it or something better. The people involved in manifesting your request will feel your energy on an energy level. (We're all connected, remember.) They will be nudged by their own spirit within to help you achieve your goals.

This is the spiritual formula for success that never fails—guaranteed!

This is the Attractor Factor!

Go back and write your script!

You're Printing Your Energy

It's worth mentioning right here that your business cards, letterhead, flyers, sales letters, and ads—everything you produce or hire someone to produce to market your business—all carry your energy in them. As a result, they will attract—or repel—the clients you say you want.

Think back to some flyer or letter you received in your mail. As soon as you glanced at it, you felt one way or another about the service. You may have had an instant feeling that said, "This looks interesting," or an instant one that told you, "Trash this."

I'm not just talking about the look of the marketing piece, although that is part of it. When you or anyone you hire creates a marketing document, they put their thoughts and feelings into what they create. People don't have to be psychic to pick up on this vibe. If you unconsciously don't believe in your product or service, that belief will appear in your marketing materials. And people will sense it. And you won't get business.

Again, feeling attracts miracles. When you know what you want, are clear about having it, and can feel the energy of what you want, you will begin to attract or pull it to you. And when you clearly feel this energy, you will create marketing pieces that convey it. Here's an example of what I mean.

When I wrote a sales letter for a software product that I totally believed in, I got staggering results. People read the letter and sensed my sincerity and the product's benefits. As a result, more than six percent of them sent in checks. In the world of direct mail marketing, that is excellent.

But when I wrote a sales letter to offer a service I did not believe in, I got nearly no replies. Why? The same writer created both letters. But my lack of belief in the second item was conveyed to people. They picked up on my vibe and just knew they had better not order.

Another example is the flyer I received to attend a workshop in Seattle. All I saw was a dark photocopy of the original flyer. So I wasn't dazzled by bright colors, fancy type, clever copy, or incredible graphics. But something about the flyer said, "Sign up for this event." I did. When I spoke to others at the seminar, all of them said they had the same feeling. Many added, "I don't even know why I'm here. I saw the flyer and knew I was supposed to be here." The people who put on the seminar were clear about what they wanted. That confidence appeared in their brochures. And the people came.

Contrast that with a company I worked for at one time that wanted to put on a seminar about Internet marketing. This company was only after profits. There was no caring in their business and no sincere desire to serve people. That attitude showed up in their brochures. When they put on their event, they expected more than 200 people to attend. Only 20 people showed up.

You can't fool the Attractor Factor.

Advertising Works

I've noticed that many people have a negative attitude toward advertising. I think that's a limiting view. An ad can help you market your business. It can become another voice working on your behalf. It can be spiritual, too.

One day, I was having dinner with Jerry and Esther Hicks, and another friend. We were talking about marketing in general and advertising in particular. My friend said, "You don't have to advertise."

"You don't have to," I said, "but you might want to. A good ad can increase your business."

"The last time we ran an ad in a magazine," Jerry began, "we got so many replies we couldn't handle them all. I dropped the ad until we hired more staff."

"It doesn't matter what you put in the ad," Esther added. "People will sense who you are and what you are offering and make a decision from that feeling."

Jerry and Esther have hired me to write their ads because they know I believe in their work. If I didn't believe in them, the ads I create for them would show it. And if they didn't believe in their work, the person they hired to create their ads would reveal that attitude.

My friend Sandra Zimmer, who runs the Self-Expression Center in Houston, also knows the power of spiritually based advertising.

Sandra consciously infuses her ads with her energy. She actually sits and meditates over her ad, sending her energy into the ad. As a result, her ads have a magnetic quality to them. She once told me that people hold on to her ads for as long as seven years. I know I had seen Sandra's ads for many years, before I finally met her in person. Although her ads didn't look different, they felt different. There was just something about her ads that made them memorable. That something was Sandra's own energy.

"Advertising is important," Sandra once told me. "But it's the energy you put in the ads that does the work. It's really the law of attraction at work."

Again, who you are inside creates the results you get outside. Your inner attracts your outer. Even your marketing pieces carry your energy. Get clear, feel the energy of what you want to do, be, or have, and you will naturally go in the direction of attracting what you want.

Jonathan's Method

Since I worked with Jonathan Jacobs for more than 10 years, seeing him almost weekly, I have a good idea of his method for creating results. As you know by now, he was able to help me, and others, achieve miracles. I think his three-step method is worth a closer look. Here's a typical session with Jonathan:

1. We meet, and he asks me what I want. This is the "setting the intention" stage. Once you decide on your outcome, the rest almost falls into place. So, Jonathan always began by focusing on your desire. *What do you want?*

   _____

   _____

   _____

   _____

   _____

2. We then focus on what is in the way of achieving my desire. Obviously, this is the "getting clear" stage of the process. Jonathan used his verbal skills to help me recognize what was blocking me from my success. *What's in the way of your success?*

   _____

   _____

   _____

_____

_____

_____

3. We then channel energy to the intention. In other words, since we had a target, and we had identified and cleared everything blocking the pathway to manifesting it, we now basically sent energy to the goal through us. *How can you receive energy or increase your energy to help you achieve success?*

_____

_____

_____

_____

_____

_____

As you can probably see, Jonathan used feeling in his last step to help magnetize the desire. That's how you use the Attractor Factor. In other words, he helped me bring in energy through my body, with the idea that it would help manifest my intention.

I'll try to explain this by using my *Chi Kung* education.

Ancient Chinese Secrets

Chi Kung, or *Qi Gong*, is an ancient Chinese healing art. It resembles *Tai Chi* in that it uses slow movements, body awareness, and the intentional channeling of internal energy to produce results. *Chi Kung* is used to heal, rebuild, improve energy, and circulation, and achieve and maintain a healthy body and mind.

You can use a simple *Chi Kung* type of exercise to pull energy into your body, aiming it to attracting your goal. It looks like this:

1. Decide on what you want.
2. Get clear of anything in the way of having the goal.
3. Bring energy into your body while holding your intention in mind.

This is easier than it may first appear. All you have to do is *breathe*. As you breathe in, imagine the air is energy. See it travel into your body and to the achievement of your desire.

Much of *Chi Kung* relies on you using your mind while you breathe and move your body. That's what I'm asking you to do here. In your mind, see your goal. Maybe you see it already accomplished. Maybe you can't see the goal, but you know on some level what it looks like when it's complete. Go there. Use your mind to experience your intention.

As you breathe, imagine the air is energy going to that mental experience. See the energy fueling it, making it live. Just pretend your energy is magic that will breathe life into your intention.

Let go. You don't need to do much more. And as you'll see in the next section on the final step in the Attractor Factor formula, letting go is very important.

Burning Desire

When I was in Australia in May 1999, I learned that many seeds don't open up and grow unless they are first burned.

In the human body, you open your seeds of desires with the heat of emotion. Whenever you feel love or fear, two very strong emotions, you are turning up the heat. That heat reaches your deeper mind and opens the seed, the image, of what you want. How you do that is through feeling.

The point of this step is that you must joyfully feel the energy of the thing you want to do, be, or have. As Joseph Murphy wrote in his little book, *How to Attract Money,* "The feeling of wealth produces wealth."

Or as William E. Towne wrote in 1920, "A thought is powerful only when it is backed by feeling. Feeling gives thought its reactiveness. To merely make an affirmation of what you desire, without faith or feeling, will accomplish little."

And Judge Thomas Troward wrote in his book, *The Hidden Power,* "Our thought as feeling is the magnet which draws to us those conditions which accurately correspond to itself."

Feel the joy of having what you want—feel it right now—and you will begin to attract it to you and you to it.

Take this moment to script something you want to be, do, or have. Remember to write this as if the intention has come into reality and you feel fantastic about it. Since you can paint this scene any way you like it, infuse it with feeling and detail and above all, have fun!

_____

_____

_____

_____

_____

_____

_____

_____

_____

The whole process of mental, spiritual, and material riches may be summed up in one word: Gratitude.

—Joseph Murphy, _Your Infinite Power to Be Rich,_ 1966

CHAPTER 16

Step Five: The Ultimate Secret

Here's a secret that may surprise you: When you want something, but can live without having it, you have upped the odds of your having it.

This is one of the ironies of life. As long as you are playfully desiring something, but not addicted to having it, the universe will most likely quickly bring it to you.

But as soon as you say, "I *must* have this," you begin to push it away. Why?

Because you are sending out an energy to repel what you say you want.

Because you are focused on need and not in the moment.

Because you haven't learned the ultimate secret, Step Five: *Let Go.*

The Ego's Love

Years ago I discovered that most of us, myself included, don't like to let go and allow because there's nothing for us to grapple with. There's no drama. Most of us feel that if we can't get in there and fight and struggle, we don't feel like we're accomplishing anything or getting anywhere. The struggle gives a sense of accomplishment. At least, you can say, "Hey, I tried."

The ego gets a big rush out of struggle. The ego gets to feel that it is doing something worthwhile. Well, that's okay. If your ego needs a pat on the back, let it struggle for some of the things that you desire. But the truth is, you don't have to struggle at all. Again, it can be another way . . . an easier way.

I used to teach a class called, "The Inner Game of Writing." It was modeled after the work of Tim Gallwey, who wrote *The Inner Game of Tennis* and co-authored several other "inner game" books. What I discovered was that we have at least two distinct beings within us, not personalities so much as aspects of our mind. Gallwey called them Self One and Self Two.

Self One can be likened to your ego, the part of you that wants to control.

Self Two can be likened to the inner master within you, the part of you that is connected to all things.

The job of Self One is to select what you want and let go.

The job of Self Two is to bring it to you.

Gallwey learned that when people learned to let go and trust, they got what they wanted more often than not, and it came much easier than if they fought for it.

The same concept works in your life. Choose what you want and let God or the Universe (whatever that means to you) bring it to you. Let it orchestrate the events that will manifest the thing you desire. Give up needing to know how you will manifest anything. Knowing how can become a limitation. If you choose to manifest something, but can't consciously see a way to create it, you may give up. The conscious mind can't see all of the possibilities. Surrender control and you free the universe to bring you whatever you want.

Tough to swallow? Then let me tell you a story . . .

Lost Secrets Miracle

When I was working on one of my earlier books, *The Seven Lost Secrets of Success,* I was obsessed. I spent two years of my life on a mission to pay homage to Bruce Barton, a man who influenced our country but somehow fell through the cracks of history.

One day, I received a call from a medical doctor in west Texas. He wanted to hire me to ghostwrite a book for him. Although I was reluctant, going to see him felt like the right thing to do. I flew there, visited with him, negotiated a contract, and flew back to Houston with a large check in my hands, a nonrefundable retainer to hire me to write his book.

Weeks passed. Then months. During this time I spent most of my energy working on my Barton book. I rarely worked on the doc's book, and never heard from him. I finally decided I should fly up to see him, and that I should present some material to him. So I made a flight reservation and started writing his book. But an odd thing happened. Whenever I called the doctor's office, no one answered the phone. This went on for days. Then, a day before my flight was to leave, someone answered the phone. It was the doctor's business manager.

"Bill, this is Joe Vitale," I began.

"Hi Joe." His voice sounded sheepish.

"What's going on? No one has answered the phone there for days."

"Well, there's been a change in plans."

"What?"

Bill mumbled something. I asked him to repeat it. I couldn't believe what I heard.

"The doc's in jail," he said.

To say I was stunned would be to lie. I was shocked. Speechless.

"The doc's in jail!?!" I blurted. "Bill, what's going on?"

"Well, he violated his parole."

Again, I was shocked.

"You mean he's been in jail *before*?!"

"Well, he sent a bomb to his ex-wife and he was caught and sent to prison," Bill explained. "He was allowed to come out and be a doctor again but he couldn't play with guns or bombs anymore."

"Don't tell me," I said.

"Yeah, they found bombs in his desk."

It took me a while to recover from this event. But I want you to notice the miracle here. When I signed a contract with the doctor, I was given a large sum of money. Nonrefundable money. Money that enabled me to work on my Barton book. And then, when the doctor went to jail, I was free from his contract. I didn't have to write his book at all. Even trying to give his money back, which I wasn't obligated to do, was pointless. The doctor was gone.

Somehow God or the Universe or the Divine (or whatever you want to call the invisible powers that be) set the stage for this grand event. Could I have orchestrated such an event? It's highly unlikely. How would I have written the ad?

"Doctor wanted: Must be ex-con, want to write a book, and be ready to go back to jail in six months so I can keep his money."

I don't think so.

Your Partner Needs Clear, Too

Again, when you know what you want and are clear, you will be drawn to the thing you want, and events will pull it to you.

Jonathan sees this happen all the time. When two doctors in Seattle couldn't agree on office space they needed, they went to Jonathan. After one session they were clear. Within 24 hours, they found the space they needed, and signed a lease for it.

I saw the same thing happen when my late ex-wife and I wanted to buy a house together many years ago (while we were still married, of course). If you are trying to manifest something that involves another person, both of you have to be clear before you'll manifest the event. I had worked on myself to buy the house I wanted. But things still weren't working out. Finally, my ex-wife went to see Jonathan. She cleared up some old beliefs she had about self-worth and money. The very next day, the real estate people called. Three days later, we moved into the house. And this was after nearly 12 months of delays!

Keep in mind that you can't blame anyone else if you aren't getting the results you want in a relationship. Remember, the outer is a reflection of your inner. Your partner is just showcasing something you believe. Change the belief in you and the outer will change.

Would you like an example from the world of business?

Change the Inner to Change the Outer

Dan Poynter is a dear friend and internationally recognized expert on self-publishing. He's written several books, including the famous *Self-Publishing Manual.* Dan also conducts weekend seminars in his home on how to self-publish and market your own book. He's been offering this seminar for over 10 years, has helped hundreds of people, but has always struggled to get people to register for the event. One day Dan called me for my help.

"Joe, I want you to write a brochure for me that is so powerful that people sign up for my seminar without my having to do a thing."

Notice what Dan was doing. He knew what he didn't want (to pull teeth to get people to come to his seminar), and he knew what he did want (to have people call and register easily and effortlessly). From those two steps, he was led to calling me. When I agreed to create a new brochure for Dan, what did he have to do?

Let go.

He had to let go. He had to trust that he hired the right guy and all would be well. Although he didn't know it, "letting go" is a key step in the Attractor Factor process. He was intuitively following it.

I designed a flyer for Dan, he loved it, and he printed it. A few weeks later, I called him and he said, "My seminar is already sold out."

"It is?!" I yelled, delighted. But Dan stopped me in my tracks.

"But it isn't due to your flyer," he said.

"It isn't?"

"The seminar sold out two weeks ago, and I only mailed out the new flyer last week. There had been a delay in the mailing."

"Then what happened?" I asked. "Why did it sell out?"

Dan didn't know. But here's my guess. As you know by now, the energy you give out brings the results you get. When Dan stated his new intention, and allowed me to create a new flyer for him, he was changing the inner signal he was sending out. *Once you change the way you are inside, the outer world changes.* Dan didn't even have to mail his flyer out. People picked up on the signals in the air and responded.

Crazy? Maybe so. But as I've pointed out throughout this book, the energy you give out attracts and creates the results you get. Change your inner energy and you change your results.

And for the record, I later saw Dan in Chicago, where he told me that due to the new brochure I'd written for him, his August seminar sold out in *June*.

My Nightingale-Conant Miracle

The following story reveals how one of my greatest dreams came true. I am sharing it with you in the hope that it will inspire you to go for your own dreams. It's all about the power of setting an intention and then letting go of it.

If you've never seen the famous Nightingale-Conant giant catalog of audiotapes on business, motivation, self-help, relationships, health, and spirituality, reach over to your phone right now and call 1-800-525-9000. Or visit their site at www.nightingale.com. Request the catalog. It's free and well worth browsing.

I had wanted to have an audio program of my own in the Nightingale-Conant catalog for many years. I wanted it for the prestige as well as for the profit. I wanted to be among their roster of greats: Tony Robbins, Tom Peters, Deepak Chopra, Bob Proctor, Brian Tracy, and Wayne Dyer.

But until autumn 1998, this desire had only been a dream. Despite the fact that I always sent Nightingale-Conant my new books as soon as they were published, I could never seem to ignite their interest in my work.

But I never gave up. I simply held onto the dream, trusted that something would give sooner or later, and kept doing my thing: Writing what I hoped were inspiring and informative books.

And then something amazing happened.

One day, a man began sending me e-mail, asking numerous questions about marketing in general and P. T. Barnum in particular. He was a fan of Barnum's and loved my book, *There's a Customer Born Every Minute.* I answered all of his questions, glad to help.

Then, one day I received a shock. The man sent me e-mail saying, "If you ever want your material considered by Nightingale-Conant, let me know. I'm their Marketing Project Manager."

You can't imagine my surprise. Or my delight.

I immediately Fed-Exed all of my books, my video, and my home study course (six audiotapes and a workbook) to my new friend at Nightingale-Conant. He didn't like anything I sent. Instead, he *loved* everything I sent. And right then and there he began the long process of selling Nightingale-Conant on me.

He became my guardian angel.

At Christmastime, he took down the star from the top of the company Christmas tree and replaced it with a photo of me.

He took pictures of me and placed them throughout the offices of Nightingale-Conant, including the men's and women's bathrooms.

After 11 months of calls, faxes, many Fed-Exes, and lots of photos of me, I am proud to announce that Nightingale-Conant is carrying its first product by me. It's called *The Power of Outrageous Marketing.* It has been a best-seller for them for about 10 years now.

And last year the same company hired me to record *The Missing Secret.* I found my contact from the previous program, let him help me negotiate a good deal for this second program, and was so impressed that I hired him. He's now my vice-president of marketing!

This amazing story illustrates many lessons:

- The power of a dream (I held my vision of what I wanted for years).
- The networking potential of the Internet (My Nightingale-Conant contact found me at my web site).
- The miracle that comes from having someone who believes in you. (My contact believes in me to a staggering degree, and told me so over and over again for 11 months.)
- The true magic that occurs when you are in alignment with your life's purpose and doing what makes your heart sing . . .
- And the power of letting go.

I'm sure there are other lessons in this story, lessons that you see and I don't. Again, I am sharing this with you in the hope that it sets your own heart on fire, awakens something in your soul, and urges you to go for—and get—your own dreams.

And here's something else to think about:

"Thy Will Be Done"

According to research done at Spindrift Foundation on the power of prayer, a "Thy will be done" prayer gets more than twice as many results as a specific "give me this" prayer. That's why it's so important to end your request for anything you want with the magic words, "This or something better."

When I was writing my book on P. T. Barnum, *There's a Customer Born Every Minute*, I went to the famous showman's grave in Bridgeport, Connecticut. I had a moving experience there, which I wrote about in my book. But what I want to share with you here is what I saw written on Barnum's gravesite marker. To my surprise, carved in his simple concrete headstone were these magical words, words that Barnum relied on throughout his colorful life:

"Not my will but thine be done."

Those magic words worked for Barnum, helping him to survive personal and professional disasters and to become one of America's first millionaires, and those words can work for you, too.

In other words, trust the universe.

Want something better?

You can ask for whatever you want to do, be, or have, but also be willing for the universe to give you something better. End all of your requests with the phrase, "This or something better," and you will be letting the universe know that "Thy will be done" is of highest importance.

Why is this so? Because the universe can see the big picture while your ego can't.

Your job is to ask for what you want, and then to act on the inner nudges you get to do things, like make phone calls, write letters, visit a certain person, or whatever. Bob Proctor, in his wonderful book, *You Were Born Rich*, puts it this way:

"Learn to follow the quiet voice within that speaks in feelings rather than words; follow what you 'hear' inside, rather than what others may be telling you to do."

The universe itself will act to move you to what you want, and move what you want to you. All you have to do is let go, while acting on your inner prompts. Let go of fear, doubt, worry, disappointment, and any other negative emotion that might make you feel low.

The famous poet and sage Rumi wrote something that may help you here: "Some things that don't happen keep disasters from happening."

Think about it. What you're being asked to do is trust. Trust that when something happens, it's good; and trust that when something you want doesn't happen, it's good, too.

Wayne Dyer has an interesting book out called *The Power of Intention*. It claims to teach you how to get whatever you want. A friend read the book and said the title should be *How to Get What You Want By Wanting What You Get*.

Exactly!

The trick to manifesting whatever you want is to trust that whatever you get is what you wanted to manifest in the first place. You attracted it. The more you can understand this balance of wanting and allowing, or desiring and letting go, the more you will be happy in every moment.

Let me explain this with a story . . .

The Swan

Terri Levine is a world-famous coach, best-selling author, and dear friend of mine. Early in 2004, she was contacted by FOX television studios about becoming the coach for one of their new shows. Terri would be seen weekly by a national television audience. Her name would become famous. She wanted to be selected as the coach, and as her marketing consultant, I wanted it for her, as well.

After weeks of interviews, e-mail exchanges, and hints from the network leading Terri to believe she was going to be the coach for the show, she got a sad call one day. She was turned down. The executives at FOX had decided to go a different route and use a different coach.

Terri was upset. You have to understand that Terri is one of the most positive people I know. She is upbeat, bubbly, cheery, and always looking for the positive in every situation. But the news of her rejection crushed her. Nothing I could say made her feel better. In time, she let go of the experience, but she would always feel disappointed.

Then, months later, the new FOX show Terri had been considered for was aired. It was about average to homely women who were transformed with plastic surgery, counseling, and coaching. Terri saw the show and was repulsed by it. She said, "It doesn't stand for anything I believe in or would want to be associated with. I'm relieved I wasn't chosen to be on it."

I sent Terri an e-mail that day that she so loved, she told me she was keeping it in her "Wisdom Folder." I had written:

"Some things that look like they are in our best interest are often not going to serve us when we see the big picture. We have to trust and let go, realizing that everything that happens is for our highest good."

The Secret of TIISG

I'm riveted by *A Lifetime of Riches,* the biography of Napoleon Hill, the author of the classic book *Think and Grow Rich.*

Not only did this man struggle for 20 years to write the definitive guide to success, but he experienced poverty, his life was threatened, his backers were murdered, he suffered from bouts of hopelessness, and his family suffered beyond all understanding.

His was not an overnight success.

One thing that stood out in Hill's life story was his ability to turn the negative into the positive. He always looked for what some people call that silver lining in the dark cloud. As I thought about Hill's life, I realized I've been noticing this ability to see the good in the bad practiced by others, too.

I was at a meeting with my friend Mark Joyner, Internet pioneer and best-selling author. I overheard Mark talking to a man who had just gone through hell due to the Federal Trade Commission. Mark listened to the man's sad story and then said, "Turn it into something good."

This was remarkable advice. It's the kind of thing Napoleon Hill would have said. It goes against what most people ever even attempt to try. The whole idea of taking whatever happens to you and turning it into something good seems, at first glance, preposterous.

But this also seems to be a key to success. I remember P. T. Barnum offering to buy a rival's elephant. He sent a telegram stating his offer. His competitors took Barnum's telegram and ran it as an ad, saying, "Here's what Barnum thinks of our elephant."

Instead of being upset, Barnum decided to join with those competitors. That gave birth to the famous Barnum & Bailey Circus. Barnum took the experience and turned it into something good.

The other day Nerissa, my love, released her first e-book at www. freevideoediting.com She had a small mistake on her site. When I went to promote her site, I used the mistake as a way to get attention for her e-book. I could have said, "Correct your site." Instead I sent out an e-mail that said, "There is a mistake on her site. If you can spot it, I'll give you a gift." This caused people to be curious, a powerful motivator. It drove traffic to her site. Sales jumped.

What I, Barnum, Joyner, and Hill are doing is the same thing: taking the so-called negative experiences in life and turning them into something good. I call this TIISG. It stands for Turn It Into Something Good.

You have the ability to do this. It's a choice. No matter what happens, take a breath and ask, "How can I turn this into something good?"

The question redirects your mind. Instead of looking at the problem, you are now looking for solutions. This is a brilliant way to learn how to operate your own brain. You become the master, not the slave, of your life.

Andrew Carnegie—that tycoon who challenged Napoleon Hill to undertake his 20-year quest to uncover the secrets of success—confessed that the principle key to his own staggering success was the ability to operate his own mind.

He told Hill, "I am no longer cursed by poverty because I took possession of my own mind, and that mind has yielded me every material thing I want, and much more than I need. But this power of mind is a universal one, as available to the humblest person as it is to the greatest."

It all begins with the basic TIISG question: "How can I turn this into something good?"

The answer will bring you new choices, happiness, and may lead to wealth you never dreamed of before.

Just remember TIISG.

What is bothering you right now that you can turn into something good?

_____

_____

_____

_____

_____

_____

_____

_____

_____

_____

_____

It's All Good

I attended Bob Proctor's three-day course called, "The Science of Getting Rich" in Denver during June 1999. It was a mind-expanding experience. I urge you to take the course live if at all possible or at least to invest in the home-study course. There are so many things you'll get out of the material that where you are now will seem like poverty after you absorb the materials and become wealthy.

But one idea that I got from Bob's course that I want to give you right now is this quote: "Everything that happens in your life is moving you in the direction of your goals."

Now think about this. That statement says that everything, without fail, without exception, is moving you toward your dreams.

So if something happens that you feel is bad, remember that it happened to move you forward. Your job is to find the positive in the negative, or at least to trust that there is a positive there, even if you can't see it at the moment.

This might be tough to accept, at first. But the truth is, it is an enlightened way of living your life. I love the statement and thank

Bob Proctor for saying it. What it tells me is that I have to let go and trust that life itself is taking me to the things I desire. And as I let go, trust, and give thanks for my life, I feel different, I radiate a different vibration to the world, and better things and experiences come to me.

Again, the whole secret is in learning to simply let go.

But what do you do?

Ever since my book, *Spiritual Marketing*, became a number one best-seller at Amazon, and then the first edition of *The Attractor Factor* went on to beat other best-selling titles, including the latest Harry Potter books, people have been writing me. Most of the time people are just praising the book. Sometimes, people have questions about the five-step process in the book for creating wealth from the inside out. By far the most common question is about Step Five, the one called "Let Go."

"But what do I *do* if I let go?" is the question I get the most. "If I let go, don't I just sit there?"

What I didn't fully explain in that book is that you usually still have to do *something* to achieve your dreams. That something might be as little as answering the phone. Or making a call. Or buying a book. Or joining an association. Or answering an e-mail. I have no idea what that action will be for you to achieve your dream. But you usually have to do something, however small or large a step. You can even see me in the movie *The Secret* urging you to take action because "the universe likes speed."

But the magic answer to the question of what action to do next is this:

You want to take what I call "Inspired Action."

Inspired Action is any action you take based on an inside nudge.

In other words, an Inspired Action is when you suddenly get a desire to drive to the store. You may have no idea why you need to go to the store right now. But something within you is urging you out the door. Follow that hunch. It may lead you to your goal. At the store, you may meet the right person. Or find the right product. Or pick up the right magazine that will lead you to completing your dream.

For example, about 20 years ago I was working for a major oil company. When I left for lunch, I always went to the food court at the closest mall. Always. Talk about being stuck in a rut.

One day, I decided to do something different. As I left for lunch that day, I felt an impulse to turn left where I always turned right. This may sound like nothing to you, but it meant the world to me. It was like leaving the planet and going to Mars. I was suddenly on an adventure.

To my sheer amazement, only a few blocks away was an Italian deli. Now try to picture this: I'm an Italian living in Texas. I hadn't had good Italian food since leaving Ohio about 20 years earlier. To stumble across an Italian deli, by accident, during lunch hour, was almost miraculous.

I went inside and met the owner. He was from Italy. He made me a sandwich that was so good I still drool today as I think about it. I was so grateful that I took his menu back to my office, shut my door, and created a whole new menu for him. I wrote new copy, designed it, and then printed him 500 copies. I then posted that new menu all over the company building.

The next day, when I went back to the deli, the owner met me with tears in his eyes. His business had been booming all day. His lunch hour was packed with customers. He didn't know how to thank me. I didn't need to be thanked. All I wanted was a sandwich.

But this miracle didn't stop there. We became friends. When my wife at the time and I needed to move and looked for a place to move to, the owner of the deli sold us his house. He wanted to move but because he built the house himself, he didn't want just anyone in it. When he learned I needed a new home, he arranged for us to buy his house. We lived in it for 10 years, and Marian lived in it right till her passing in 2004.

And all because I took Inspired Action!

What are you being nudged to do from within?

_____

_____

_____

_____

_____

_____

_____

Watch the Signals

Once you state your intention and work the other steps in the Attractor Factor process, you need to watch the signals you get and act instantly on them when you see them.

When I was working for a major oil company and hated my job, I used to pray for a way out. This was 20 years ago and I felt lost. I felt trapped in my nine-to-five prison. I would drive 35 miles each way, to and from a job I hated so much I would cry as I drove. It was pretty sad. But I stated my intention to break free. I then looked for the signals.

Every day, I would pass a street named Quitman. I never thought much of it, until I realized it was a signal for me. The sign was on the freeway for people to know where to exit. But for me it meant, "Quit, man."

And I did quit my job. I've been happier ever since. Today, I'm a well-known author, speaker, Internet celebrity, and so much more. All because I took Inspired Action.

Infinite Mind

Here's another example: While writing this book a dear friend paid us an unscheduled visit. You have to realize that this is highly unusual. We live in the hill country outside of Austin, Texas. We are not easy to get to. And we don't usually appreciate people dropping in unannounced. After all, we work at home and would prefer not to be interrupted. I could be doing a radio show by phone, or Nerissa might be editing a video project. Our home is usually buzzing with activity.

But our friend called at the right time, saying she was in the area, so we told her to come over. The conversation was mostly about energy, remote viewing, mind over matter, and other such esoteric talk. During our conversation, our friend raved about a book called *Infinite Mind*. She told us she read and reread the book, underlined passages, and thought it was pure genius.

I immediately took that as a signal for me to get the book. Why? Because the whole situation reeked of synchronicity. The fact that our friend appeared while I was writing this seemed odd. The conversation directly applied to some of the principles in *The Attractor Factor*. And the book seemed like a must-have for my research.

I immediately took Inspired Action. As soon as our friend left, I ran upstairs, jumped online, and ordered the book from Amazon for overnight delivery. Not only that, but while in this buying mode I also ordered *Manifesting Your Heart's Desires, Book I* and *Manifesting Your Heart's Desires, Book II*. They all turned out to contain key information to help me better communicate the Attractor Factor process to you.

And all this from an innocent event that others might have dismissed!

The Red Flags Theory

Years ago I was going to co-author a book called *The Red Flags Theory*. It's the theory that as you go through life, there are signs to go forward, pause, or even stop and retreat. They are a little like center lane bumps on the highway telling you to get back into your lane. I call them green, yellow, and red flags.

The key is to pay attention to the clues, or flags, and act on them. When you do, life seems to flow at a smooth rate. When you don't, you hit jolting bumps, scary rapids, and/or unforgiving walls.

I was telling some friends about my red flags theory over lunch. One of them had gotten himself into a tangled business relationship. As I explained that before he got into the tangle there were probably yellow flags to alert him of problems ahead, he asked for an example.

I remembered that decades ago I took on a client who ended up being a nightmare. I finally had to fire him, return his money, and wish him well. It was a very unpleasant experience. When I reflected on why I signed on with him in the first place, I realized that there were yellow flags on the field from the first day I met him but I didn't pay full attention to them.

Those yellow flags were things like an uncomfortable feeling in my stomach; noticing an odd statement or odd behavior; feeling a tiny shudder when he said something about someone else that seemed negative or inappropriate. I didn't pay close attention to those yellow flags because this client was paying me a great deal of money, and I needed it (or thought I did) at the time.

So I let the promise of big money help me ignore or rationalize the warning flags.

But yellow flags turn into red flags if you don't do something about them. Ultimately I had to end my relationship with that client.

As I told this story to my friends, they nodded. They realized there were hints, clues, and flags all along the way, in every relationship, coming in every moment.

The point is to awaken, be responsible, and act on them.

A yellow flag doesn't mean stop; it means explore the caution. If you can't resolve it or shake it, you might have to get out of that game.

Here's another example:

Donny Deutsch recently interviewed Donald Trump on his CNBC show, *The Big Idea*. In it The Donald said he once got the flu when he was about to close a deal to buy a newspaper. Donald explained that he never gets sick, but he got terribly sick on the day of the deal. He took it as a sign not to go through with it. As it turned out, it was the right decision. Being a newspaper publisher is not The Donald; being a real estate tycoon is.

The flu was a red flag to stop.

I have no idea if Donald Trump received yellow flags before the day of the deal, but I bet he did. You don't get a red flag unless you've ignored all the yellow ones.

And that's the point: Be alert to the yellow flags.

Of course, green flags are the good signs that say this is the way to go. But if you don't act, you may get yellow and then red flags on those deals, as well. Often I won't get a green flag (or any flag) until *after* I've taken action.

This is a little like being at a football game. There's no reason to toss a flag on the field *before* the game begins. But once it starts, look for the flags. Same in life. I've often begun something because it felt right. After I took action, the game is afoot. From that point on I have to pay attention, and act, on all signs.

Also, as new information becomes available and relationships grow, new flags may also appear. Life isn't static. The game isn't over. This is why you have to *stay awake* in every moment.

As I've said here, there, and even on Larry King's TV show, the great goal of life is to awaken. Flags help you tune in to this moment; and this moment is all there is.

Here's one final example:

Because I'm traveling more these days, I decided to get a laptop connect card so I could use my laptop virtually anywhere to connect to the Internet. I went to my current phone service provider but he couldn't determine what card I needed for my particular laptop.

Yellow flag.

I told him I would return with my laptop in hand so he could look at it and give me the right connect card. I returned, he took one look, and said he didn't have the card I needed, even though my card is a standard one and should be in stock.

Yellow flag.

He went on to say I would have to go to a larger city, probably Austin or San Antonio, to get the card I wanted. Since I had no plans to go to either city, and needed the card today for a trip I'm making tomorrow, I passed on his suggestion.

Note that these yellow flags don't mean I shouldn't get a laptop connect card; they simply mean (so far) not to get one with my current phone service provider.

I sat in the car and made a few phone calls to local stores of competing phone service providers, seeing who had the card I needed. After three calls (notice I'm taking action) I found a friendly woman who assured me she had the card in stock.

Green flag.

She told me her name is Chelsea, which is the name of one of our cats.

Green flag.

I went over to her store, went inside, and was greeted by the friendliest staff.

Green flag.

No waiting. No hassles. No deposit, or card fees, or much else.

Green flags.

And while I was there, one of my favorite waitresses of all time breezed into the store, saw me, and rushed over to give me a hug.

Green flag.

I now have the Internet connect card I need and I feel *great* about the experience.

Mission accomplished.

I still don't know if I'll ever write a book about my red flags theory, but I'm hoping this helps you remember that there are clues in every moment telling you if you're on course.

Pay attention.

And act.

How to Do This

So here's how to make Inspired Action work for you:

Step One. Set an intention. An intention is your declaration about your dream, or goal, that you want to be, do, or have. This is your request of your subconscious, unconscious, and the universe itself. The clearer your intention, the better your results. One of my intentions was "I intend to have a best-selling audiotape program with Nightingale-Conant." Another was "I intend for my *Spiritual Marketing* book to become a number one best-seller at Amazon." Yet another was "I intend to find a new place to eat lunch." Write it here:

_____

_____

_____

_____

Step Two. Follow your hunches. Watch the signals. Listen to your intuition. If you get a desire to make a plan of action, so be it. Do it. But if you get a desire to go for a walk, or to watch television, or to surf the Web, then do that. You never know where your Inspired Action will take you, but because you set an intention (Step One), your intuition will find a shortcut to your dreams. Write actions that seem inspired here:

_____

_____

_____

_____

_____

_____

Inspired Action works because your ego can only see limited terrain while the universe can see it all. Your ego might say, "Write a business plan." Inspired Action comes from the bigger picture, which you can't always see until you've taken the actions you're being inspired to take.

Finally, the more you can quiet your mind, still your thoughts, and relax your body, the more you will hear the inner voice nudging you in the direction of your dreams.

When it speaks, move.

That's Inspired Action.

Do it, and you'll find amazing new shortcuts direct to the fulfillment of your stated desires. It's an easy path, more fun, more relaxed, and usually more profitable, than planned action and constant struggle.

Try it and see.

A Secret about Money

Let me tell you a secret about money.

One day Pat O'Bryan, a wonderful Texas musician well known in Europe, walked into a master mind group we are in and announced, "One day I'm going to write a book titled *The Myth of Passive Income.*"

He was joking. Everyone laughed. He had been working hard on his site at www.InstantChange.com and realized from firsthand experience that there is little passive about passive income.

I heard an opportunity.

"You ought to write that book right now," I said.

Everyone shut up. They looked at me.

"It's a great idea," I explained. "People think passive income is doing nothing all day and making money while you sleep. It isn't quite like that. So let's blow the whistle and tell people the truth."

Pat was beginning to learn how to act when an opportunity popped up.

"I'll do it," he said.

We met in the parking lot after the group meeting. He asked, "Would you go ahead and write a letter asking people making money online if they would contribute an article to our book? We just want to know what a typical day for them is like. I bet they don't sit around doing nothing."

Suddenly I was the co-author in this project. Well, I see opportunities and jump on them, too. I agreed.

I went home, went to my computer, and drafted a letter. It was simple. I asked successful people online if they would tell us what a day was like in their "passive" world. I sent the letter to Pat. He approved it almost instantly. I then sent it out to every list owner I knew. This all happened within maybe three hours.

Within 24 hours we had wonderful articles by David Garfinkel and Tom Antion. Later the same day I heard from Jim Edwards, Yanik Silver, Jo Han Mok, and other online giants, all agreeing to send articles for our book.

Now note what happened here:

A spontaneous joke became a project. That project began to take form within three hours. And within one day the book was being written—and not by Pat *or* me.

This process is how I created such moneymaking digital products as my online e-classes, several bestselling e-books, and even a few online promotional campaigns. I came up with the ideas and within minutes acted on them. The result: Success.

So what does money like?

Money likes speed.

That's the secret few know about money.

Money comes to those who act fast. If you think, wonder, question, doubt, plan, meet, discuss, or in any other way drag your feet, money goes to the next person in line.

If you want to know how I've managed to write so many books and articles, it's because I act fast. This very section is an example. Twenty minutes ago I got the idea to write something about "money liking action." I thought I should write it some day. Then I thought, "Why not *now*?"

Well, here you go.

It's done.

You now know the secret, too. When you get an inspired nudge to take action, then *take action*. Don't wait. Act. Act *right now*.

What are *you* waiting to do?

Tend Your Garden

Many people say they don't want to take any action, that they just want to "Let go and let God."

That reminds me of the story of the man with a beautiful garden in his backyard. One day a man walked by, saw it, and stopped to admire it.

"You have an amazing garden here," the stranger said.

"Thank you," said the owner.

"It's really God's garden, isn't it?"

"Yes, it is," replied the owner. "But you should have seen it when God had it all by Himself."

The point is, God (Universe, Spirit, or whatever name feels right for you) provides us with the basics, and we have to do something with what we've been given. If we just allow things to grow in the backyard, we'll have a jungle, not a garden. Someone has to tend to the earth.

Take Jesus, for example. According to Bruce Barton, author of the 1925 best seller, *The Man Nobody Knows*, Jesus was a business-man. He "hired" 12 employees, inspired them, and sent them out to spread his message. That's sound marketing. That's Inspired Action.

Or take Phineas Parker Quimby, the man credited with being the father of New Thought or modern spirituality. Martin Larson calls Quimby "the Advertising Therapist" in his book, *New Thought or a Modern Religious Approach: The Philosophy of Health, Happiness, and Prosperity* (New York: Philosophical Library, 1985):

From 1847 to 1859, then, the tireless, searching Quimby went from town to town offering mental therapy through the power of faith. He distributed a brochure in 1855 which repudiated the mesmeric (hypnosis) technique and which read in part: "Dr. P. P. Quimby would respectfully announce . . . that . . . he will attend to those wishing to consult him in regard to their health, and, as his practice is unlike all other medical practices, it is necessary to say that he gives no medicine and makes no outward applications, but simply sits down by the patients, tells them their feelings and what they think is their disease. If the patients admit that he tells them their feelings, etc., then his explanation is the cure; and if he succeeds in correcting their error, he changes the fluids of the system and establishes the truth or health. The truth is the cure."

As you can see, even the great father of metaphysical healing handed out flyers in order to get new business. He didn't sit and do nothing.

The point is, letting go doesn't mean do nothing. It means take action based on your inspiration. If you feel moved from within to make a call, or run an ad, or take a walk, or build a community, then do so. Just have the spirit of nonattachment as you do. Nonattachment is letting go.

Again, when you want something and are fine if you get it or not, then you are most likely going to receive it.

You must let go of your *attachment* to success to attract success.

Go to the Light

Letting go doesn't mean giving up.

When I went to Italy in 2004, I visited many people and places, from Michelangelo's tomb in Florence to the Pope in the Vatican.

I found Italy to be a country rich in ancient history but poor in current prosperity. I met some snooty people and some warm ones.

Sister Mary Elizabeth is one of the warm ones. She's the personal secretary to the Mother General of the Sisters of St. Filippini order, which serves very poor women and children in third-world countries. She is on my e-mail list, and a fan of my books. She once told me my ideas, as expressed in the e-books *Hypnotic Writing* and *Hypnotic Marketing,* helped her raise funds to feed homeless and starving children around the world. It was a very gratifying thing to hear, to be sure.

But odd things began to happen. While in Rome, I checked my e-mail. I was stunned to see an e-mail from my sound engineer, telling me the master audio tapes for a program I had invested thousands of dollars to create, had vanished. He had no explanation. He runs one of the best studios in the world, and he lost the masters! And here I am, on the other side of the planet, unable to do a thing about it. I couldn't believe it.

Things got even stranger. We hired a driver in Italy to take us to Pompeii and Naples. We had a great day. But at the end of the day, while unloading the car, he suddenly told me he wanted more money than agreed on. It made the entire day feel ugly.

Later that night, we went out to eat. It was our last evening in Rome. We had a nice dinner, but when we went to pay, we were told by an unfriendly French waitress speaking only Italian, that their credit card machine was down. Well, we had no cash. We ended up leaving, promising to send them money for our meal.

We got back to the States safely, but the strange world seemed to stay with us. I was told I owe thousands of dollars in back taxes on property I own. My agent was supposed to negotiate a deal with a publisher and ended up getting fired over it.

We decided to go to Las Vegas and see some shows to relax. But on the flight there, I had chest pains and couldn't breathe very well.

I thought I was having a heart attack. We landed safely but the chest pains stayed with me. The next day the house doctor at The Venetian hotel took one look at me and sent me to the emergency room. I had never been in any hospital before, so this was scary. And with my chest pains, I thought I was never going home again. Several hours later, and $5,000 lighter, I was told I had asthma.

We returned home but the strangeness continued. One day, while I was typing a chapter in this very book, an entire sentence repeated itself on my screen. At first I thought I imagined it. I deleted the sentence. But as I watched the screen, the sentence retyped itself on my screen. Talk about bizarre! I assumed I had a virus and shook my head.

What in the world was happening here?

The Truth

One day I drove out of town and spent the day with my chiropractor and dear friend, Dr. Rick Barrett, author of several books, including, *Healed by Morning*. I needed to chill, to relax, to get some distance. I told him about these misadventures. I was feeling stressed to the max as I relayed all of what I just shared with you. I added, "I feel like I picked up a curse in Italy. Nothing has been right since."

Rick looked right at me and said, "Maybe this all ties in."

"Huh?"

"Maybe you are being attacked by the dark forces," he explained. "You went to Rome, went to the Vatican, and saw the Pope, which are all holy things. And you are focused on writing your new book, which could truly change the world."

"Yes? Yes?"

"Well, maybe your move into the light is causing the dark to try to stop you."

"I'm not sure I follow."

"Whenever we go to Mexico to do our mission work, something bad happens," he explained. "Me, my wife, other doctors, and other volunteers, are planning to go to some truly impoverished areas and donate our time, medicine, and practice to help people there. It's a good cause. Yet every time we plan it, something happens. One time, I fell off a ladder one week before going. Another time a woman was denied entry into Mexico because her papers weren't in order. It just seems like when you go to the light, sometimes the dark comes after you."

I didn't agree with his assessment. From an Attractor Factor viewpoint, I'd say a part of us was showing its ugly head. When he fell off the ladder, it was the part of him that resisted the good another part of him wanted to do. He attracted the experience.

It's the same with me. As I grew closer to completing this book, I almost sabotaged my own efforts to make it a success. No evil force was out to get me. It was simply a part of me that resisted my intention.

Dr. Valerie Hunt, writing in her book, *Infinite Mind,* put it this way: "To acknowledge diabolical entities that possess power in and of themselves without the person's participation, I believe is inaccurate and destructive." She adds, "It assures protection from uncovering one's unfinished business, because one is looking in the wrong place."

In short, I had to get clear. I had to find out why a part of me was resisting what I wanted to attract. I did that, too, or else you would not be reading this finished book.

But back to the conversation with Dr. Barrett.

"How do we reinforce ourselves so the light wins?" I asked.

"You have to tell yourself that nothing will stop you, that you won't give up, that you won't give in," Rick answered. "Sometimes you just have to turn it over to God or the Universe and say, 'I don't see the way.'"

And there's the secret: *You maintain your overall goal and you move toward it,* always being sensitive to something better being offered, but you are not attached to the outcome, either.

The Ultimate Secret

Again, *the ultimate secret to attracting whatever you want is to want it without needing it.* When you are detached from the outcome, you disconnect from everything that could sabotage your success. The Attractor Factor kicks into overdrive when you state your intention and are happy whether you achieve it or not. This is a delicate balance. But it's the major secret to how the universe works.

In other words, in the world of everyday reality, struggling to achieve something causes the opposite forces *within yourself* to kick into play. But when you come from an inner place of serenity, and you go with the flow toward your wishes, you have upped the odds of your achieving them. Your peace will attract peace.

As Deepak Chopra wrote in his book, *The Spontaneous Fulfillment of Desire,* "Intention is not simply a whim. It requires attention, and it also requires detachment. Once you've created the intention mindfully, you must be able to detach from the outcome, and let the universe handle the details of fulfillment."

In short, you fully activate the Attractor Factor when you *let go.*

> Miracle mindedness means behaving like someone who is fearless, well-intentioned, innocent, and, ultimately, invulnerable. She or he listens within for guidance and follows any and all impulses toward loving and constructive action, however bizarre and inappropriate they may appear to the ego.
>
> —CAROLYN MILLER, *CREATING MIRACLES: UNDERSTANDING THE EXPERIENCE OF DIVINE INTERVENTION*

CHAPTER 17

The Million Dollar Secret Formula

"What's the hardest part of creating life the way you want it?" a friend asked me over lunch.

I thought for a moment and replied, "Learning to stop figuring out *how* you will get what you want."

My friend looked confused.

She asked, "What do you mean?"

"If you try to figure out how you will get that new car, or that new house, or that new relationship, you'll limit yourself to what your ego can see and do," I explained. "Turn your goal over to your unconscious, which is connected to the spirit of everything and everyone, and let it bring the goal to you and you to the goal. Just follow your inner promptings, and act on the opportunities that come your way, and you'll get there."

Well, I'm not sure if my friend understood what I was saying. But a few days later, I was sitting in a limousine, being driven to have dinner with eight wealthy, wonderful, self-made people. All of these people started with nothing. Many of them started as I had, with empty pockets and hope in their hearts.

As I sat in the limo, a part of me couldn't believe I was there.

"How did I get here?" I remember thinking to myself. "I'm in a beautiful limo, with beautiful people beside me, going to have a beautiful dinner that some other beautiful person is going to pay for.

I'm just a nobody kid from Ohio who left home to find fame and fortune. I used to dig ditches, drive trucks, work in the dirt, the rain, and the heat, and for never enough money to pay my bills. How'd I get in this limo?"

As I thought about it, I knew the secret was the five-step formula I've revealed to you in this book. It's the Attractor Factor. In short, the secret to increasing your business, finding your love, achieving better health, or manifesting whatever you want is:

1. Know what you don't want.
2. Select what you do want.
3. Clear all negative or limiting beliefs.
4. Feel what it would be like to have, do, or be what you want.
5. Let go as you act on your intuitive impulses, and allow the results to manifest.

Yes, that's it.

Truth is, there's no one way to achieve anything in this world. Some people get new cars by winning them, others by struggling to pay for them, others by happily paying for them, others by other means.

What I told my friend at lunch is the truth: You can't orchestrate the world to do your bidding. Instead, state your intentions and let the world arrange itself to bring your goals to you.

In other words, you don't manufacture your outcomes, you participate in them. And you participate best when you allow your inner spirit to do most of the work.

I was in that limo because I didn't plan to be in it.

I allowed, acted, trusted, and accepted.

I followed the five-step formula.

I activated the Attractor Factor.

And when the limo pulled up, I got in.

Six Key Points

Before we end this book, let's go over some final key points in the Attractor Factor process:

1. *You are totally responsible for your experiences in your life.*

   That doesn't mean you caused them. But on some level you attracted them. You are responsible for them. That's not good or bad. Simply use the experiences to learn about yourself. Get clear, and choose what you prefer to experience.

2. *You are absorbing beliefs from the culture itself.*

   If you are watching movies about violence, or reading the papers, or watching the news, you are filling your mind with the very vibe that will attract more of what you soaked up. Mother Teresa said she would never attend an antiwar rally. Why? Because it contains the very energy that creates more war. Watch what you absorb. Choose what you want to attract. Be aware.

3. *You are not ruler of the earth, but you have more power than you ever realized.*

   You can move mountains with the right thought and action. Keep a balance of ego and spirit in your life, always striving to let your ego obey spirit.

4. *You can change your thoughts.*

   This often feels impossible to believe because it's not normal for the vast majority of people. But what you think is largely habit. Start noticing what goes through your head. If you don't like it, start consciously changing it. Choose new thoughts.

5. *You can do the impossible.*

   What you believe to be the restraints of time and space right now may simply be the limits of our current understanding. No one knows what is impossible. If you have an inclination to try something new and different, then so be it. Go for it. Make it so. You may be creating a path never seen before. Dare something worthy.

6. *Whatever image you add feeling to will manifest.*

If you fear something, or love something, you are adding energy to it. Anything you fear or love will tend to be attracted into your life. Choose your passions wisely.

When Your Limo Pulls Up

Finally, I can't find any better way of ending this chapter than with this quote from Frances Larimer Warner, written in 1907. When I was interviewed on a late-night talk show one evening, they asked me to read this quote to them twice. Then they were silent for a moment while the meaning of these words hit home. I'll end this book with those same words, and wish you Godspeed in making all your dreams come true.

And when your limo pulls up, get in!

> If we plant a seed in the ground we know that the sun will shine and the rain will water, and we leave it to the Law to bring results....Well, the desire you image is the seed, your occasional closing of the eyes in imagery is the sun, and your constant, though not anxious, expectation is the rain and cultivation necessary to bring absolutely sure results.
>
> —Frances Larimer Warner, *Our Invisible Supply: Part One*, 1907

CHAPTER 18

The Shocking True Story of Jonathan

Nearly every day, I get a call, an e-mail, or a letter from someone asking, "What happened to Jonathan?"

Every person asking the question marveled at the stories of my miraculous and even shocking work with Jonathan Jacobs (not his real name), and now wants to meet the man himself.

The thing is, Jonathan is no longer available. I'll tell you why, but you had better brace yourself. This may not be easy to read.

Jonathan clearly made a difference in my life. He was my miracles coach and best friend for more than 10 years. The stories you read in this book are all true. Jonathan was a true helper in cocreating miracles for me, and for lots of other people.

But Jonathan was also human. Along the way, he started to let his ego take control of his success. I noticed little things at first. In conversation, he appeared more smug. He wanted the attention on himself. And he talked about his work more than most people wanted to hear. I let that slide, because I was too involved in enjoying the results I was getting from my work with him.

But it got worse. He started to have intimate relations with a few of his female clients. At one point he was working at a clinic, doing his healing work, and was fired for inappropriate conduct with his clients. I supported him during that dark phase of his life, because he was my friend.

But it didn't stop there. Jonathan lost his father, and went into a depression. He considered suicide. I was his lifeline and did my best to help him. I went and stayed with him. I counseled him. I used the very healing methods I learned from him to help him. After a few months, Jonathan came around, moved back into life, and started to see clients again.

But he was still stuck in his self. He again seduced his female clients. At least one was married, and her relationship with Jonathan caused her to fall into depression over her own guilt.

But even that didn't end this downward spiral into hell.

The turning point for me came when one day Jonathan manipulated and then molested the friend closest to me in my life at that time. Words cannot convey how badly this hurt me. I felt betrayed. My best friend, my guru, had become a criminal.

The woman he molested couldn't handle this experience. Her healer and friend had manipulated and molested her. You can imagine what it did to her thinking. She called the suicide hotline. She called the rape crisis hotline. She began a long series of bouts with deep depression, then car accidents, then hospital visits, and more, ending with a near-fatal car accident.

It didn't stop there for her, either. She then saw medical doctors who kept prescribing medication to numb what she was feeling. Later, the medications caused her to have seizures. She was hospitalized repeatedly, and nearly died in the emergency room. At one point, she actually flat lined.

It was a horrible time.

During it, Jonathan hid. He never offered help. He never apologized. And he disappeared from our lives.

My guru had stabbed me and left me bleeding. The pain was beyond words. I had to seek counseling myself. Even today, the memory still stings. This is my first time to write about the experience in such an open way.

By now, you should know I tend to look at life's experiences as a symbol. So I wondered why this happened. Why did Jonathan become evil? Why did he hurt me and others who loved him? What was the positive in this negative? How could I *turn this* into something good?

I remember reading a helpful passage in one of my favorite books, *Breaking the Rules* by Kurt Wright. It goes like this:

"Have you ever noticed how easy it is to look back on events that happened a year or more in the past and see the perfection in them? For most of us this is true even for situations which seemed tragic, horrible, or even devastating at the time. Now, if it is possible to see the perfection in those things a year later, doesn't it make sense that the perfection must be there in the moment it happens, too?"

Wow! What a freeing statement! It causes you to look for the positive in everything, and to look for it *right now*.

So I turned my light on the situation with Jonathan. All I could conclude was this was a gift of freedom. For over 10 years I had turned to Jonathan when I needed help. Well, now it was time for me to be my own healer, my own best friend, and my own guru. I was free.

I feel better than ever before. I am grateful for Jonathan helping me during my time of need, and I wish him well, wherever he is. I no longer want or need him in my life, but I'm grateful for the time we had together.

As for my abused lady friend, she died on October 2, 2004. She was my wife. She never fully recovered from the betrayal, the pain, or the humiliation of her experience with Jonathan. She tried to heal herself, and she tried to forgive him, but for the last three years of her life, she suffered. She only found peace in death.

As you can imagine, my life wasn't peachy during that time. I certainly kept busy, but I also kept working on myself. I knew I had to forgive. Forgiveness is the greatest transformative tool there is. But I admit it took me at least a year to not cry every day.

Today, I'm at peace. My adventures continue and my life is one of magic and miracles. How do I stay clear and focused? I work with several people these days to keep myself on track. Most of them are listed in the back of this book.

There are other healers around, of course. My only advice is to trust your intuition, and not become addicted to a healing or healer. The goal is freedom. The only path is your connection to Spirit.

Trust yourself.

CHAPTER 19

The Experiment: Intentional Meditation Foundation

Will you join me in transforming the world?

I am looking for people all over the world to help lift the energy of the planet. With enough people practicing the Attractor Factor and using the meditation I plan to teach below, we can reduce crime, lower violence, and raise the wealth and prosperity of everyone near us.

When I was on a radio show one night and announced my colossal plan to change the world, I was amazed to later hear from people in Africa, India, Ireland, New Zealand, Australia, and all over the United States—all volunteering to help.

I got the idea for this rather noble project while reading *Permanent Peace: How to Stop Terrorism and War—Now and Forever* by Robert Oates. That book reveals 19 scientific studies that proved when groups of people meditate, the crime and violence in their area goes down. Oates writes:

"The basic idea is simple to state: Like ripples on a pond radiating outward from a pebble's splash, ripples of orderliness and harmony radiate outward from concentrated groups of meditation experts. And the evidence for this idea has been repeated and is statistically significant. Not only do signs of social disorder go down—such as violent crime, fires, traffic accidents, warfare, and terrorism—but signs of coherence and progress go up. Patent applications, for example, stock market levels, and economic indicators have all been shown to rise."

Notice his last sentence. It suggests that meditation helps increase wealth. With that in mind, I decided to create a global set of "hubs" where people learn how to meditate to intentionally attract wealth. The idea is, the more you help yourself, the more you also help those around you. And as you help them, you help the planet.

This is the noble purpose of the Intentional Meditation Foundation. It is a nonprofit foundation designed to teach a specific meditation technique to people all over the globe, with the purpose of lowering violence and increasing wealth wherever it is practiced. At the core of this movement is a 30-day event I'm calling The Experiment.

When I told a close friend that I planned to run a 30-day experiment to see if meditation could raise the prosperity level of the people meditating as well as influence everyone near them, she asked me something interesting.

"Do you care that you are running this experiment during a war, when people are worried about their jobs, their next payday, and maybe even their lives?"

"Actually, that's *why* I'm running this experiment," I replied.

This brief conversation intrigued me because her question assumed that outward events have the control. On the contrary, your income doesn't have to be affected by war, recession, pay cuts, or layoffs. You don't have to be a victim of circumstances. In my mind, outward events are simply the result of what we have already done inside ourselves.

I'll repeat that: *Outward events are simply the result of what we have already done inside ourselves.*

Maybe we attracted our current economic situation unconsciously, but we certainly attracted it. There is no right or wrong in that perspective. It simply is.

Now the really wonderful thing is that once you realize you are the creator, you can create the kind of life you prefer.

And that leads me to the subject of this chapter.

I'm asking for people to help me in what I am calling The Experiment. This 30-day event is designed to bring you more money, almost by magic, but only if you do three things:

1. Record where you are now in your finances, and then, when The Experiment is over, record the changes.
2. Meditate every day for 20 minutes using the technique I'm about to teach you.
3. Act on the insights that you receive and/or the opportunities that come your way afterward.

That's it.

Before I tell you the "IM" technique, let's cover a few basics to set the stage for what is about to happen.

1. *You are the cocreator.* Just as I pointed out to my friend, you are the predominant creative force in your life. What is happening to you is being created in part by you. You are attracting it. This is good news. It means you can change those appearances to match what you consciously prefer. It also means you can be, do, or have anything you can imagine, because the person responsible for any of it is you.

2. *Your belief creates your reality.* If you do this IM technique every day but still believe it won't work for you, then it won't work for you. You have to believe that change is possible. Belief rules. Intention is king. We are belief-beings and the results are belief-creations. Change your beliefs, and you change your life.

3. *Your feelings are the fuel.* Your feelings are what fuel your beliefs, desires, hopes, and dreams. When you worry, you are fueling a belief in a negative outcome. When you have faith, you are fueling your belief in a positive outcome. Your feelings are the motivators that make things happen. A belief without feeling is a thought. With feeling, it's an intention.

4. *Whatever you say after "I Am" defines you.* You create yourself by how you define yourself. Ask yourself, "Who am I?" and pay attention to your answers. That is what you are creating. Change your answers, and you change your results. In fact, it would be enlightening to see what you are telling yourself right now. This self-talk is creating the life you have! Write down some "I am" statements and see if any surprise you:

Now let's look at the IM process itself.

"IM" stands for *Intentional Meditation.* Most meditation is not request-oriented. That is, the meditation is simply a quieting of the mind. In and of itself, that is wonderful.

I once had a T-shirt that read "Meditation is not what you think." Exactly! If you're thinking, you're not meditating. Traditional meditation is beyond thinking, or behind it.

But *Intentional* Meditation is a departure from traditional meditation. In the IM method, you are focused on a specific outcome. You *are* thinking, and you are thinking with feeling. An IM is a request to the universe, through your conscious intent, to attract a particular result.

In other words, traditional meditators would sit and simply watch their thoughts. That is the meditation of my T-shirt: "Meditation is not what you think." It is a wonderful method. I encourage you to do it.

The Beatles made a form of meditation popular in the sixties called "TM," or Transcendental Meditation. In TM you are given a mantra, or special phrase, to repeat over and over again as you sit. This mantra keeps your mind busy so your being can settle down and relax. TM is powerful. When people used meditation to lower crime rates, as reported in 19 separate studies in Oates' book, they were doing TM.

IM is different.

IM is focused on achieving a result. You go into the meditation with a mental request and a feeling, which you amplify in your meditation. In other words, an IM might be something like this:

"I see myself at the end of our 30-day experiment with my business goals for the month achieved, I'm feeling great, smiling, maybe singing or whistling, as I feel the exhilaration of having magically attracted more money easily and effortlessly."

The statement is your intention.

Your intention is what you use as a type of mantra in your meditation.

Are you with me?

I'll walk you though an IM method to help make this clearer for you:

1. *Decide on what you want to achieve.* Make it believable to you. Remember, belief rules. If you don't believe you can do it, you probably won't. Let it be a stretch, but be honest with yourself, too. Again, what do you want to achieve at the end of the 30 days? How much more business or income? Write it here:

_____

_____

_____

_____

2. *Write it down in one clear statement.* For example, "At the end of the 30-day experiment, I have an extra $15,000 in the bank from unexpected sources." Or maybe "At the end of the 30-day experiment, I have 20 new clients." Write it down now.

_____

_____

_____

_____

3. *Feel what it will be like to have achieved your intention.* If you already had what you say you want, what would that feel like now? Get into those feelings. Relish them. Roll around in them. How would you look? How would you act? How would you smile? Feel the feelings now.

_____

_____

_____

_____

_____

_____

That's it.

In short, here it is again:

You simply take your intention (what you wrote down that you want), and you take the feelings of already having accomplished it (feel the success now) and spend 20 minutes a day soaking it up—pretending it's all happening now.

Again, that's it.

So, how does this simple method work? How does it make your intentions come true?

In short, you are putting in a request with the universe. You are placing your order. Because you are clear about what you want, and you feel what you want, you have streamlined the process. The universe will hear you and will begin to orchestrate events to help you attract your intended desire. All you have to do is pay attention and act on your hunches. Trust the process.

As I mentioned earlier, 19 separate studies proved that meditation can lower the crime rate. Those studies were all about Transcendental Meditation. In short, the meditators created a peaceful field, which radiated out and calmed everyone—including many potentially violent people.

In the IM formula that I just described to you, you are quieting the mind as in meditation, and even merging with all that is, but you are also placing a request with the universe. That request will radiate out and reach the people who can help you achieve it. From there, magic happens. I know much of this may seem strange, but I'm calling it an experiment so you can find out, with me, just how powerful this system can be.

Now, if you want a few more resources to help you understand this process, here are some great ones:

1. Sign up for Mike Dooley's "Notes from the Universe" at www .tut.com. His messages will help you stay focused on your goals. They are free.

2. If you're interested in the research about the 19 studies where meditation lowered crime rates, get the book *Permanent Peace* by Robert Oates.

3. If you believe it's difficult to get money into your life, start the flow by giving money. That's right—give some away. This is explained in my book, *The Greatest Money-Making Secret in History!*

4. Visit www.mrfire.com/IntentionalMeditationFoundation.com/ index.html.

5. Consider hiring a coach. See www.miraclescoaching.com.

Remember what you have to do:

1. Write down where you are in terms of current income, and after The Experiment write down your results.
2. Meditate using the IM method 20 minutes every day.
3. Act on the impulses, ideas, and opportunities that come your way.

Is this easy or what?
Yes, you can create change in your life.
It all begins right now.

> We must not make ourselves dependent on any particular *form* of wealth, or insist on its coming to us through some particular channel—that is at once to impose a limitation and to shut out other forms of wealth and to close other channels; but we must enter into the *spirit* of it.
>
> —JUDGE THOMAS TROWARD, *THE HIDDEN POWER*, 1902

CHAPTER 20

Common Questions (with Answers)

Can I attract a specific person? I
have my eyes on someone I really like.

It is a violation of free will to attract a specific person, so the
answer is no. After all, you are trying to find a match for yourself based
on what you ego can see in your circle of friends and coworkers. That's
a small group. The universe can see the big picture. There are six bil-
lion people on the planet, so chances are astronomically high that
there is a better match for you out there than the person you are thinking about. The wiser approach is to note the qualities you like in the
person you are attracted to. That will help attract the right person to
you. So focus on the characteristics of what you think you would like,
not on an actual person.

*What if I'm desperate? I am out of work and about to be thrown
out of my apartment.*

I understand. What you have to do is find a way to find peace
right now. You might need to ask for help, pray, take any job you can
get, borrow money, make a deal with your landlord for late payment, or something else that will help your immediate situation. As
you do that, you must also find the spirit of gratitude for what you do
have already. As much as I feel for your situation, as I've been there,
I also know you can be sincerely grateful for something in your life,

if only your life itself. When you feel gratitude, you begin to shift your energy and you'll begin to attract more peaceful new moments.

How can I end war?

The easiest answer is to understand peace begins with you. If you are angry or anxious about war, you are actually sending out the signal that attracts more war. You want to come from a place of inner peace. There are 19 scientific studies (as reported in the book *Permanent Peace*) that prove without question that when people meditate in a group, they help lower the crime and violence in that immediate area, as well as increase the prosperity of the same area. I would suggest you form such groups. If you don't feel so inclined, then at least spend time every day in silence, in peace, in appreciation of your life. That energy will help neutralize war.

What's the fastest way to attract whatever I want?

Appreciate what you have. An attitude of gratitude will speed up the attraction process. Beyond that, I'd say there are three things: (1) Know what you want; (2) Take action to attract it; and (3) Let go of any desperation or need for it. In short, you will attract faster if you don't need what you'd like and you take action to manifest it. It sounds contradictory, but action and letting go are the two essentials to success. You still have to get and stay clear of any limiting blocks within you, but action can often override them.

Am I to blame for everything I've attracted?

No. You attract your life experiences due to unconscious programming, rarely to any premeditated conscious desires. I advise people to accept responsibility for what occurs but not any blame or guilt.

What about people who attract disasters?

Again, we attract our life experiences due to a wide variety of unseen and unconscious processes. I have no idea what lurks in someone's history to attract a flood or a fire or any other kind of challenge.

When something happens, it's wise to handle it while looking for the hidden "attractor" belief that may have triggered it. Again, no one is doing this consciously. But our unconscious mind is packed with limiting beliefs and self-esteem issues, and maybe even past life baggage. I don't honestly know. None of this is cause for alarm, blame, or guilt. The idea is to awaken, choose what you do want, and take action toward it. Life goes on. It's just so much better when you're awake.

What's the ultimate secret to attracting whatever I want?

Get clear. When you are clear of any beliefs within you regarding what you want to attract, you'll attract it or something better. Also, be happy with what you have while taking inspired action out of this moment. Happiness is what you ultimately want and happiness is yours right now. Look around and enjoy. It doesn't mean you won't take action to create even better moments; it means your appreciation of this moment will attract even better moments, based on your vibration and your action. Be here now. Be happy now. Heaven is here.

When someone has hurt you, how do you forgive them? Have you forgiven Jonathan? If you have forgiven him, where did you go in your heart and mind to forgive him?

As I said in this book, yes, I've forgiven Jonathan. I did it with the quote I gave earlier, from Kurt Wright, about realizing that it's all good. True forgiveness is when you realize nothing bad happened in the first place. It may take time to forgive, but you can do it in an instant with the right mind-set. That mind-set is one of love.

If your five-step formula works, why don't you attract hair?

You have to want it to attract it. I don't care if I have hair on my head or not. Your question implies that baldness is bad. It's not. Some of the sexiest people alive are bald, such as actors Sean Connery and Bruce Willis. Some people even shave their head to become bald. If I wanted hair, I'd find a way to attract it. The real question is, what do *you* want? Instead of imagining what I should want, what is your own desire?

I read on your blog that you were burglarized in Los Angeles. Did you attract that?

You attract everything. So do I. My hotel room was broken into and someone stole my laptop, iPod, and cash. They left jewelry and expensive leather jackets. This is relevant because only weeks before I had been thinking about buying a new laptop and iPod. The criminals took what I was ready to let go of. And the cash they got was cash I give away to servers and homeless people. In short, I attracted an experience that fit exactly what I unconsciously wanted. Had I been more conscious at the time, I would have simply bought a new laptop and iPod, and given the money away. This is why we need to awaken. Until we do, our unconscious is in charge and may create/ attract unpleasant experiences to help us get what we really want.

Is giving a good way to attract wealth?

I read a fascinating study that proves giving makes you rich. The article states, "More giving doesn't just correlate with higher income; it *causes* higher income." (Italics mine.) See the article at www.port folio.com /views/columns/2007/10/15/Charity-Makes-Wealth. After that, go read my book, *The Greatest Money-Making Secret in History*. And then give some money away.

What is necessary to change?

Two key things: Understanding that you can do it, and knowing that it is worth the effort. Assuming you want to change anything at all in your life, you have to believe that you can do it and you have to believe it is worthwhile to do. If you don't believe you can do whatever it takes to change, you won't even try. If you don't believe the end result of change is worth it, you won't even begin the process. Again, you can do it and it's worth doing. Those are essential first steps to lasting change.

How is Spiritual Marketing *different from* The Attractor Factor?

Spiritual Marketing was the early version of *The Attractor Factor*. The latter has been greatly enriched, expanded and revised. The five steps in both are the same.

How do I let it go, if I am meditating on it?

What you let go of is your attachment to the end result, not the desire itself. When you can desire something without needing something, you are in a powerful magnetic field to attract the very something you desire. You simply can't need your desire. If you do, you're coming from desperation, which will attract more desperation.

I need money to pay someone like a coach to help me get clear but I don't have any money. Who can help me get clear if I can't afford to pay them?

You don't need anyone to get clear. You can use this book, or the methods in my other books, such as *The Key*. Thinking you "need" someone is a belief. Yes, I believe that you grow faster with a coach, and that's why I created my Miracles Coaching program, but you don't need someone to help you. You simply need to help yourself.

Okay, I've tried everything. I've read your books, I've watched The Secret, *I spent thousands of dollars on yagnas and still nothing works! How come?*

Actually, it all works—unless you block it. What you're getting is what you are wanting. Accept it, love it, and choose a new direction. Remember, you have counterintentions within you that block your conscious desire from coming to you. Get clear of them and you are free. Getting clear takes moment by moment awareness and everything you can throw at it. Don't give up.

How can I figure out what I really want in my life and how to start getting it? You say follow your passion and the money will come but I have no idea what I love or what I'm passionate about. Help!

You always know what you are passionate about when you are ruthlessly honest with yourself. Pretend you won the lottery and have three hundred million dollars in your bank. What would you do? After you spend money on cars and toys, what would you do with yourself?

How can I focus on positive things through good feelings when everything in my life is going wrong and I'm surrounded by all this negativity?

First, you have to understand nothing is going wrong. Your perception of the event is what is making it feel lousy. See it all with love and you're at peace and even appreciate it all. Second, do what you need to get back to feeling grateful for what you have. You are lucky to be alive. Many aren't. You are lucky to be able to read these words. Many can't.

How do you maintain when you encounter crazy drivers, rude people, and just the other negative people you can't help but encounter in the world?

You love them. As you love all you see, you begin to notice they disappear from your experience. Don't wait for the drivers to change; you change.

When does everything start coming together? So far nothing has changed. One month, four months? Longer?

How do you know nothing has changed? Most of your programming is unconscious, so there could be changes there. Also, if you are concerned or impatient, then that is a sign you're not clear. Being clear would mean you're happy now, and that state of peace would attract what you want, or something even better. Truth is, time is a human concept. Everything happens when it happens. Enjoy the moment.

Can you help me get out of debt? Can you offer me a loan and I'll pay you back?

This is thinking there is only one way to solve a problem or attract a result: me. Don't wait for me or anyone else for you to take continual action. Don't just ask one person and stop right there. Look beyond me and keep going. If you are open and willing to constantly take inspired action, the Universe will help you when the time is right. I'm no longer able to answer all the e-mails and requests I receive, so don't even look in my direction. But look within and ask for guidance. Then act on what you receive.

What do you think about children who were born sick? How did they attract sickness? Are the parents responsible for it?

Each of us comes into this world with an agenda. It's programming. Who knows why some children were born sick? But they're here now, so heal them. Your responsibility is to handle all that is in your experience. It doesn't matter how it got there. It's there. Now heal it.

I'd like to create a clear vision of what success looks like and, I know you'll think this is silly, but I really haven't ever been exposed to it. So, I need some help from my heroes. I want to know if there is something you have that helps commemorate your achievements in life. Did you get awards? Do you have letters from important people? What does a big house have inside of it?

I often reward myself when I accomplish something. Sometimes it's a new pair of shoes. Or a car. Or a trip. Or a piece of furniture. This helps me anchor the feeling of success and remind me of it later when I look at the item I bought. I don't always have to buy a reminder, either. This could be something like a drinking glass I was given when I was on Donny Deutsch's TV show. Or the photo of me and Larry King taken when I was on his show.

How do I stay inspired?!?!?

By focusing on what your heart wants.

Does the law of attraction override karma, or does karma override the law of attraction?

Karma is the law of attraction.

How come when I acted on a hunch, it didn't lead me anywhere?

Where did you expect it to lead you? It may have taken you right where you needed to go, but you judged it as wrong. Trust in life means you trust all that happens is for your highest good.

What are the eight words you mention that can forever change my life?

See the front of this book: "You never have to worry about money again."

I didn't quite get the part explaining the muscle test; are there any other resources I can go to, so I can get clear about that?

See www.goodhealthinfo.net/herbalists/muscle_testing.htm and www.geocities.com/sunmoonessences/muscle.html. You might also read *Muscle Testing* by Serafino Amoroso.

My spouse just left me. Can I "wish" him back to me again?

No. That is a violation of your spouse's free will. Instead, focus on the part of you that he represents. Love that inner part of you and he will come back, or not, but you will be at peace and ready for more love.

How does Zero Limits reconcile with the Law of Attraction?

Zero Limits points to the Divine. Come from there and all you do will be pure Attractor Factor. I say there are three stages of awakening. The first is victimhood. Attractor Factor appeals to the second stage, where you awaken to your power. Zero Limits is the third stage, where you surrender and work with the Divine. They are simply stepping stones on the road to the enlightenment—to being right here, right now, at total peace.

I want to know if I caused my husband's death. Can you think yourself to death?

People often think themselves to death. If you don't monitor your thoughts and choose the ones that support you, you can choose the ones that kill you, sometimes over time, sometimes instantly.

But no, you cannot think another person to their death. I'm sorry you lost your husband. You cocreated the experience of his loss, but you did not create his death. He had his own life. You have yours. The time you had together was a great gift. Remember it.

Do you still use a coach?

Absolutely. I have miracles coaches to help me keep growing and awakening, just as people go to my own Miracles Coaching program. We all need support to attract miracles. You can do it alone, but it's so much easier and faster with your own coach.

BIBLIOGRAPHY

Aleksiuk, Michael. *Power Therapy: Maximizing Health through Self-Efficacy.* Kirkland, WA: H&H Publishers, 1996.

Amoroso, Serafina. *Muscle Testing.* Bloomington, IN: AuthorHouse. 2006.

Atkinson, William Walter. *Thought Vibration, or The Law of Attraction in the Thought World.* Chicago: New Thought Publishing, 1906.

Ball, Ron, et al. *Freedom at Your Fingertips.* Fredericksburg, VA: InRoads Publishing, 2006.

Barton, Bruce. *What Can A Man Believe?* New York: Bobbs-Merrill, 1927.

Behrend, Genevieve, and Vitale, Joe. *How to Attain Your Desires by Letting Your Subconscious Mind Work for You, Vol.1.* Garden City, NY: Morgan-James Publishing, 2004.

———. *How to Attain Your Desires, Vol 2: How to Live Life and Love It!* Garden City, NY: Morgan-James Publishing, 2005.

Bender, Sheila Sidney, and Sise, Mary. *The Energy of Belief: Psychology's Power Tools to Focus Intention and Release Blocking Beliefs.* Santa Rosa, CA: Energy Psychology Press, 2008.

Bowen, Will. *A Complaint Free World.* New York: Doubleday, 2007.

Braden, Gregg. *The Divine Matrix: Bridging Time, Space, Miracles, and Belief.* Carlsbad, CA: Hay House, 2006.

Bristol, Claude. *The Magic of Believing.* New York: Pocket Books, 1991

Bruce, Alexandra. *Beyond the Secret.* New York: Disinformation Company, 2007.

Butterworth, Eric. *Spiritual Economics: The Principles and Process of True Prosperity.* Lee's Summit, MO: Unity, 1993.

Byrne, Rhonda. *The Secret.* New York: Atria Books/Beyond Words, 2006.

Callahan, Roger. *Tapping the Healer Within: Using Thought-Field Therapy to Instantly Conquer Your Fears, Anxieties, and Emotional Distress.* New York: McGraw-Hill, 2002.

Canfield, Jack, and Switzer, Janet. *The Success Principles: How to Get from Where You Are to Where You Want to Be.* New York: Collins, 2006.

Casey, Karen. *Change Your Mind and Your Life Will Follow.* New York: Conari Press, 2005.

Chopra, Deepak. *The Spontaneous Fulfillment of Desire.* New York: Harmony, 2003.

Coates, Denise. *Feel It Real! The Magical Power of Emotions.* Los Angeles: Denise Coates Publishers, 2006.

Coppel, Paula Godwin. *Sacred Secrets: Finding Your Way to Joy, Peace and Prosperity.* Unity Village, MO: 2008.

Cornyn-Selby, Alyce. *What's Your Sabotage?* Portland, OR: Beynch Press, 2000.

Craig, K.C. *Placing Your Order: Steps for Successful Manifestations.* Fairfax, VA: RMS Publications, 2007.

Dahl, Lynda Madden. *Beyond the Winning Streak: Using Conscious Creation to Consistently Win at Life.* Woodbridge Group, 2000.

———. *Ten Thousand Whispers: A Guide to Conscious Creation.* Woodbridge Group, 1995.

———. *The Wizards of Consciousness: Making the Imponderable Practical.* Woodbridge Group, 1997.

Deutschman, Alan. *Change or Die: The Three Keys to Change at Work and in Life.* New York: Reagan Books, 2007.

Di Marsico, Bruce. *The Option Method: Unlock Your Happiness with Five Simple Questions.* Walnut Grove, CA: Dragonfly Press, 2006.

Doré, Carole. *The Emergency Handbook for Getting Money Fast!* San Francisco: Celestial Arts, 2002.

Doyle, Bob. *Wealth beyond Reason.* Duluth, GA: Boundless Living, 2004.

Dwoskin, Hale. *The Sedona Method: Your Key to Lasting Happiness, Success, Peace and Emotional Well-Being.* Sedona, AZ: Sedona Press, 2003.

Dyer, Wayne. *Manifesting Your Destiny.* New York: HarperCollins, 1997.

———. *The Power of Intention: Learning to Co-Create Your World Your Way.* Carlsbad, CA: Hay House, 2004.

Eker, T. Harv. *Secrets of the Millionaire Mind: Mastering the Inner Game of Wealth.* NY: Collins, 2005.

Ellsworth, Paul. *Mind Magnet: How to Unify and Intensify Your Natural Faculties for Efficiency, Health and Success.* Holyoke, MA: Elizabeth Towne Company, 1924.

Evans, Mandy. *Travelling Free: How to Recover from the Past.* Encinitas, CA: Yes You Can Press, 2005.

Fengler, Fred, and Todd Varnum. *Manifesting Your Heart's Desires, Book I and Book II.* Burlington, VT: HeartLight, 2002.

Ferguson, Bill. *Heal the Hurt that Sabotages Your Life.* Houston, TX: Return to the Heart, 2004.

Ford, Debbie. *The Dark Side of the Light Chasers.* New York: Riverhead Books, 1998.

———. *Why Good People Do Bad Things: How to Stop Being Your Own Worst Enemy.* New York: HarperOne, 2008.

Gage, Randy. *Why You're Dumb, Sick & Broke . . . And How to Get Smart, Healthy & Rich!* Hoboken, NJ: John Wiley & Sons, 2006.

Gaines, Edwene. *The Four Spiritual Laws of Prosperity.* PA: Rodale Press, 2005.

Gallwey, Tim. *The Inner Game of Tennis.* New York: Random House, 1997.

Gene Landrum, *The Superman Syndrome: The Magic of Myth in The Pursuit of Power: The Positive Mental Moxie of Myth for Personal Growth*. iUniverse, 2005.

Gillett, Dr. Richard. *Change Your Mind, Change Your World*. New York: Simon & Schuster, 1992.

Gilmore, Ehryck. *The Law of Attraction 101*. Chicago: Eromlig Publishing, 2006.

Goi, James. *How to Attract Money Using Mind Power*. West Conshohocken, PA: Infinity Publishing, 2007.

Goldberg, Bruce. *Karmic Capitalism: A Spiritual Approach to Financial Independence*. Baltimore, MD: Publish America, 2005.

Grabhorn, Lynn. *Excuse Me, Your Life Is Waiting: The Astonishing Power of Feelings*. Charlottsville, VA: Hampton Roads, 2003.

Gregory, Eva. *The Feel Good Guide to Prosperity*. San Francisco: LifeCoaching, 2005.

Hall, Philip. *Jesus Taught It, Too: The Early Roots of the Law of Attraction*. Alberta, Canada: Avatar, 2007.

Harris, Bill. *Thresholds of the Mind: Your Personal Roadmap to Success, Happiness, and Contentment*. Beaverton, OR: Centerpoint Research, 2002.

Hawkins, David. *Devotional Nonduality*. Sedona, AZ: Veritas Publishing, 2006.

Hawkins, David. *I: Reality and Subjectivity*. Sedona, AZ: Veritas Publishing, 2003.

———. *Power vs. Force: The Hidden Determinants of Human Behavior*. Carlsbad, CA: Hay House, 2002.

———. *Transcending the Levels of Consciousness*. Sedona, AZ: Veritas Publishing, 2006.

Helmstetter, Shad. *Self-Talk for Weight Loss*. New York: St. Martin's Press, 1994.

———. *The Self-Talk Solution*. New York: Pocket Books, 1987.

Hicks, Jerry and Esther. *Ask and It Is Given: Learning to Manifest Your Desires*. Carlsbad, CA: Hay House, 2004.

———. *Ask and It Is Given: Learning to Manifest Your Desires*. San Antonio, TX: Abraham-Hicks, 2004.

———. *The Law of Attraction: The Basics of the Teachings of Abraham*. Carlsbad, CA: Hay House, 2006.

———. *Sara and the Foreverness of Friends of a Feather*. With an introduction by Joe Vitale. San Antonio, TX: Abraham-Hicks, 1995.

———. *What to Say When You Talk to Yourself*. New York: Pocket Books, 1982.

Hogan, Kevin. *The Science of Influence*. Hoboken, NJ: John Wiley & Sons, 2004.

Holmes, Ernest. *Creative Mind and Success*. San Francisco: Tarcher, 2004.

———. *Science of Mind*. San Francisco: Tarcher, 1998.

Houlder, Kulananda and Dominic. *Mindfulness and Money*. New York: Broadway, 2002.

Hunt, Valery. *Infinite Mind*. Malibu, CA: 1996.

Jahnke, Roger. *The Healing Promise of Qi*. New York: McGraw-Hill, 2002.

Joyner, Mark. *Simpleology: The Simple Science of Getting What You Want*. Hoboken, NJ: John Wiley & Sons, 2007.

Kaa, Sri Ram. *2012: You Have a Choice!* Tijeras, NM: TOSA Publishing, 2006.

Kahler, Rick, and Fox, Kathleen. *Conscious Finance: Uncover Your Hidden Money Beliefs and Transform the Role of Money in Your Life*. Rapid City, SD: FoxCraft: 2005.

Kaufman, Barry Neil. *To Love Is to Be Happy With*. New York: Fawcett, 1985.

Kennedy, Dan. *No B.S. Wealth Attraction for Entrepreneurs*. Entrepreneur Press, 2006.

Kramer, Carolyn Miller. *Creating Miracles: Understanding the Experience of Divine Intervention.* Tiboron, CA: 1995.

Kristof, Aziz. *The Human Buddha: Enlightenment for the New Millennium.* New Delhi, India: Kristof, 2006.

Landrum, Gene. *Paranoia and Power.* Morgan-James Publishing, 2008.

Lapin, Jackie. *The Art of Conscious Creation.* Charleston, SC: Elevate, 2007.

Lapin, Rabbi Daniel. *Thou Shall Prosper: Ten Commandments for Making Money.* Hoboken, NJ: J. Wiley & Sons, 2002.

Larson, Christian D. *Your Forces and How to Use Them.* London. Fowler, 1912.

Larson, Melody. *The Beginner's Guide to Abundance.* Booklocker.com, 2007.

Levenson, Lester. *No Attachments, No Aversions: The Autobiography of a Master.* Sherman Oaks, CA: Lawrence Crane Enterprises, 2003.

———. *The Ultimate Truth About Love & Happiness: A Handbook for Life.* Sherman Oaks, CA: Lawrence Crane Enterprises, 2003.

Lichtman, Stuart, and Joe Vitale. *How to Get Lots of Money for Anything FAST.* E-book, 2002.

Lipton, Bruce. *The Biology of Belief: Unleashing the Power of Consciousness, Matter and Miracles.* Mountain of Love, 2005.

Losier, Michael. *Law of Attraction.* Victoria, Canada: Losier Publications, 2003.

Love, Lisa. *Beyond the Secret: Spiritual Power and the Law of Attraction.* Charlottesville, VA: Hampton Roads, 2007.

Mackenzie, Kathleen. *Not Manifesting? This Book Is for You!* Denver, CO: Outskirts Press, 2007.

Martin, Art. *Your Body Is Talking, Are You Listening?* Penryn, CA: Personal Transformation, 2001.

McTaggart, Lynne. *The Intention Experiment: Using Your Thoughts to Change Your Life and the World.* New York: Free Press, 2007.

Murphy, Dr. Joseph. *The Power of Your Subconscious Mind.* New York: Bantam, 2001.

Myss, Caroline. *Anatomy of the Spirit.* New York: Three Rivers Press, 1997.

Neville, Goddard. *Immortal Man.* Amarillo, TX: DeVorss & Company, 1999.

———. *Immortal Man: A Compilation of Lectures.* Camarillo, CA: DeVorss & Company, 1999.

———. *The Law and the Promise.* Camarillo, CA: DeVorss & Company, 1984.

———. *The Power of Awareness.* Camarillo, CA: DeVorss & Company, 1983.

———. *Your Faith Is Your Fortune.* Camarillo, CA: DeVorss & Company, 1985.

Neville, Goddard, and Vitale, Joe. *At Your Command.* Garden City, NY: Morgan-James Publishing, 2005.

Norville, Deborah. *Thank You Power: Making the Science of Gratitude Work for You.* Nashville, TN: Thomas Nelson, 2007.

Oates, Robert. *Permanent Peace.* Institute of Science, Technology and Public Policy, 2002.

———. *Permanent Peace: How to Stop Terrorism and War—Now and Forever.* Fairfield, VA: Oates, 2002.

O'Bryan, Pat, and Vitale, Joe. *The Myth of Passive Income: The Problem and the Solution.* E-book, 2004. *www.mythofpassiveincome.com.*

———. The Think and Grow Rich Workbook is a free e-book based on the classic by Napoleon Hill. E-book, 2004. *www. InstantChange.com.*

Orr, Leonard. *Breaking the Death Habit: The Science of Everlasting Life.* Berkeley, CA: North Atlantic Books, 1998.

Patterson, Kerry. *Influencers: The Power to Change Anything.* New York: McGraw-Hill, 2008.

Pauley, Tom. *I'm Rich Beyond My Wildest Dreams, I Am, I Am, I Am.* New York: Rich Dreams, 1999.

Ponder, Catherine. *The Dynamic Laws of Prosperity.* Camarillo, CA: DeVorss & Company, 1985.

———. *The Dynamic Laws of Prosperity.* Amarillo, TX: DeVorss, 1985.

Proctor, Bob. *You Were Born Rich: Now You Can Discover and Develop Those Riches.* Tornoto, Canada: LifeSuccess Productions, 1997.

Rafter, Mark. *The Wealth Manifesto: Transforming Your Life from Survive to Thrive.* Auburn, CA: New Knowledge Press, 2008.

Ray, James Arthur. *The Science of Success: How to Attract Prosperity and Create Harmonic Wealth through Proven Principles.* Sun Ark Press, 1999.

Ressler, Peter, and Mitchell, Monika. *Spiritual Capitalism: How 9/11 Gave Us Nine Spiritual Lessons of Work and Business.* New York: Chilmark Books, 2007.

Ringer, Robert. *Looking Out For #1.* New York: Fawcett, 1985.

———. *Winning Through Intimidation.* New York: Fawcett, 1984.

Ritt, Michael, and Kirk Landers. *A Lifetime of Riches: The Biography of Napoleon Hill.* New York: Dutton, 1995.

Roazzi, Vincent. *Spirituality of Success: Getting Rich with Integrity.* Dallas, TX: Namaste, 2001.

Roberts, Jane. *The Nature of Personal Reality: Specific, Practical Techniques for Solving Everyday Problems and Enriching the Life You Know.* CA: New World Library, 1994.

Rutherford, Darel. *So, Why Aren't You Rich?* Albuquerque, NM: Dar, 1998.

Ryce, Michael. *Why Is This Happening to Me—Again?* Theodosia, MO: Ryce, 1996.

Sage, Carnelian. *The Greatest Manifestation Principle in the World.* Beverley Hills, CA: Think Outside the Book, 2007.

Scheinfeld, Robert. *Busting Loose From The Money Game: Mind-Blowing Strategies for Changing the Rules of a Game You Can't Win.* Hoboken, NJ: John Wiley & Sons, 2006.

———. *The 11th Element: The Key to Unlocking Your Master Blueprint for Wealth and Success.* Hoboken, NJ: John Wiley & Sons, 2004.

Shumsky, Susan. *Miracle Prayer: Nine Steps to Creating Prayers that Get Results.* Berkeley, CA: Celestial Arts, 2006.

Staples, Dr. Walter Doyle. *Think Like A Winner!* Hollywood, CA: Wilshire, 1993.

Tipping, Colin. *Radical Forgiveness: Making Room for the Miracle.* Marietta, GA: Global 13 Publications, 2002.

———. *Radical Manifestation: The Fine Art of Creating the Life You Want.* Marietta, GA: Global 13 Publications, 2006.

Truman, Karol. *Feelings Buried Alive Never Die . . .* Olymbus, UT: 1991.

Tuttle, Carol. *Remembering Wholeness.* Salt Lake City, UT: Elton-Wolf Publishing, 2003.

Vitale, Joe. *Adventures Within: Confessions of an Inner World Journalist.* AuthorHouse, 2003.

———. *The Attractor Factor: Five Easy Steps for Creating Wealth (or anything else) from the Inside Out.* Hoboken, NJ: John Wiley & Sons, 2005.

———. *Buying Trances: A New Psychology of Sales and Marketing.* Hoboken, NJ: John Wiley & Sons, 2007.

———. *The Greatest Money-Making Secret in History.* 1st Books Library, 2003.

———. *Hypnotic Writing.* Hoboken, NJ: John Wiley & Sons, 2007.

————. *The Key: The Missing Secret to Attracting Whatever You Want.* Hoboken, NJ: John Wiley & Sons, 2007.

————. *Life's Missing Instruction Manual: The Guidebook You Should Have Been Given at Birth.* Hoboken, NJ: John Wiley & Sons, 2006.

————. *The Missing Secret: How to Use the Law of Attraction to Get Whatever You Want, Every Time.* Audio program. Niles, IL: Nightingale-Conant, 2008.

————. *The Seven Lost Secrets of Success.* Hoboken, NJ: John Wiley & Sons, 2007.

————. *There's a Customer Born Every Minute: P.T. Barnum's Amazing 10 "Rings of Power" for Creating Fame, Fortune, and a Business Empire Today—Guaranteed!* Hoboken, NJ: John Wiley & Sons, 2006.

Vitale, Joe, and Ryan, Mark. *Attracting Wealth: Magnetizing Your Unconscious Mind for Prosperity: Subliminal Manifestation DVD #4.* Austin, TX: Hypnotic I Media, Inc., 2007.

Vitale, Joe, and Len, Ihaleakala Hew. *Zero Limits: The Secret Hawaiian System for Wealth, Health, Peace, and More.* Hoboken, NJ: John Wiley & Sons, 2007.

Waldroop, James, and Butler, Timothy. *The 12 Bad Habits that Hold Good People Back.* New York: Random House, 2000.

Wattles, Wallace D. *How to Get What You Want.* Publisher unknown; circa 190-?.

————. *The Science of Getting Rich.* New York: Penquin/Tarcher, 2007.

Wilber, Ken. *Quantum Questions: Mystical Writings of the World's Greatest Physicists.* Boston: Shambhala, 2001.

Wilde, Stuart. *The Trick to Money Is Having Some.* Carlsbad, CA: Hay House, 1995.

Wojton, Djuna. *Karmic Healing: Clearing Past-Life Blocks to Present-Day Love, Health, and Happiness.* Berkeley, CA: Crossing Press, 2006.

Wright, Kurt. *Breaking the Rules.* Boise, ID: CPM, 1998.

Web Sites

www.miraclescoaching.com
www.theclearingaudio.com
www.advancedclearingaudio.com
www.attractanewcar.com
www.zerolimits.info
www.moneybeyondbelief.com
www.AttractorFactor.com
www.MyProsperitySecrets.com
www.emofree.com
www.BobProctor.com
www.InstantChange.com
www.BeyondPositiveThinking.com
www.richbits.com
www.OptionMethodnetwork.com
www.TUT.com
www.Centerpointe.com
www.totalsuccess4u.com
www.dreamsalive.com
www.WealthBeyondReason.com
www.MrFire.com
www.yagna.by-choice.com
www.jyotish-yagya.com
www.caroltuttle.com
www.Abraham-Hicks.com
www.prosperitynetwork.com

Healers, Mentors, Coaches

See www.miraclescoaching.com

Ann Harcus   anntaylor@innerhealing.com

Anya Wendt   anya@mentor-team.com

Bill Ferguson	bill@billferguson.com
Kathy Bolden	kjbolden@earthlink.net
Mandy Evans	mandy@mandyevans.com
Dr. Roopa Chari	info@charicenter.com
Karol Truman	Karol@healingfeelings.com
Mark Ryan	Mark@MarkJRyan.com
Carol Tuttle	carol@caroltuttle.com
John Burton	jkburton@charter.net

Abundance and gratitude, 187–188

Addiction versus desire, 207

Action. *See* "Inspired Action"

Advertising, spiritual, 199–201

Advanced Hypnotic Writing (Vitale), 101

Adventures Within (Vitale), 37

Aerosmith, 1

Aesop Marketing, 2

Affirmation, Gamblers Anonymous, 36

Alignment

  of beliefs, conscious and uncon-
    scious, 141–143

  with life's purpose, 214

*AMA Complete Guide to Small Business
  Advertising, The* (Vitale), 61, 86

Amaroso, Serafino, 264

Amazing Kreskin, The, 46

Amazon.com, 221

American Management Association, 86

American Marketing Association,
    61, 86

American Statesman (newspaper), 97

Anatomy of the Spirit (Myss), 154–155

Angels, 138–141

Ancient Egypt, 22

Anthony, Dr. Robert, 3, 57, 86–87,
    118–119

Antion, Tom, 231

Ask and You Shall Receive (Morency),
    112–113

Attention to signals, 225–26. *See also*
    Awareness; Consciousness

Attitude:

  dismissive, 55–58

  playful, 20

  positive mental (IQ test), 9–10

Atkinson, William Walker, 17, 21

Attraction, law of:

  compared to Newtonian physics,
    22–23

  conscious versus unconscious
    attraction, 7–80

Attractor Factor, The (Vitale), 26, 25–54,
    178, 221, 260–261

Attractor Factor, steps to:

  case study, 17–20

  clearing, as "missing secret,"
    135–182

  "do wants," 91–134

  "don't wants," 83–89

  "feel what you want as if you already
    had it," 183–205

  five-step formula, 240

  key points, 241–242

  letting go, 207–235

  testimonials, 25–54

Austin Family (magazine), 97

Awareness, 23, 226. *See also* Attention;
    Consciousness

Babson, Roger, 63

Babylon, 22

Barker, Raymond Charles, 134

Barnum, P. T., 4, 86, 129, 213, 215, 218

Barrett, Dr. Rick, 235

Barton, Bruce, 137–139, 209, 232

Beatles, the, 251

Beliefs. *See also* Emotions; Desires;
    Feelings
  absorbed from culture, 241
  in alignment, 141
  clearing of negative, 135–136,
    147–150, 152–155, 161–163
  clearing through using the "Script,"
    179–182
  conscious choice of, 151
  conscious and unconscious in con-
    flict, 142
  as creators of reality, 111–112, 249
  as excuses, 107
  as hindrances to receiving, 142,
    159–160
  about money, healing of, 68,
    149–150, 167–169
  hidden, and disapproval as a sign
    of, 56
  meaning, as ascribed by belief, 145
  negative, 19, 110
  as power for healing, 109, 111
  remote healing and, 152–153
  results that are experienced, 155–156

Behrend, Genevieve, 70

Beyond Positive Thinking (Anthony), 3,
    57, 87, 118

BIG Austin, 97

Big Business of Life (Parlette), 73

Big Idea, The (television show), 3, 129

Blotnick, Scrully, 63

Blues Brothers, 129

Bolden, Kathy, 152–153

Bond, James, 1

Branson, Richard, 87

Bray, Stephen, 47–49

Breaking the Rules (Wright), 245

Breathing, in *Chi Kung* exercise, 203

Breen, Jean M., 32

Broken Trail (film), 26

Business interests versus
    spirituality, 64

Caffrey, Ann Marie, 7–15

Canfield, Jack, 84

Carnegie, Andrew, 219

Cars:
  case study of Attractor Factor, 17–20
  manifesting, 1, 18–20, 42, 98–103

Carter, Jimmy, 104

Change Your Mind, Change Your World
    (Gillett), 56

Change:
  healing of pneumonia through
    changing message, 188–189
  of inner signal to change outer
    world, 212
  necessity of, 260
  "Turn It into Something Good"
    (TIISG), 218–219
  world as affected by the
    individual, 177

Chi Kung (*Qi Gong*), 202–203

Chopra, Deepak, 95, 213, 237

Circle of activity, 85

Clarity:
  of both partners, 210–211
  clearing energy to allow
    manifestation, 152–172
  dissolving objections and
    excuses, 110
  of intentions, 95, 110, 201
  in marketing materials, 198–199

Classrooms, virtual:
  e-classes, 99–103
  excuses for not attempting, 105–106
Clearing:
  beliefs that hinder manifestation,
    147–149
  in Jacobs's three-step method, 201
  as "missing secret" of Attractor
    Factor, 135–182
  of past events that drain energy,
    153–155
Cocreation of reality, 9–80, 249
Consciousness:
  choice of beliefs, 151
  versus unconsciousness, 77–80,
    108–109, 111
Complaints:
  creating "do wants" from "don't
    wants," 94–96
  in daily life, 83–84
  "don't wants," 88–89
  worksheet for 180-degree
    turnarounds, 95–96
Connections:
  broadening the networking
    base, 85
  e-mail lists, 104–105
Connery, Sean, 259
*Creating Miracles: Understanding the
  Experience of Divine Intervention*
  (Miller), 237
Creativity:
  life created from perceptions,
    108–109
  world as created by self, 177
Credentials, 105–106
Cummins, Kent, 96–98
Curiosity versus need, 18

Dell Computer Corporation, 50
Dempsey, Jack, 104
Desires. *See also* Beliefs; Emotions;
    Feelings
  versus addiction, 207
  admitting what you truly want,
    118–119
  "burning" the seeds of, for growth,
    203–204
  versus "hungry ghost" cravings,
    114–115
  as motivation, 115
  playful attitude toward, 207
Deutsch, Donny, 3, 129
Di Marsico, Bruce, 145
Dismissing, 55–59
"Do wants," 91–134
Donovan, Jim, 42–43
"Don't wants," 83–89
Dooley, Mike, 254
Dossey, Larry, 139
Doubts, 19, 80, 171, 180
Dreams:
  power of holding a vision, 214
  seeing as already fulfilled, 196–197
Dyer, Wayne, 163, 131, 213

eBay, 106
E-books, free online, 105
*E-Code: 47 Surprising Secrets for
  Making Money Online Almost
  Instantly* (Vitale), 104
E-classes, 99–103
Economy, created by beliefs, 248
Edwards, Jim, 231
Ego:
  in balance with spirit, 241
  as barrier to intentions, 95, 208, 229

Einstein, Albert, 9

Electrical system, 193

Ellsworth, Paul, 74

E-mail:

    as tool for networking, 86, 104–105

Emotional pain:

    expressing versus suppressing, 164

    hot buttons, from past experiences,
      161–163

Emotions, power of, 186–187, 203–204.
    See also Beliefs; Desires; Feelings

Energy:

    attraction based upon, 85

    channeled toward intention, 202

    clearing energy, case studies,
      157–164

    drained by past events, 154–155

    of emotions, 187–187

    given, and results, 189

    low, and negativity, 83

    Jacobs, Jonathan, on, 154

    patterns, 155–156

Evans, Mandy, 35, 62, 145–146, 187

Excuses:

    as beliefs, 107, 112

    as number-one mistake people make,
      103–108

    worksheets, 107–108

Executive mentoring program
    (Vitale), 115

Experiences versus lessons, 194–195

Experiment, The (intentional
    meditation), 248–250

Faith:

    versus negativity, 84

Faith and Inspired Action (IQ test),
    11–12

Fear. *See also* Negativity

    of admitting desires, 119

    of driving, case study of, 153–154

    releasing, case study of, 157–158

    releasing grudges, case study of,
      159–160

    as a stumbling block, 19, 84

Federal Trade Commission, 218

Feelings Buried Alive Never Die . . .
    (Truman), 156, 179, 182

Feelings. *See also* Beliefs; Desires;
    Emotions

    attention to, 135

    attracting miracles, and promotion,
      198–199

    caused by perceptions, 145

    in concert with thoughts, 204

    as "fuel" for manifesting, 250

    Goddard, Neville, and imaging,
      183–184

    hurts from the past, 135, 161–163

    imagery, and adding energy to, 242

    resolving past by using the "Script,"
      179–182

Feld, Kenneth

Ferguson, Bill, 160–163

Fiction, or nonexistence of, 185–186

Financial straits, 257

Five-step process:

    using to do good in the world, 115

    in *Spiritual Marketing*, 174–175

"Flags," or signals, 225–229

Focusing on true desires, imagery
    exercise, 116–117

Forgiveness, 163, 245, 259

Freedom, 110, 246

Free will, 264

Freud, Sigmund, 142

Fundamentals of Prosperity
  (Babson), 63

Gage, Randy, 81–82, 87
Gallant, Velma, 44
Gallwey, Tim, 208
Gamblers Anonymous, 36–37, 115
Garfinkel, David, 231
Gilbert, Dr. Richard, 56
Gilman, Stephen, 33
Gitterle, Marcus, 172, 174
Giving:
  as cause of wealth, 260
  donating to causes, 5
  versus greed, 121
Goal-setting:
  "assuming the feeling of the wish
    fulfilled," 184
  to achieve income stream, 2
  in "Attractor Factor" IQ quiz, 8
  Proctor, Bob, on, 220
  in testimonial to *Spiritual
    Marketing*, 49
  higher levels of participating with
    people, 87
  turning over to the unconscious, 239
  writing as a tool to achieving, 120–121
Goddard, Neville, 183–187
Goethe, 190–191
Gossip, 83, 87–88
Gratitude:
  as antidote for financial straits,
    257–258
  attitude of, to propel attraction
    process, 258
  for countering negativity, 262
  energy of, and shifting of outlook,
    187–188

feelings of, for generating
    forgiveness, 163
  worksheet, 74–75
Gravity, law of, 22
*Greatest Money-Making Secret in
    History!, The* (Vitale), 35, 254, 260
Greed, antidote, 121
Griffith, Andy, 191
Growth, stunted by dismissive
    attitude, 55
Guaranteed Outcome Marketing
    (Vitale) (formula), 101

Haeske, Roger, 34
Hager, Brad, 94
Handbook to a Happier Life
    (Donovan), 43
Hansen, Mark Victor, 84
Happiness:
  in present moment, 259
  shortcut to whatever you want, 3
Harcus, Ann, 34–35
Harris, Philip, 22
Hawaii State Hospital, 176
Hawkins, Dr. David, 131
Heal the Hurt That Sabotages Your Life
    (Ferguson), 160
Healed by Morning (Barrett), 235
Healing:
  of cancer, 110
  ho'oponopono (Hawaiian healing
    method), 175–179
  Hindu healing rituals (*yagyas* or
    yagnas), 172–175
  Jacobs, Jonathan, 68, 110
  of pneumonia, 188–189
  and prayer, 139
  remote, 152–153

Healing (*Continued*)
  Chi Kung (*Qi Gong*) exercise, 203
  Schneider, Meir, 67, 68
  of self, to heal others, 175–179
Henderson, Karin, 49–50
Hicks, Jerry and Esther, 195, 200–201
Hibbler, Bill, 38
Hidden Power, The (Troward),
  204, 255
Hill, Napoleon, 32, 217, 219
Hoffman, Christy, 35–37
Holmes, Ernest, 172
Homelessness, 67
Ho'oponopono (Hawaiian healing
  method), 176–179
Hoover, J. Edgar, 104
Houlder, Dominic, 114
House, Paul, 32
Hovey, Rich, 19
How to Attract a New Car (Vitale), 2
How to Attract Money (Murphy), 204
*How to Create an E-book in Only
  7 Days* (Vitale), 2
"How to Think Like God" (Vitale)
  (seminar), 119–120
Hypnotic Marketing (Vitale), 132, 234
Hypnotic Writing (Vitale), 2, 101, 234
Humphrey, Lucius, 197
Hungry ghosts (neurotic cravings),
  114–115
Hunt, Dr. Valerie, 236
Hutchens, Becky, 37–38

"I am" statements, 250
"I love you": statement for healing self
  and others, 177–179
Illusions:
  outer versus inner reality, 74

*I'm Rich Beyond My Wildest Dreams,
  I Am, I Am, I Am* (Pauley), 102
Imagery exercise:
  for expressing, versus suppressing,
    energy, 163–165
  from "How to Think Like God,"
    119–120
  with Stuart Wilde, 116–117
Imagination:
  excuses, imaginary versus real, 107
  Goddard, Neville, on power of, 183
  and visualization, experience of a
    reader, 46–47
Imagining the outcome, 190–191
Immortal Man (Goddard), 195
"In the moment," 207
Incentives, 105
Income stream, 2
Infinite Mind (Hunt), 224
Inner Game of Tennis, The (Gallwey),
  208
"Inner Game of Writing, The" (Vitale)
  (class), 208
Inner self:
  change of inner signal changes outer
    world, 212
  as source of peace, 160
Insanity, criminal, and Hawaiian
  healing method, 175–176
Insecurity, as a block to prosperity, 62
Inspiration as intention, 129–130
"Inspired Action," 221–229, 262–263
Intelligence quotient:
  Prosperity IQ quiz (Gage), 81–82
  Attractor Factor IQ quiz (Caffrey),
    7–15
Intentional Meditation Foundation,
  247–255

Intentions:
case study of attracting a car, 98–103
Chopra, Deepak, on, 95, 237
versus counterintentions, 166, 261
Cummins's, Kent, experiences of, 96–98
"Dare something worthy" motto, 102
and feelings, 250
and Hindu healing rituals (*yagyas* or *yagnas*), 174–175
as inspirations, 129–130
and "Inspired Action," 228–230
setting, and letting go, 212–214
stating to the universe, 140
testimonial to power of, 46
Winfrey, Oprah, on, 98
writing on card for carrying, 134
Interconnectedness, 156, 160, 177
International marketing, 106
Internet marketing, 86, 99–103, 104–106, 214
Iqbal, Faisal, 44–46
Italy, author's visit to, 233–235

Jacobs, Jonathan, 68, 109, 110, 137–138, 140–141, 147, 153, 154, 156–160, 193, 243–246
three-step method for creating results, 201–202
Jesus Christ, 21, 232
Jesus Taught It, Too: The Early Roots of the Law of Attraction (Harris), 22
Joy, as part of manifestation process, 196, 204
Joyner, Mark, 2, 218
Jung, Carl G., 109

Karma
clearing through Hindu ritual (*yagyas* or *yagnas*), 174–175
questions on, 263–264
Katie, Byron, 169–171
Kaufman, Barry and Suzi, 67
Kennedy, Dan, 48
Kent Cummins Magic Camp, The, 97
Key, The (Vitale), 3, 21, 27, 141, 261
King, Larry, 3, 185, 191, 227
Knievel, Evel, 86, 104

Lack, experience of, 68, 81
Lakeway Breakfast Club, 97
Larson, Martin, 232
Law of Attraction, 77–79, 264
Law and the Promise, The (Goddard), 183
Law of Success, The (Hill), 32
Leap, The (film), 3
Learning:
versus dismissing, 55–58
Learning Access, The, 31
Lemberg, Paul, 102
Len, Dr. Ihaleakala Hew, 176–179
Lessons versus experiences, 194–195
Letting go:
asking for help, 211–212
ego and struggle, 208
versus giving up, 233–235
"Inspired Action," 221–223
and meditation, 261
nonattachment, 233
playful attitude, 207
power of, 214
and prayer, 215–216
and trust in the universe, 220–221

Levenson, Lester, 4–5, 59
Levine, Terri, 216–217
Levinson, Jay Conrad, 86
Life interests, pursuit of, versus pursuit
  of money, 63–64
Lifetime of Riches, A (biography of
  Hill), 217–218
Light versus dark forces, 233–237
Limitations:
  authority figures and self-limitation,
    187
  ego hindrances to "letting go,"
    239–240
  versus expecting miracles, 114
  versus letting go, 208
  overcoming beliefs in, 241–242
  removing inner, 119–120
  and unconscious beliefs,
    142–143, 259
Lind, Jackie, 25–27
Livesay, John, 32–33
Lord, Walter, 185
Love:
  absence of, blocking
    manifesting, 163
  mindset of, 259
  for self, as method of loving and
    healing others, 177–179
  toward negative people and
    events, 262
Luck, 10, 98
Lying to oneself, 151

Magic of Change, The (Cummins), 96
Magnetic attraction:
  of desire, for manifestation, 202
  life created from perceptions,
    108–109

Man Nobody Knows, The (Barton), 232
Manifest Your Destiny (Dyer), 163
Manifesting Your Heart's Desires, Book I
  and *Book II*, 224
Manifesting:
  cars, 1, 17–20
  elements, key, 20
  versus fear, 19
  IQ test (Caffrey), 7–15
  by letting go, 208, 216
Marketing:
  and advertising, 200–201
  materials as projections of feelings
    and energy, 198–199
  small businesses, 61
Materialism:
  energy as basis for material
    forms, 156
  versus spirituality, 17, 103
Meaning, ascribed by belief, 145
Media:
  abstaining from, 84–85
  affect on visualization, 77–78
Meditation:
  Experiment, The, 248–250
  Intentional Meditation Foundation,
    247–255
  to reduce crime and violence, 247–248
Mentors, 140–141
Miller, Carolyn, 237
Millionaire (magazine), 94
Mindfulness and Money (Houlder), 114
Mind Magnet, The (Ellsworth), 74
Mindset of love, 259
Miracles:
  author's experiences, 1–6, 214
  expecting, versus limitations,
    113–114

Miracles Coaching program (Vitale), 113, 115, 140, 214, 261, 265
Missing Secret, The (Vitale) (audio-program), 141
Mitchell, Chris, 29–32
Mok, Jo Han, 231
Money:
  attracting, 61–65
  clearing doubts about receiving, case study of, 158–160
  likes speed, 231–232
  patterns of problems with, 165–166
  versus spirit, 63
  study of pursuing money versus pursuing life interests, 63–64
Money Beyond Belief (Vitale and Yates), 2
Moody, Elinor, 84
Morency, Pierre, 112–113
Morningstar, Jonathan, 188–189
Mother Theresa, 241
Mozumdar, A. K., 80
Mulholland, John, 104
Murphy, Dr. Joseph, 45, 77, 156, 204, 205
Muscle testing, 130–133, 264
Muscle Testing (Amoroso), 264
Mustard seed, 171
MySpace.com, 28
Myss, Caroline, 154–155

Natural law of reciprocal action, 70
Nature of Personal Reality, The (Roberts), 21
Needs:
  versus desire, 261
  as repelling desired outcomes, 207
  unacknowledged, 109–110

versus curiosity, 18
Negativity:
  abstaining from, 84–85
  daily life, 83
  "don't wants," 88
  media coverage, 77–80
  seeing with love, 262
Networking:
  higher levels of, 85–87
Network Marketing (book-and-tape series), 36
New Thought, or a Modern Religious Approach: The Philosophy of Health, Happiness, and Prosperity (Larson), 232–233
Newton, Sir Isaac, 22–23
Newtonian principles, 22–23
Nightingale-Conant (audiotape programs), 39, 213–214
Night to Remember, A (Lord), 185
Nonattachment. *See* Letting Go
"Notes from the Universe" (Dooley), 254

Oates, Robert, 247, 254
O'Bryan, Pat, 230–231
Oden, Nerissa, 1–6, 218
Ogilvy, David, 47–48
180-degree turnarounds of thoughts, 95, 107–108
On the Beam (Humphrey), 197
Opportunities:
  avoid dismissal of, 55–59
Oprah, 160
Option Institute, 67
Option Method (Di Marsico), 145
Opus, The (film), 3
Our Invisible Supply (Warner), 69–70, 242

Outcomes, nonattachment to, 237, 240
Out of This World (Goddard), 183
Out-picturing of inner pictures, 77, 79

Panoz Esperante GTLM (car), 18–20
Parlette, Ralph, 73
Participation in versus manufacturing
  of outcomes, 240
Partners, and clearing energy
  together, 211
Passion, 261–262
Past:
  clearing through use of the "Script,"
    179–182
  clearing energy of past events, case
    studies, 157–163
  letting go of, 154–155
Patterns. *See also* Beliefs
  beliefs about money, 165–166
  betrayal, case study of, 166–167
  fear of driving, 153–154
  hurt feelings and emotional pain,
    161–163
  recurring, and worksheet for
    examining, 168–169
Patterson, Charles Brodie, 71
Patterson, Floyd, 91–92
Pauley, Tom, 102
Peace:
  and ending war, 258
  and meditation, 254
Peace Pilgrim, 92–93
Penguin Publishing Group, 29
Perceptions:
  life created from our, 108–109
*Permanent Peace: How to Stop
  Terrorism and War—Now and
  Forever* (Oates), 247, 254, 258

Persistence, 9
Personal best, 91
Peters, Tim, 213
*Philosophiae Naturalis Principia
  Mathematica* (Newton), 23
Positive, the, in the negative, 217–223
Possibilities, recognizing versus
  dismissing, 55
Power vs. Force (Hawkins), 131
Power of Intention, The (Dyer), 216
Power of Outrageous Marketing, The
  (Vitale) (audio program), 39, 214
Power of Your Subconscious Mind, The
  (Murphy), 45
Poynter, Dan, 211–212
Prayer:
  power to heal, 139–140
  power of "Thy will be done," 215
Present moment and attracting energy,
  197–198
Problems:
  created by individual, 111
  countered by "Inspired Action,"
    262–263
  as projections of self upon the
    world, 177
  patterns of, 165–169
Proctor, Bob, 156, 163–164, 213,
  215, 220
Programming:
  fiction novel as cause of Titanic
    disaster, 185–186
  and question about karma, 263
  unconscious beliefs and attracting
    life experiences, 258
Project for a Scientific Psychology
  (Freud), 142
Projection, universe as a camera, 191

Promotion:
  business cards, 61
  as your energy in print, 198
  turning negatives into good
    experiences, 218
Prosperity IQ, 81–82
Prosperity Power Institute, 82
Psychology, winning, 33
Public Broadcasting System (PBS), 61
Purposeful action:
  unacknowledged needs, 109–110

Qi Gong (*Chi Kung*), 202–203
*Question Your Thinking, Change the
    World* (Katie), 170
Questions and answers, 257–265
Quimby, Phineas Parker, 232–233
Quizzes:
  Prosperity IQ quiz (Gage), 81–82
  Attractor Factor IQ quiz (Caffrey), 7–15

Reality, 21
Red Cross, The, 61
Relationships:
  and the Attractor Factor, 257
  healing of, 67
Responsibility:
  and healing of others, 176
  key point of Attractor Factor, 241
  personal, and law of attraction, 77
Rituals (*yagyas* or *yagnas*), 172–175
Roberts, Jane, 21
Robbins, Tony, 111, 185, 213
Robb Report (magazine), 18
Rodriguez, Laura V., 33–34
Rooney, Jackie, 27
Rumi, 216
Ryan, Mark, 46–47

SamWitch shops, 96–97
Schneider, Meir, 67
Science of Getting Rich (Proctor)
    (seminar), 163–164, 220
Scott, Michele, 28–29
"Script, the" (Truman), 179–182
Scripting, 195–202
Secret, The (film), 3, 21, 27, 28, 166,
    221, 261
Sedona Institute, 5
Sedona Method, The, 4–5
Seitz, Katie, 27–28
Selection of thoughts for
    visualization, 186
Self-defense mechanism, 56
Self-esteem issues, 259
Self-Expression Center, Houston, 200
Self-help materials, 57. *See also*
    Web sites
Self-improvement:
  Beyond Positive Thinking (Anthony), 3
  personal best, for athletes, 91
  to raise vibration and effect upon
    world, 178–179
  worksheet, 92
Self-love, as tool for healing self and
    others, 177–179
Self One and Self Two, 208
Self-Publishing Manual (Poynter), 211
Self-respect, 102
Self-sabotage, 57, 146, 194–195, 236
Seminars:
  Internet e-class in place of, 99–103
September 11, 2001, 38–39
Service:
  to the world, 62, 167, 234
  using wealth to help others,
    102–103

Service (*Continued*)
  wishing others well, as an antidote to greed, 121
Seth material (Roberts), 21
Seven Lost Secrets of Success, The (Vitale), 138, 209
Sherwood, Liz, 25
"Shore Leave" (*Star Trek* episode), 69
Signals:
  change of inner signal changes outer world, 212
  "flags," 225–229
  inner, and instant action, 223
Simon and Schuster, 29
Silver, Yanik, 25, 102, 231
Socrates' advise on gossip, 87–88
Sister Mary Elizabeth, 234
Sisters of St. Filippini order, 234
Speed and money, 221, 231
Spindrift Foundation, 215
Spirit, connection to, 246
Spirits, 138–141
Spirituality:
  in balance with ego, 241
  energy as basis for material forms, 156
  versus materialism, 17, 103
  "New Thought" or modern spirituality, 232
  talk by author, 171
Spiritually based advertising, 200–201
Spiritual Marketing (Vitale), 32–42, 87, 98, 174, 221, 260–261
Spontaneous Fulfillment of Desire, The (Chopra), 95, 237
Success, unconscious obstacles to, 109–110
Suffering, Byron Katie on, 170

Sugarman, Joe, 86
Suppression of feelings and emotions, 156
"Surgery, karmic," 172–173
Surrendering control, 208
Symbols:
  case study of attracting a car, 17
Synchronicity, 224

Target, the (IQ test), 7–9
"Tend your garden," 232–233
Testimonials:
  Bray, Stephen, 47–49
  Breen, Jean M., 32
  Donovan, Jim, 42–43
  Gallant, Velma, 44
  Gilman, Stephen, 33
  Haeske, Roger, 34
  Harcus, Ann, 34–35
  Henderson, Karin, 49–50
  Hibbler, Bill, 38–41
  Hoffman, Christy, 35–37
  House, Paul, 32
  Hutchens, Becky, 37–38
  Iqbal, Faisal, 44–46
  Livesay, John, 32–33
  Mitchell, Chris, 29–32
  Reader from Farmington, Arizona, 33
  Rodriguez, Laura V., 33–34
  Rooney, Jackie, 25–27
  Ryan, Mark, 46–47
  Scott, Michele, 28–29
  Seitz, Katie, 27–28
  Sherwood, Liz, 25
  Worchester, Missi, 42
  Zappa, John, 50–54
There's a Customer Born Every Minute (Vitale), 4, 86, 106, 213, 214

Think and Grow Rich (Hill), 217
Thought control (IQ test), 12–14
Thought forms, 197, 204
Thoughts Become Things (TUT), 45
Thoughts:
  choosing new, 241
  examining the focus of, 88
  worksheet, 89
Thought Vibration (Atkinson), 21
Ticker Tape Toilet Paper, 53
TIISG. *See* "Turn It into Something
  Good"
Titanic, the, 185
Tonight Show with Jay Leno, 98
Tools and techniques (IQ test), 14–15
"Top 20 Self-Defeating Beliefs"
  (Evans), 146
Towne, Elizabeth, 89
Towne, William E., 204
Tracy, Brian, 120, 213
Transcendental Meditation (TM),
  251, 254
*Travelling Free: How to Recover from
  the Past by Changing Your Beliefs*
  (Evans), 145
Trick to Money Is Having Some, The
  (Wilde), 116
Troward, Judge Thomas, 5, 204, 255
Truman, Karol, 156, 179, 181, 182
Trump, Donald, 86, 104, 185
Trust:
  case study of, 157–158
  and letting go, 216
  of the universe, 215, 220–221
Turbocharge Your Writing (Vitale), 39
Turkish Psychological Association, 48
"Turn It into Something Good"
  (TIISG), 218

TUT. *See* Thoughts Become Things
Tuttle, Carol, 45
Tyler, Steven, 1

Unconscious manifestation, 79, 194–195
Universe and you, diagram, 142

Victory Over Myself (Patterson), 91
Virgin Records, 87
Vitale, Marian, 1–2, 153–154, 222
Voice, quiet, within, 215, 229–230

Wall Street (film), 78
Wants versus needs, 237
Warner, Frances Larimar, 69, 242
Wealth:
  affect of meditation on, 248
  Carnegie, Andrew, on, 219
  increased by giving, 260
  using to help others, 102–103, 248
  wishing others well, as an antidote to
    greed, 121
Web sites
  www.amazon.com, 221
  www.attractanewcar.com, 2
  www.BeyondPositiveThinking.com, 57
  www.thebookcoach.com, 43
  www.ecommerceconfidential.com, 41
  www.freevideoediting.com, 218
  www.geocities.com/sunmoonessences/
    muscle.html, 264
  www.goodhealthinfo.net/herbalist/
    muscle_testing.htm, 264
  www.HypnoticWriting.com, 2
  www.InstantChange.com
  www.IntentionalMeditation
    Foundation.com, 47
  www.itstimetogetrich.com, 31

Web sites (*Continued*)
www.jimdonovan.com, 43
www.menieres-disease.ca, 50
www.miraclescoaching.com
www.mrfire.com/IntentionalMeditati
onFoundation.com/index
.html, 254
www.myprosperitySecrets.com, 82
www.myspace.com, 28
www.nightingale.com, 57, 213
www.peacepilgrim.net/pphome.htm
www.portfolio.com/views/
columns/2007/10/15/Charity-
Makes-Wealth, 260
www.rudlreport.com, 41
www.sedona.com, 5
www.7dayebook.com, 2
www.smart-attractor.com, 7, 15
www.TheHealthyShop.com, 42
www.thework.com, 170
www.tut.com
www.welcomechanges.com, 44
www.yagna.by-choice.com, 174
Weight loss, and counterintentions,
166, 167
What Can a Man Believe? (Barton), 139
Wilde, Stuart, 116, 156
Willis, Bruce, 259
Wimberley, Texas, 2–3, 39, 41
Winfrey, Oprah, 98
Worchester, Missi, 42
Worksheets:
"I am" statements, 250
"assuming the feeling of the wish
fulfilled," 184, 191–192
clearing and aligning, 144
dreams, and experiencing as already
fulfilled, 196–197

examining focus of thoughts, 89
examining recurring patterns,
168–169
excuses, real versus imaginary,
107–108
expressing emotions, versus
suppressing, 164–165
"Inspired Action," 223, 228–229
intentional meditation (IM) steps,
252–253
muscle testing, 133–134
new beliefs that you want to instill in
yourself, 151–152
180-degree turnaround of "don't
wants" into "do wants," 95–96
selecting what you truly want, 112,
113, 118
thoughts infused with feelings,
204–205
thoughts of gratitude, 74–75,
188, 189
thoughts inspired by Peace
Pilgrim, 93
thoughts for a new life, 70–71
thoughts of opportunities that you
may have been dismissing, 58–59
thoughts of self-improvement, 92
"Turn It into Something Good"
(TIISG), 219–220
"The Work," by Byron Katie, 171
writing down desired goal(s), 130
writing down "wants," 120–121
"Work, The" (Katie), 169–171
Worry, manifesting as reality, 193–194
Wright, Kurt, 245, 259
Writing. *See also* Worksheets
exercise, for clearing negative energy,
163–165

for manifesting desires, 120–121, 195–202

for turning "don't wants" into "do wants," 95

Yagyas (or *yagnas*), 172–175

Yates, Brad, 2

You Can Receive Whatsoever You Desire (Moody), 84

Your Infinite Power to Be Rich (Murphy), 205

Your Invisible Power (Behrend), 70

You Were Born Rich (Proctor), 215

Zappa, John, 50–54

Zero Limits (Vitale), 3, 175, 178, 264

Zimmer, Sandra, 200–201

One of the standout stars of the hit movie *The Secret,* Dr. Joe Vitale is president of Hypnotic Marketing, Inc. and president of Frontier Nutritional Research, Inc., both companies based outside of Austin, Texas.

He is author of the No. 1 best-selling books *The Key: The Missing Secret to Attracting Whatever You Want,* and *Life's Missing Instruction Manual.* He also recorded the best-selling Nightingale-Conant audio programs, *The Power of Outrageous Marketing* and *The Missing Secret: How to Use the Law of Attraction to Get What You Want Every Time.*

He's also written *Zero Limits, The E-Code, Meet and Grow Rich, There's A Customer Born Every Minute, The Seven Lost Secrets of Success, Hypnotic Writing, Your Internet Cash Machine, Inspired Marketing,* and *Buying Trances,* all for John Wiley & Sons.

Once homeless and living in poverty, Joe is now considered one of the pioneers of Internet marketing. He has made millionaires and helped create online empires. Due to his work in *The Secret,* and to the success of his books, he is now becoming known as a self-help guru. He's often called the Buddha of the Internet.

His main web site is www.mrfire.com.

Special Offer

How to Easily and Quickly Attract the Life You Want with Your Own Miracles Coach

Finally Overcome the Internal Roadblocks that Prevent You from Attracting the Results You Want with the Help of Dr. Joe Vitale's Miracles Coaching Program

You need to be *clear* to achieve the results you want. If there are any counter intentions within you, consciously or unconsciously, you will not attract the results you really want. If you do achieve them, it will be temporary and you will lose them.

So, how do you get *clear*? How do you get rid of the roadblocks and go to warp speed, right to whatever it is you're trying to attract?

Obviously, you can use the roadmap in this book, but if you want even faster results, and/ or if you want some personal direction, you may need a Miracles Coach. For a limited time, you can apply to be mentored at the web site below.

For details, please see

www.miraclescoaching.com

FREE!
"Beyond the Attractor Factor"

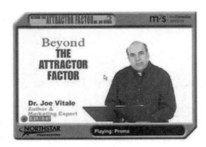

As a special thank you for purchasing *The Attractor Factor: Second Edition*, you can have FREE access to Dr. Joe Vitale's, 75-minute presentation, "Beyond the Attractor Factor," a multimedia seminar online.

Dr. Vitale will show you how to:

- Create more of what you want
- Never worry about money again
- Quit struggling
- Use your complaints as a springboard to success
- Snap out of the cultural trance created by TV, radio, and newspapers
- Take "inspired action"
- Use conscious co-creation
- Employ the questioning process to open up roadblocks
- Stop lying to yourself
- Take conscious control of what was previously unconscious
- Nevillize your goals
- Practice EFT (Emotional Freedom Technique)
- Use the power of intention
- Get what you want or something better
- Benefit from inspired action instead of controlled action

This is a special FREE offer that may be removed at any time without advanced notice.

Sign up today at...

http://beyondattractorfactor.com/AF

Also, sign up for Dr. Joe Vitale's FREE newsletter "News You Can Use" at...

http://www.mrfire.com/newsletter-subscribe.html